FIGHTING FOR TIME

by
Glenn H. Worthington

Introduction
by
Brian C. Pohanka

Burd Street Press

First Printing, 1932
Second Printing, 1985   *(Revised Edition)*
Third Printing, 1988
Fourth Printing, 1994

In respect for the scholarship contained herein, the paper used in this book meets the guidelines for permanence and durability of the Committee on Production Guidelines for Book Longevity of the Council on Library Resources.

This Burd Street Press publication is printed
by arrangement with
Beidel Printing House, Inc.
63 West Burd Street, Shippensburg, PA 17257 USA

For a complete list of available publications,
please write
Burd Street Press
Division of White Mane Publishing Co., Inc.
P.O. Box 152
Shippensburg, PA 17257 USA

The Library of Congress has Cataloged the Hardback Edition
of this Work as follows:

ISBN 0-942597-71-0
(previously ISBN 0-942597-08-7 and ISBN 0-932751-03-2)

88-20742
CIP

PRINTED IN THE UNITED STATES OF AMERICA

INTRODUCTION
by Brian C. Pohanka, 1985

"They were the saviors of Washington." So General Lew Wallace judged the Federal soldiers who fought and died July 9, 1864, at the battle of Monocacy, Maryland. And History has in large measure confirmed Wallace's opinion of the stand made by his 7500 men against nearly twice that number of Confederates commanded by General Jubal A. Early. The bloody fight waged on the rolling fields that flank this muddy river gave fatal pause to the last major Confederate invasion of the North; an invasion designed to bolster the waning fortunes of the South, but one that sputtered to an inconclusive finale three days later, before the defenses of Washington. Monocacy was a Confederate victory, but it was also a Confederate defeat.

If the historical significance of Monocacy is undenied, it was as a bitter soldier's battle that the fight was best remembered by the enlisted men who wore the blue and gray. "It was one of those fights where success depends largely upon the prowess of the individual soldier", wrote that peerless Southern warrior, General John B. Gordon. Isaac Bradwell of the 31st Georgia concluded, "This battle...was conducted by private soldiers, each man acting independently." Lieutenant M. J. Stearns of the 106th New York said simply, "Every man tried to do his best against great odds."

And, if Monocacy was not an especially costly battle by Civil War standards, it was a particularly fierce one. General Gordon stated, "I recall no charge of the war, except that of the 12th of May against Hancock (at Spotsylvania), in which my brave fellows seemed so swayed by an enthusiasm which amounted almost to a martial delirium." This frenzy on the part of the combatants elicited similar comments by John Worsham of the 21st Virginia, one of Stonewall Jackson's old veterans, who described Monocacy as "the most exciting time I witnessed during the war." — "The men", said Worsham, "were perfectly wild." In suffering defeat at Monocacy both sides stood to lose much. Time and again regiments reduced to handful of men by the terrible bloodletting of the Wilderness campaign advanced into the vortex of fire that swept the fields of the Worthington and Thomas farms.

Yet, when all is said and done it is the strategic importance of Monocacy that makes that July day so memorable. Early decided to rest his command following the engagement. He marched all day on the 10th, his men straggling badly. On July 11 he reached the outskirts of Washington, but concluded his forces were in no condition to risk battle. On July 12 he threatened the city's defenses with some half-hearted attacks which were countered by two divisions from the Federal VI Corps — troops who had arrived on the 11th and 12th. The attacks were called off, Early withdrew and recrossed the Potomac on July 14.

Had Lew Wallace not delayed Early at Monocacy, the Confederates could have reached Washington a day earlier than they did, before the arrival of Grant's veteran troops. Whether they could have taken the city is of course a matter of conjecture — however, the chances for success would certainly have been far greater facing untrained militia and garrison troops.

Perhaps U. S. Grant best summed up the importance of Monocacy when he wrote,

> "General Wallace contributed on this occasion, by the defeat of the troops under him, a greater benefit to the cause than often falls to the lot of a commander of equal force to render by means of a victory."

*****

Despite the historical significance of the battle of Monocacy, *Fighting for Time* remains the only book-length study of the engagement. As such it is a mandatory source for any student of the events of July 9, 1864. And, if we tolerate an occasionally rambling and digressive passage, there was no more natural author for such a book than Glenn Howard Worthington. For as a child of six Worthington had watched wide-eyed through the cellar windows of his family home as the tide of battle swept through his front yard. He had glimpsed heavy booted feet and kersey trousers flashing past, had heard the rattle and thunder of musketry and the crashing roar of Confederate artillery deployed adjacent to the house. These were memories still very much alive, when, nearly 70 years later he compiled his history of that day.

Glenn Worthington was born in the Urbana District of Frederick County, Maryland, on April 22, 1858. His father, John T. Worthington, was a prominent farmer — a slaveholder and Democrat; his mother, Mary R. Simmons Worthington, daughter of another local farmer. He was educated at the public schools of the neighborhood, and, from 1872 to 1876, at Frederick City College. After moving to Chicago and briefly considering a career in business and then Insurance, young Worthington returned to Frederick where he became a schoolteacher while pursuing a degree in law. In May, 1887 he graduated from the University of Maryland Law School, and the following year was appointed School Examiner for Frederick County, a position he held for four years, and in which he excelled.

On April 30, 1890, Glenn Worthington married Julia Alvey, the daughter of Judge Richard Alvey of Hagerstown. Five of their children would live to maturity: two sons and three daughters. Having decided to devote full time to a burdgeoning law practice, in 1899 Worthington was nominated by the Democratic Party and elected State's Attorney of Frederick County. He held this position to 1904, in the meantime serving as a Member of the State Board of Education. In 1907 he was appointed Chief Judge of the Sixth Judicial Circuit of Maryland, and in the same year a member of the Court of Appeals. During the First World War, Worthington served as Chairman of Frederick's Selective Service Board. In later years Judge Worthington was a highly regarded pillar of the Frederick community, a scholarly and dignified gentleman proud of his service to his native state. He died on August 7, 1934 at the age of 76, and was buried in the family plot at Mount Olivet Cemetery, Frederick.

*****

The movement to properly preserve and commemorate the battlefield of Monocacy can perhaps be traced to Lew Wallace, who wished to gather together the remains of the Federal soldiers slain there, and erect over their mass grave a monument with the inscription, "These men died to save the National Capital, and they did save it." The remains were taken elsewhere and by 1904 there had yet to take place any substantative action to preserve the battle site. Speaking at the ceremonies held on the 40th Anniversary of the battle, General William H. Seward, Jr. said,

> "The project of raising some enduring monument to those who fell here, and to commemorate the battle itself, is a noble and patriotic object, which, after the lapse of forty years, should be done and done well and done now..."

However, with the exception of some regimental monuments, nothing of note had transpired by 1928, when Confederate veteran Isaac Bradwell wrote,

> "Gettysburg was on a much larger scale than Monocacy, and there are memorials all over the ground to commemorate the event, but the latter was even more important in consequence as to the result of the war...By all means let the government make this place a memorial park."

Eventually a Congressional bill was introduced, and passed, with a suggested appropriation of 50,000 dollars to acquire the battlefield acreage. But, a Depression era Congress virtually emasculated the proceedings by reducing the sum to a mere 5,000 dollars.

It was in reaction to this turn of events that Judge Worthington set out to acquaint the public with the historical significance of the battle. His book, published two years before the Judge's death, was the product of several years of historical research. His goal was plain. As he stated in his Conclusion, "Would it not create a patriotic shrine to appropriately mark the battlefield, lay out drives and walks and erect a monument there...?"

As it was the battlefield languished in obscurity for 40 more years, during which time Interstate Route 70-S (now known as Route 270) was cut through the swale between the Worthington and Thomas farms, effectively bisecting the area in which the heaviest fighting occurred.

The plan to preserve the Monocacy battlefield revived largely through the efforts of the late Congressman Goodloe E. Byron, in whose district it was located. On January 21, 1974 Congressman Byron introduced a Bill to establish the Monocacy National Battlefield Park, supplanting the earlier Congressional action. In due time this was approved, and the 1934 act amended to enlarge the park's boundaries. Additional boundary modifications were made in 1978 and 1980. The boundary now contains 1670 acres and includes the bulk of the area in which the main battle was waged.

The action to preserve Monocacy is timely indeed in light of the battlefield's location in the rapidly expanding urban corridor between Washington and Frederick. Central to the development of the battlefield park will be the use of scenic easement to maintain the integrity of the park boundaries against the specter of urban sprawl. Equally important will be the integration of picnicking and camping facilities within the historic areas, as the site is one of natural as well as historical significance, ideal for hiking and canoeing. Development of the park is in its early stages. Eventually, over the next several years and through three distinct phases, the battlefield will be appropriately interpreted with trails, signs, overlooks and a National Park Service visitor's center.

Surely only a scant few of the many thousands of travelers who daily pass along the highway realize that they are driving through a significant site in the annals of American military history. But now we may finally hope to see preserved and commemorated what Glenn Worthington termed, "The battle that saved the National Capital from capture and mayhap the Union itself."

BRIAN C. POHANKA
Alexandria, Virginia
October 6, 1984

GLENN WORTHINGTON

FIGHTING FOR TIME

OR

The Battle That Saved Washington and Mayhap the Union

A story of the War Between the States, showing how Washington was saved from capture by Early's army of invasion, and how that achievement contributed to the preservation of the Union, with many stories and incidents of the invasion hitherto untold.

BY

GLENN H. WORTHINGTON
FREDERICK, MARYLAND

"Even as a traveller passes unmoved over fields of fame, or through cities of ancient renown, — unmoved because utterly unconscious of the lofty deeds which there have been wrought, of the great hearts which spent themselves there."

PRINTED AND PUBLISHED UNDER THE SANCTION OF
THE FREDERICK COUNTY HISTORICAL SOCIETY
OF FREDERICK, MARYLAND

PRESS OF
DAY PRINTING COMPANY
600 EAST LOMBARD STREET
BALTIMORE, MD.
1932

DEDICATION

—

CONTENTS

CONTENTS

CONTENTS

viii

CONTENTS—APPENDIX

LIST OF ILLUSTRATIONS

MAPS

FIGHTING FOR TIME

OR

THE BATTLE THAT SAVED WASHINGTON AND MAYHAP THE UNION

PRELIMINARY STATEMENT

The preparation of this book was begun after a bill providing for the establishment of a "National Military Park at the Battlefield of Monocacy, Maryland," had been introduced in the Seventieth Congress, had passed the House and was pending in the Senate with encouraging prospects of its passage by that body at the December session, 1928. However, the bill did not pass the Senate until the spring of 1929, and then the sum authorized by the House bill was reduced from $50,000 to $5,000, and the bill so altered in its form as to make it in fact a new bill. As amended the bill was concurred in by the House and signed by the President, March 1, 1929. The appropriation was granted by the Seventy-first Congress and became available July 1, 1930.

The sum finally appropriated ($5,000) is so inadequate to any proper marking of the battlefield that it is really negligible. The State of Pennsylvania alone has erected a monument to its three regiments which participated in the battle that must easily have cost $6,000, or more, when both labor and material were much cheaper than now; New Jersey has a monument that cost $4,500, and that would probably cost at present prices, $8,000 or $9,000; Vermont has a smaller but handsome monument to its hard-fighting Tenth Regiment of Volunteers, and the local chapter, Daughters of the Confederacy, has erected a large boulder, appropriately inscribed, to the weary, worn but heroic soldiers of the South who fought here so valiantly.

If the National Government is to notice this battle-field at all, surely it will do so in a way worthy of this great nation and appropriate to the vital importance of the sanguinary struggle that took place there at so critical a moment. For the sake of historical accuracy, and as a matter of general interest, it seems desirable that a more compact and comprehensive account of the invasion of Maryland by Gen. Jubal A. Early in July, 1864, should be available than has hitherto been the case. I have therefore persisted in my purpose to prepare such an account.

An examination of the books on the subject found in the Congressional Library at Washington and in the Peabody Institute Library at Baltimore disclosed many first-hand partial accounts which, it seemed, if collected, would show in a striking way the progress of the invasion and establish beyond cavil the fact that the courageous stand taken by General Wallace at Monocacy actually saved the disastrous consequences of the capture of the seat of Government by the enemy, and possibly saved the disruption of the Union.

The *Official Records of the Union and Confederate Armies,* published by the Government, were among the books examined, and therein were discovered copies of many original letters and telegrams bearing directly on the subject, written by the leading participants on both sides during the progress of the invasion. These, it was considered, have an especial interest for the present-day wayfarer as well as for the student of American history. These letters and telegrams are scattered through several volumes of the "Official Records," though found chiefly in Volume 37, Series 1, Parts 1 and 2, and are not readily accessible to the average reader. By collecting these together and putting them in proper order of sequence with explanatory and descriptive text, it was thought a more vivid picture could be presented than by a mere narrative statement of the happenings of those stirring and eventful days.

Benedict, in his *Vermont in the Civil War,* says:

"The Battle of Monocacy occupies much less space in history than it deserves. It was a stout and most creditable fight; and though a defeat in name and in fact, it accomplished as much as many a victory, for it delayed Early's march upon Washington two days."

When the danger of the fall of Washington had passed the attention of the nation was directed to subsequent happenings, and adequate stress has seldom been given this battle by the historian; though General Grant in his *Memoirs* has paid General Lew Wallace the tribute of his high commendation for Wallace's achievement. And Benson J. Lossing in his *History of the Civil War,* after briefly describing the battle, says:

"So ended the Battle of Monocacy, in the ultimate defeat of the few national troops there engaged, but in triumph for the National cause, for the check given the flushed invaders by Wallace in that gallant fight of eight hours which gave time for reinforcements to reach Washington, saved the Capital. So declared the Secretary of War and the Lieutenant-General. But for that check of thirty hours, the Capital would have been Early's prize and a heap of blackened ruins its possible fate. In view of all these circumstances, the Battle of Monocacy appears as one of the most important and brilliant of the war."

Perhaps no one was better able to weigh the importance of the bloody encounter fought at Monocacy on

July 9, 1864, than L. E. Chittenden, Register of the Treasury during Mr. Lincoln's administration, who evidently gave much study to the subject and who has written an interesting book entitled, *Recollections of President Lincoln and His Administration.* (1901.) In this book Mr. Chittenden considers all the evidence pro- and con concerning the battle and its consequences, and in the course of his discussion says:

"If that (battle) fought at Monocacy did delay General Early so as to save the Capital from assault and probable capture, it was one of the decisive battles of the world, and with the events which immediately followed it, deserves a much more complete account than it has hitherto received." (Page 390.)

Further on he says, in substance and effect, that the battle did delay Early long enough to save the Capital and that it was fought "over one of the bloodiest fields of the war." He concludes as follows:

"When the children of the republic are asked what it was that brought Early's campaign to naught and saved the Capital, let them be taught to answer: 'General Wallace and his command at the Battle of Monocacy, and the arrival of the Sixth Corps within the defences of the Capital.' "

In Sergeant Tirrell's *History of the Fourteenth New Jersey,* the author says:

"Every drop of blood shed at Monocacy, every life lost, was sacrificed in a noble cause. Those fallen heroes . . . if they could only know that their lives saved our National Capital from destruction, would willingly exclaim: 'I die content, I gave my life to my country.' "

The same meed of praise may justly be bestowed upon Early and his cohorts, for his undertaking was one displaying military skill and daring, and his followers fought valiantly, many laying down their lives in a cause they believed to be just and right.

Many bigger battles were fought during that four years of civil strife, with greater numbers of casualties, but these were chiefly battles of attrition, or the wearing away of the armies of the Confederacy, while this battle, in its direct and immediate results, saved the fall of the Capital of the Nation, and the ignominious flight or capture of the heads of Government, and you who read may find that indirectly and mediately it saved the Union. With the object in view of establishing by a fair, honest and accurate marshaling of facts, the tremendous importance of the battle fought at Monocacy River, near Frederick, Maryland, on July 9, 1864, the task of compiling the data concerning the whole of Early's invasion, was undertaken. It has been a task involving no small amount of labor and research, but it has also been one of absorbing interest. Will any impartial reader of the facts and circumstances gathered together in the following pages doubt the truth of the last words of Gen. Lew Wallace in his official report concerning those of his command who fell at Monocacy: "These men died to save the National Capital, and they did save it."

GLENN H. WORTHINGTON.

Frederick, Md.

CHAPTER I

A BRIEF REVIEW

In order to understand the significance and importance of the Battle of Monocacy, it will be helpful to be reminded of some leading events of the war transpiring within a few months previously, to serve as a background to the narrative of that battle and the events directly flowing from it.

Viewed merely as a battle between contending forces, it resulted in a decisive victory for the Confederates, and an overwhelming defeat for the Federals, but viewed with respect to its immediate consequences, it was a great victory for Gen. Lew Wallace and the Union cause; more decisive than Antietam, Shiloh, or Gettysburg.

GRANT IS MADE LIEUTENANT-GENERAL

A bill restoring the grade of lieutenant-general of the United States Army was passed by the Congress, and became a law on February 26, 1864.

The nomination of Gen. U. S. Grant to the position thus created was sent to the Senate on March 1, and confirmed the next day.

The commission of the new lieutenant-general was handed to him at the Executive Mansion on March 9, 1864, by President Lincoln himself, in the presence of his cabinet, the general's eldest son, Frederick D. Grant, those of his staff who were with him, and a few visitors.

Prior to this time only two persons had ever held the
high rank of lieutenant-general of the United States
Army; these were George Washington and Winfield
Scott, the latter only by brevet; that is, as to him, it
was merely an honorable title.

The Confederate Government was not so frugal of
rank and title, and several commanders of her armies
were made lieutenants-general, notably Generals Jackson,
Johnston, Longstreet, Early and Ewell.

This commission to General Grant placed him in
command of all the Union forces in the field, subject
only to the orders of the President himself, who by the
Constitution is Commander-in-Chief of the Army and
Navy of the United States, and of the militia of the several States when called into actual service of the United
States.

On June 3, 1862, Gen. Robert E. Lee had been made
"General" and put in command of the Army of Northern
Virginia, and at the time of Grant's appointment as
lieutenant-general he was commanding an experienced
Confederate force, numbering perhaps 70,000 to 80,000
men in all.   This force was concentrated in large part
between Fredericksburg, on the Rappahannock, a few
miles below its junction with the Rapidan, and Richmond on the James.

"ON TO RICHMOND"

It was the strategy of Grant's campaign from the
time of his appointment as general-in-chief of the Union
Army to capture Richmond, the Confederate capital.
"On to Richmond" was the slogan throughout his whole

army, and the cry throughout the country. To this end he sent Gen. Benjamin F. Butler with a large force up the James River to get as near to Richmond as practicable and to threaten it from that direction.

General Sigel was sent into the Shenandoah Valley to cut off the supplies which were being furnished the Confederate Army from that source. The Shenandoah Valley, or the "Valley of Virginia," as it was generally called, is a fertile and productive valley, and during the war was frequently referred to as the "granary of the Confederacy."

Shenandoah Valley To Be Made A Desert

In his correspondence with the War Department, General Grant said that this valley should be made a desert as high up as possible, so crows flying over it would have to carry their own provender with them. (See *Official War Records Serial No. 71*, pp. 301, 329.) While this may appear harsh, it was, perhaps, a legitimate war measure intended to reduce the Confederacy by starvation.

Grant's own part of the plan of campaign was to march directly on Richmond from the north with a very large force and to whip Lee on his own ground—"between the Rapidan and Richmond."

Wilderness—Spottsylvania—Cold Harbor

A most sanguinary engagement took place between the two armies at the Wilderness on May 5-6-7. In this battle the nationals lost 18,000 men, of whom 6,000 were taken prisoners. The Confederate loss was heavy, but much smaller, about 11,000.

Then from the 8th to the 18th of May took place the battle of Spottsylvania Court House. Here the Union loss was reported to be about 30,000 men, while the Confederate loss was very much less, perhaps not 8,000, all told.

Then followed the battle of the North Anna River from May 23 to 27, which again was indecisive.

Then occurred on June 1, 2 and 3 the second battle of Cold Harbor, within twenty-five miles of Richmond.

Of this battle it is said by Gen. Thomas W. Hyde in his book, *Following the Greek Cross,* at page 211:

"That we lost 15,000 men and the enemy but 1,500 is commentary enough."

Even before this disaster to the Union arms, Butler, operating on the James River, had been driven from Drury's Bluff back to Bermuda Hundred, and there was effectually "bottled up" by forces under the Confederate General, Beauregard. Also the news had come in from the Valley that Sigel had been badly defeated at New Market and was retreating down the Valley.

So that with the repulse at Cold Harbor the campaign generally was not progressing favorably to the Union cause. Indeed one disaster followed another in rapid succession. Butler was driven back. Sigel was routed and Grant himself suffered losses in three great battles almost equal to the whole of Lee's effective army. Even the campaign in Georgia had not gone favorably, for on June 27 Sherman had been defeated at Kenesaw Mountain by the Confederate forces under Gen. Joseph E. Johnston. The losses to the Federal forces in these battles were not less than 60,000 men, while those of the Confederacy were scarcely one-half as many.

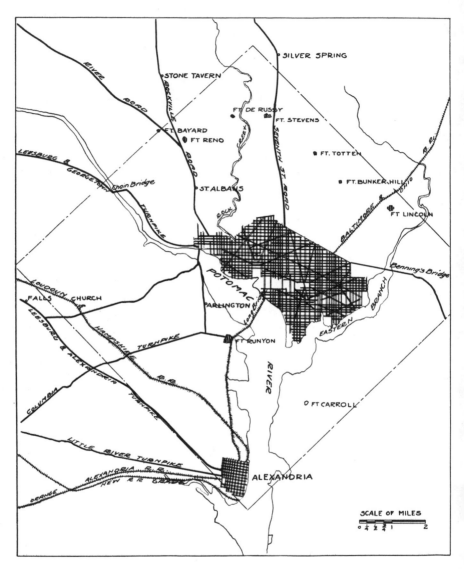

DEFENSES OF WASHINGTON

Map showing the outlines of the District of Columbia and some of the outlying forts, of which there were about 50 in all constituting, with breastworks, ditches, palisades and abatis, the defenses of Washington. Fort Stevens was the point of attack of Early's Army of Invasion.

General Grant now resolved to abandon the plan of taking Richmond from the north side and to move his army to the south side of the James; and, because Petersburg was a railroad centre, from which supplies could be sent to Richmond, he destroyed the railroads thereabouts, and undertook to capture that place by siege.

In June, 1864, he established his headquarters at City Point on the James River, at the mouth of the Appomattox, about ten miles from Petersburg, and invested the latter place with all the Federal forces he could gather together.

Garrison Withdrawn From Washington

Among others, he withdrew the trained army defending the National Capital. Early in the war, Washington had been made ready against any attack of the enemy by the erection of a series of outlying defenses. These defenses consisted of fifty-three widely separated forts located on every side of the city—north, east, south and west—and embracing a perimeter of perhaps forty miles in extent. Some of these forts were on the Virginia side of the Potomac and the others along or near the boundaries of the District of Columbia, on the Maryland side of the river. To properly man these defenses, a force of at least 25,000 trained soldiers was deemed necessary, and approximately such a force had been maintained there, but General Grant persuaded President Lincoln that in case of emergency he could send troops from City Point in time to repel any attempt that could possibly be made to capture the city.[1] He stated to the President that he would keep transports in the James River, close to City Point, where his headquarters were, under banked fires, ready to start with troops quickly for Washington, upon notice that they were needed there for the protection of that city. He stated that he could transport a large force within thirty-six hours.

These assurances had induced the President to permit these trained soldiers to be withdrawn from the fortifications around Washington and to be added to the forces then besieging Petersburg. The distance from the Federal lines before Petersburg to Washington, by way of City Point, was more than 250 miles, and the water route, from City Point down the James River to Hampton Roads, and thence up the Chesapeake Bay and Potomac River to Washington, was the only practicable route. As the army investing Petersburg was ten or more miles inland from City Point, is was necessary for Grant to send word to General Meade, who was in immediate command of the besieging forces, to send in to City Point such troops as were required to be transported. Such troops as were called for were obliged to march these ten or fifteen miles to City Point where they could embark on the transports, there being no ready means of conveyance to that place.

From thirty-six to forty hours were, in fact, required from the time a message was received from Washington by General Grant at City Point until a loaded transport could tie up at the dock in either Baltimore or Washington, and that too, without allowing for any mishap or misadventure. Thus Washington was left practically defenseless because, except for the clerks, convalescents, citizen volunteers, a portion of the Veteran Reserve Corps, and the remnant of the garrison, there were none within reach to man the fortifications.

As has been stated, a part of the strategy of Grant's

campaign of 1864, was the desolation of the Valley of Virginia by a force under General Franz Sigel. But Sigel had been badly defeated at New Market by a Confederate army under General John C. Breckinridge[2] on May 15, 1864. From Spottsylvania Court House where Lee was at grips with Grant, the former sent the following message to the victor at New Market:

Spottsylvania Court House,
May 16, 1864.

General J. C. Breckinridge:

I offer you the thanks of this army for your victory over General Sigel. Press them down the Valley, and if practical, follow him into Maryland.

R. E. LEE,
General.

Soon thereafter General Sigel was superseded by General David Hunter, who assumed command of the Department of West Virginia, on May 21, 1864.

EARLY TO THE RESCUE

Hunter was successful in driving the Confederate forces under Breckinridge, operating in the Valley, toward Staunton, Lexington and Lynchburg.

On the 18th of June he was threatening Lynchburg which was then quite a storehouse of supplies for the Confederate Army. Breckinridge's force was inadequate for the defense of that city.

To prevent the capture of Lynchburg and the valuable supplies stored there, General Lee, on June 16, sent from the defenses around Petersburg to the aid of Breckinridge, a force of Confederates under General Jubal A. Early, an experienced officer who had shown himself to be a resourceful and energetic campaigner.

General Jubal A. Early was born in Franklin County, Virginia, November 3, 1816. He graduated from West Point in 1837, and the same year, served in the second Seminole War in Florida. In 1838, he resigned his commission in the army and studied law. Later, however, in 1847, he served as major-general of volunteers in the war with Mexico.

At the outbreak of the Civil War, he was appointed colonel in the service of the Confederate States. He was considered one of the boldest and most enterprising Confederate generals. At Gettysburg, he commanded a division of Lee's army.

He died in Lynchburg, Virginia, March 2, 1894. Before his death, he prepared a short autobiography explaining his part in the war of the rebellion and especially his attack upon Washington. This autobiography, with notes by his niece, Miss R. H. Early, was published by the Lippincott Company, Philadelphia, in 1912.

EARLY'S UNDERTAKING

Although the Union Army besieging Petersburg was a formidable one and numerically stronger than the forces under Lee, the latter evidently felt that the recent reverses and heavy losses sustained by Grant's army at the Wilderness, at Spottsylvania Court House, at Cold Harbor and other places, would tend to somewhat demoralize his plans and his troops for the time being, and therefore that he could spare Early's Division from the defense of Petersburg long enough at least to enable Early's and Breckinridge's combined commands to repel Hunter's

GENERAL JUBAL A. EARLY

attack upon Lynchburg. Early was also directed to drive Hunter out of the Valley, or to capture his whole army, if possible, and if successful, Early was to move down the Valley, cross the Potomac into Maryland and threaten Washington from the north. It was also at the same time suggested by General Lee to Early that if the opportunity offered, the latter should send a cavalry force to liberate the Confederate prisoners held at Point Lookout; and these might then, he thought, be organized into an effective army corps to co-operate with Early in case he should be successful in capturing Washington.

These views were expressed by General Lee to General Early in a personal conference between them at Petersburg, but the only orders given Early by his superior were that he should proceed at once to Lynchburg to the aid of General Breckinridge, and after Hunter had been disposed of, he was to use his own judgment and be governed by circumstances as to going down the Valley, crossing the Potomac into Maryland, menacing Washington, and capturing it, if possible.

(Note)—The significance of the plan of releasing the prisoners at Point Lookout will be more readily understood if a brief description of that prison camp be given. As the conditions prevailing at the camp are not generally known, a more detailed description will be given than necessary for merely an understanding of the design of releasing the prisoners, as a matter of general interest. This description is derived largely from an account written by a visitor to the camp in November, 1864.

---

(1) in his *Defences of Washington*, Gen. J. G. Barnard, at page 108, says:

"Grant had withdrawn all the experienced and highly efficient artillery regiments which had constituted the garrison of the defences, the result being that in June and July, 1864, the Capital presented a tempting object of attack."

At another place in his book General Barnard says: "When in July, 1864, Early appeared before Washington all the artillery regiments which had constituted the garrisons of the works and who were experienced in the use of artillery had been withdrawn and their places partly filled by a few regiments of 100 days men just mustered into the service." . . . "Hence it became necessary to find other troops to oppose Early. One division (Ricketts') was, as we have seen, detached on the 5th of July, from the lines before Petersburg and sent to Baltimore, where it arrived in time to bear the brunt of the battle of Monocacy. (Page 113.) The other two divisions did not receive their orders until the 9th and did not reach Washington until 2 P. M. on the 11th, barely in time. A part of the 19th Corps, just arrived at Fort Monroe from Louisiana, was likewise dispatched to Washington and arrived at the same time."

JOHN CABELL BRECKINRIDGE

(2) John Cabell Breckinridge was born near Lexington, Kentucky, January 21, 1821. He studied law and began to practice his profession at Lexington in 1844. In 1847 he was chosen major of a volunteer regiment for the Mexican War. He afterwards served as a member of the State Legislature, and for four years, 1851-1855, as a member of Congress. In 1856 he was nominated for vice-president of the United States, with James Buchanan, and was elected. He served as Vice-President during Buchanan's administration from 1857 to 1861. In 1860 he was nominated by one wing of the Democratic Party for President, with Gen. Joseph Lane of Oregon for Vice-President. Stephen A. Douglas of Illinois and Hershel V. Johnson of Georgia were nominated by another wing of the same party. John Bell of Tennesssee and Edward Everett of Massachusetts were nominated by the American Party, and Abraham Lincoln of Illinois and Hannibal Hamlin of Maine by the Republican Party.

It became the duty of Vice-President Breckinridge to preside over the joint meeting of the two Houses of Congress at the counting of the electoral vote. He opened in the presence of the two Houses the sealed envelopes containing the electoral vote of each State, and the votes were then counted. Breckinridge declared the result as follows: For Lincoln and Hamlin, 180; for Breckinridge and Lane, 72; for Bell and Everett, 39; for Douglas and Johnson, 12. Vice-President Breckinridge declared Lincoln and Hamlin duly elected.

After his defeat for the Presidency the Legislature of Kentucky elected Breckinridge United States Senator from that State. He served in the Senate from March 4, 1861, to December of the same year, when he withdrew because of harsh criticism of his utterances on the rights of the States, and entered the Confederate Army. He was made a major-general in 1862 and took part in a number of battles, including that of Monocacy, July 9, 1864. At that time he was commanding a separate corps of two divisions, Gordon's and Echols', under General Early. It was he who directed General Gordon to ford the Monocacy with his division and drive Gen. James B. Ricketts and his command from the defensive position occupied by it on the Thomas farm. He himself crossed the Monocacy and kept close to the front. Near the close of the war he was appointed Secretary of War in the Cabinet of President Jefferson Davis, and held that position when the Confederacy fell in April, 1865. Soon after he departed for Europe, but returned to his native State and died there, in Lexington, May 17, 1875. He was but 35 years of age when elected Vice-President, the youngest man who ever held the position. He was an exceedingly eloquent and forceful speaker and of commanding presence. Alfred Seely Roe, in his book entitled, *History of the Ninth New York Heavy Artillery*, says that he saw General Breckenridge on horseback and that he thought him the handsomest man he had ever seen. General Breckinridge was perhaps one of the ablest and most outstanding of the leaders of the Confederate cause. His son, Clifton R. Breckinridge of Lexington, Kentucky, born in 1846, served as a member of Congress for many years and as Minister to Russia during Cleveland's second administration. He is still living at the advanced age of 85 honorable years.

CHAPTER II.

POINT LOOKOUT PRISON CAMP

Point Lookout is a long, flat, narrow headland projecting into the waters of the Chesapeake Bay and Potomac River at their confluence about ninety miles below Washington. It is located at the southern extremity of St. Mary's County in Southern Maryland, and is bordered on the north by a grove of tall pine. At a little distance is Point Lookout Lighthouse whose bright light has been kept constantly burning at night for many years to warn pilots and seafaring men to beware of the projecting headland and of the somewhat shallow waters surrounding it.

It was here that the Federal Government established during the Civil War an extensive camp for the confinement of captured Confederate soldiers, and other prisoners. There were no barracks for the use of these unfortunates but all lived in tents during their confinement. The prison camp proper embraced a considerable area of land enclosed by a high plank fence, and there were besides, outside the enclosure, the commandant's headquarters, hospital buildings and store houses.

THE TENTS OF THE PRISONERS

Within the enclosure the ground was laid off into squares by streets running east and west and by others crossing these at right angles, and running north and south. On these squares facing the streets were erected thousands of tents which were intended as shelters for the prisoners.

THE TENTS

The tents were of three kinds: 1. The common A tent. 2. The wall tent. 3. The Sibley tent.

The last was found to be unsuitable, however, because so many men could be packed into it that it proved to be unhealthy for them.

A few built themselves framed and weather-boarded houses out of cracker boxes, of which a great many were brought to camp.

THE STREETS

There were three parallel streets one way, and perhaps a dozen intersecting streets. The streets were about twenty-five feet wide with a shallow ditch on each side, the middle being higher than the sides in order to drain off the waters from the rainfall. Each street was given a name. There was a Market Street, a Baltimore Street, a Wall Street, and so forth. The bed of the streets was packed hard by the feet of the men.

The whole body of prisoners was apportioned off into divisions and companies, 100 men to a company. Ten companies to a division, lettered from A to K. Thus making one thousand men to a division. In the summer of 1864, there were between 17,000 and 18,000 Confederate prisoners held here.

THE ENCLOSURE

The prison camp enclosure was directly upon the bay shore. It was quadrangular in shape, fenced on

three sides with a plank fence about fourteen feet high
with a parapet or observation platform arranged on the
outside, about four feet from the top for sentries who,
when on duty, could see over the top all that transpired
within. This platform extended completely around the
three fenced sides, and sentries with loaded rifles were
kept constantly walking back and forth on this raised
platform, day and night, so as to keep a strict watch
over the conduct of the prisoners; and a large number
of Federal guardsmen were kept always available for
succor at the slightest emergency call.

On the fourth side, that is on the water front, the
fence was much lower and no sentries were mounted
there. There were, on this side, two openings in the
fence leading to platforms extending some distance over
the water, and intended to serve certain hygienic purposes. Though there was no platform on this side, and
no marching sentinels, yet there were armed guards,
strategically located, constantly watching to prevent
escape, and three gunboats stood by in the bay a short
distance off the shore, their marines and crews ever ready
and watchful that no prisoner take French leave.

The main entrance to the enclosure was from the
west side opposite the bay shore or water front. This
entrance was made by leaving a space about twelve or
fourteen feet wide, and ten feet high, in the plank fencing
and fitting to the opening thus formed, a big double gate
which swung to and fro on hinges, affording ingress and
egress for horses and wagons; and there was also a
smaller gate for pedestrians.

This entrance was well guarded by a corporal's guard
always on duty; there was also a guardhouse close by;
and a regiment of negro infantry, some cavalry and a
battery of artillery were encamped immediately opposite.

The Commandant's Headquarters

The headquarters of the commandant in charge of the camp was a neat frame building just on the edge of the grove of tall pines which marked the Point from afar. In front of his house was a seawall built along the line of the beach, and upon this wall paced day and night, with monotonous tread, a sentinel right about facing and going through sundry mysterious motions with his musket, each time he turned.

Not far from the commandant's house was a double cottage used by the provost marshal of the camp as his business office and headquarters.

There was also in the vicinity a wretched barracks where boarders could be accommodated after a fashion. At times, relatives and friends came to visit the prisoners within the enclosure, and these could be, in a manner, accommodated at the barracks. Of course, these visitors were admitted only after scrutiny and questioning by the guard and sometimes they were required to be vouched for by some one known to the officer in charge.

The visitor from whose account of his visit to the camp in 1864, this description is largely taken, says:

"After the spring of 1864, no one was admitted, unless now and then a fanatic impersonating an honorable calling, with a black valise and a white tie, to lecture the prisoners on the ungodliness of secession, and to feed their hungry bellies with a goodly stock of tracts and pious admonition."

The Hospital

Outside the enclosure containing the prisoners were several long buildings used as barracks for convalescents, mess-room and for commissary purposes, while near the water were erected the several large wards of a general hospital, all the wards divergent from a central, covered, circular walk, from which access was convenient to every ward.

Indeed, the plan of the hospital was like a great wheel, the hub of which was roofed over and surmounted by a huge tank of fresh water, and the spokes of which were the several one-story structures used as wards for the sick and feeble of both armies, but mostly for the sick among the Confederate prisoners, of whom a large number were always present.

THE WHARF

There was a makeshift of a wharf at one side, extending some distance into the water, where vessels, desiring to load or unload, made fast. It was a sloppy, dirty wharf where came army wagons, soldiers, officers and gangs of shiftless and dismal-looking negroes clad in cast off uniforms. These would help to discharge cargoes in an indifferent, careless way, as if it were very little concern of theirs.

Sometimes a fog would settle down over the place and stay for hours, indeed at times, for days. At other times the sun shone brightly and the surface of the broad expanse of the mingling waters of the Potomac River and Chesapeake Bay, danced in wavelets in the sunlight. The distant Virginia shore could be seen on these clear days, but it offered little in the way of hope of escape for the unhappy prisoners, for it was several miles away, and the vigilance of the guards and sentries was unceasing.

Inside The Enclosure

But we have not yet been inside the enclosure except to note the streets and tents. The enclosure was of many acres extent, and that part of it, next to the entrance, about one-third of the whole, was divided off from the rest of the enclosed ground by a ditch and a sentry walk, across which no prisoners were permitted to come, except by leave and under observation.

This upper third was devoted to commissary buildings and mess-rooms for the prisoners; one mess-room for each division, and large enough to accommodate 300 men at a meal at one time. So that the mess had to be set three or four times in order to feed a division. As the men were usually fed but twice a day, this entailed no great hardship on the cooks and kitchen force.

Each company and each division of these prisoners was put in charge of a Confederate sergeant who was deemed trustworthy, and who mustered the men, called the roll, selected certain of them for special duty and acted as their representative with the authorities.

For these services, these sergeants were given certain privileges, extra rations and sometimes were favored with a parole that made them free for a time at least.

Inside the enclosure, beyond the mess-rooms was an open space, then the sentry walk along side the ditch, after that the pumps and wells, then another open space, and after that came the prison camp proper.

As already stated, this was laid off into streets and squares, with tents facing the streets, and certain of the squares assigned to each division, and marked or numbered so that given the division number and company letter, any prisoner sought could speedily be located.

THE PRISONERS

Here were to be seen the unfortunates who had been captured during the war. Many of them were mere lads, and some from almost every State in the Confederacy. They were mostly spare and sallow-looking fellows, with a woe-begone expression in their eyes that told of hardships long endured and of almost complete abandonment of hope. There they were sauntering about or standing, singly or in groups, talking, staring and *scratching*. Some were barefoot, others with badly worn shoes, shoes out at the toes, rundown at the heel, soles worn through. Only a small number wore fairly good footgear. Some were in their shirt sleeves, some in worn and torn garments, the rents tied together with string as best they could.

Some in cool weather wore blankets like a Mexican poncho, or for want of a blanket, an old quilt, or piece of carpet.

Their headgear was also motley. Some were to be seen wearing the blue kepi, others the stove pipe, yonder was a Quaker broad brim, there a Scotch cap, and still others wore non-descript slouch hats of all shades of color, black, brown, gray, weather beaten, torn, bandless, dirty. A few wore embroidered, velvet smoking caps, soiled and threadbare, but worn jauntily, nevertheless, and some others were bareheaded.

Altogether the prisoners inside the plank fence presented a motley scene, and one likely to excite sympathy. They looked so forlorn, woebegone, hopeless and helpless.

And over it all was the dirtiness and the drabness of everything. The tents themselves were weatherbeaten, brown and dingy, the garb of the soldier prisoners was faded and dirty, and the men grimy. Now and then could be seen one who seemed too gentle for his rougher comrades. A mother's boy petted, and unused to hardship. Too miserable, wretched and unhappy to survive very long such surroundings.

All were scratching, scratching, but obtaining scant relief from the pests that infested their clothing. At nearly all times, when the weather would permit, could be seen seated under the lea of the plank fence fifty or sixty of them, with their shirts off, busily engaged in trying to remove their tormentors one by one.

The food served in the mess-rooms was chiefly bread, a bit of meat and bean soup, served with little variation except occasionally a little cabbage or potato.

THE SUTLER'S BOOTH

Just outside the fence near the entrance gate was a sutler's booth with an open counter toward the gate, through the bars of which the sutler's offerings could be seen from inside. Here, when permitted to stand just inside the gate, would come a motley bunch to gaze longingly for hours at a cheese, a link of sausage or a jar of striped stick candy. They had no money, yet they seemed fascinated by the sight of the, to them, appetizing things to eat, which they craved and hungered for, but could not get. There they stood for hours looking wistfully, longingly, futilely, unavailingly. Oh, the misery of it all.

Two men sought their liberty by a foolhardy undertaking, attempting to dig a tunnel for escape under the highboard fence, They were caught in the act and promptly shot, as a warning to others like-minded.

Such is the "want and woe of war."

In connection with the aforegoing description of the prison camp at Point Lookout, a few excerpts from the diary of a prisoner there will be interesting.

Excerpts from The Diary of Bartlett Yancey Malone, a prisoner at Camp Lookout, Maryland. Edited by William Whatley Peerson, Jr.

The diary seems to be free of comment but records things as they happened, or as Malone understood them. He appears to have had no hard feelings toward anyone.

Malone writes that he was a private or top-sergeant in Company H, Sixth North Carolina Regiment. His own spelling and manner of speech is followed:

He says, "I was born January 22, 1838, in Caswell County, N. C. I inlisted June 18, 1861."

"October 5, 1863. One of the Yankee senternels shot one of our men the other day, he soon died. He shot him in the head for peepen threw the cracks in the planken."

"25 Dec. 1863. The 25th was Christmas day and was clear and coal and I was both coal and hungry, all day. We only got a peace of Bread and a cup of coffee for Breakfast and a small slice of meat and a cup of soup and five crackers for dinner. Supper I had none."

"16th Dec. 1863. A Yankee captain shot his pistol among our men and wounded five of them. Sence one has died. He shot him for crowding around the gate. The Captain's name was Sids. Him and Captain Patison and Sergeant Finegon was the three boss men of the prisoners' camp."

"The 31st which was the last day of '63 was a rainy day. And maby I wile never live to see the last of '64. And theirfour I will try to do better than I have. For what is a man profited if he shal gain the whole world and loose his own soul, or what shall one give in exchange for his Soul."

"1st Jan. 1864-5. at Point Lookout, M.D.   The morning was plesent but toward eavening the air changed and the nite was very coal.   Was so coal 5 of our men froze to death before morning.   We all suffered a great with coal and hunger two of our men was so hungry they killed a rat and cooked and eat it."

"6th Jan.   9 men died at Hospital today."

"The 10th was a nice day and I saw the man today that makes coffens at this plaice for the Rebels and he sais that 12 men dies here every day, that is averidgs 12."

"The Commandant at this point is named *Marsto*."

"22nd Jan.   I feasted today on crackers and coffee."

"17th Feb.   It was so cool we had to lye down and rap up in our blankets to keep from freazing for we had no wood to make fire."

"February 24.   too of the prisoners got killed the nite of the 24 they attempting to get away.   We were guarded 8 to 8 by 2nd & 5th & 12th N. H. Regiment until February 25 when 26th N. C. Negro Regiment was plaised guard over us."

"March 18.   Our beds at this plaise is composed of sea feathers, that is we gather the small stones and lye on them."

"O it was so coal the 18th."

"20th of March a Yankee Sergeant named Young shot one of our officers today for jawing him."

Sometimes Malone like Silas Wegg dropped into poetry.   Here are some examples:

> "Where ere you roam
> What ere your lot
> Its all I ask
> Forget me not."

> "All I lack of being a whale
> Is a water spout and a tail."

"May your days be days of pleasure
     May your nites be nites of rest,
May you obtain life's sweetest treasure
     And then be numbered with the blest."

"His purposes will open fast
     Unfolding every hour
The bud may have a bitter taste
     But sweet will be the flower."

"April 12. The 3rd Md. Negro regiment was plaised on guard around prison camp."

"When the Negrows from Carolina arrived they wore their knapsacks and when they was put on poust they peeled them off and laid them down at the end of the lines. And some of our men stole two of them. And when the negrow found it out he sais to the next one on poust. Efrum, white folks has stold my knapsack aredy. The other one sais they done stold mine too, but I a'int caring for the knapsack: All I hate about it is loosing Sophys Garotipe."

"One day two commenced fooling with their guns they had their guns cocked. Presently one of the guns went off and shot the other one threw the brest. he fell dead the other sais:—Jim, Jim git up from dar you ain't hurt you jist trying to fool me."

"29th Another Negro kill himself Shot himself in the mouth with a gun."

DIARY OF BARTLETT YANCEY MALONE

The excerpts from this diary and the description of conditions in the prison camp are not given place here as reflecting on the management of the camp or the treatment of the prisoners. At both North and South there were instances of brutality and inhumanity toward these unfortunates, but in the main it was the desire on both sides to treat prisoners humanely. Sometimes those in charge of these war-time prisons were cruel by nature and these had little regard for the comfort or welfare of those subject to their caprice, but such instances were the exception and not the rule, it is believed.

Malone's descriptions of conditions at Point Lookout prison camp are so artless and straightforward, and his method of spelling and of expression, so unique, that the excerpts from his diary, which was discovered in the Library of Congress, were deemed worthy a place in this history as expressive in an illuminating way of camp atmosphere and environment.

CHAPTER III

EARLY MOVING

In the summer of 1864 there were approximately 17,000 Confederates held at Point Lookout as prisoners of war, and it was these prisoners who, it was hoped, might be liberated and organized to co-operate with General Early in case he should succeed in capturing Washington.

In a letter written to President Jefferson Davis about this time, Lee mentioned what was in his mind in regard to those prisoners. Extracts from his letter follow:

Headquarters, Army of Northern Virginia,
June 26, 1864.
His Excellency, Jefferson Davis,
President Confederate States.

Mr. President—I have the honor to acknowledge the receipt of your letter of 25th inst.

General Hunter has escaped Early, and will make good his retreat. . . . . If circumstances favor I should recommend Early's crossing the Potomac. I think I can maintain our lines here against General Grant.

Great benefit might be drawn from the release of the prisoners at Point Lookout, if that can be accomplished. I think the guard there might be over-powered, the prisoners liberated and reorganized and marched immediately on the road to Washington.

Of the Marylanders connected with the army, I consider Colonel Bradley T. Johnson the most suitable for leader. . . . . At this time as far as I can learn, all the troops in the control of the United States are being sent

to Grant, and little or no opposition could be made by
those at Washington. . . . .
Very respectfully,
Your Excellency's obedient servant,
R. E. LEE,
General.

LEE TO DAVIS

That General Lee was giving much thought to the
possibilities of an attack upon Washington and the releasing of the prisoners at Point Lookout is shown by another
letter written by him to the President of the Confederacy
three days later:
Headquarters, Petersburg,
June 29, 1864.
His Excellency, Jefferson Davis,
President Confederate States.

Mr. President—I enclose for perusal a letter received
today from General Early. His general plan of action
is in conformity to my original instructions and conversation with him before his departure. . . . . The success of General Jos. E. Johnston, announced in the morning journals, besides its good general effect, will favor
Early's movement.
If it could be united with a release of the prisoners
at Point Lookout the advantages would be great. I believe the latter only requires a proper leader. Can one
be found? There will be time to shape Early's course
when he reaches the Potomac, as circumstances require. . . . .   R. E. LEE,
General.

The views of the commanding general expressed in
his letters to the President of the Confederacy concerning
Washington and Point Lookout were the same views
previously expressed by him to General Early at their
interview near Petersburg

TELEGRAPHED BRECKINRIDGE

After this interview Early immediately started his
corps (which had been formerly Ewell's) for Lynchburg
by way of Charlottesville. At the latter place Early sent
General Breckinridge the following telegram, which shows
somewhat the energy of the man:

Charlottesville, Va.,
June 16, 1864.
Gen. Jno. C. Breckinridge,
Lynchburg, Va.

See that railroad agents use promptness, energy and
dispatch. I will hold all railroad agents and employees
responsible with their lives for hearty co-operation with
us.

J. A. EARLY,
Lieutenant General.

Early arrived at Lynchburg with part of his forces on
June 17, 1864, at about one o'clock P. M. General Lee
at Petersburg, being anxious concerning the outcome of
Hunter's menace to Lynchburg, sent General Early the
following:

Headquarters, Army of Northern Virginia,
June 18, 1864.
Gen. J. A. Early,
Lynchburg, Va.

Strike as quick as you can and if circumstances
authorize, carry out original plan.

R. E. LEE,
General.

The original plan as we have seen was for Early to
dispose of Hunter, march down the Shenandoah, cross
the Potomac into Maryland, capture Washington, liberate the Confederate prisoners at Point Lookout, and

join them, when organized, to his own forces, thereby more than doubling them.

In reply to his telegram of the 18th of June, General Early sent Lee the following:

> New London, Va.,
> 9.30 A. M.,
> June 19, 1864.

General R. E. Lee.

General—Last evening the enemy attacked my lines in front of Lynchburg and was repulsed by the part of my command which was up. The enemy is retreating in confusion. If the cavalry does its duty, we shall destroy him.

> J. A. EARLY,
> Lieutenant General.

HUNTER RETREATS FROM BEFORE LYNCHBURG

Hunter, however, escaped into the mountains and his army was not destroyed. A little more than a week later General Hunter, from the mountains of West Virginia, sent to the adjutant-general at Washington the following message:

> Loup Creek near Gauley, W. Va.,
> June 28, 1864.

Adjutant General U. S. Army.

General—Running short of ammunition and finding it impossible to collect supplies while in the presence of the enemy, believed to be superior to our own forces in numbers, and constantly receiving reinforcements from Richmond and other points, I deemed it best to withdraw, and have succeeded in doing so, closely pursued by the enemy, but without serious loss, to this point.

> D. HUNTER,
> Major General, Commanding.

In his *Defenses of Washington* Major-Gen. J. G.
Barnard, at page 91, in speaking of Hunter's retreat
from the Valley of Virginia, says:

"But after crossing the mountains, the most expeditious route for that officer was to strike the Ohio, and
ascending by water to Parkersburg, to take the Baltimore
and Ohio Railroad. Low water in the river and breaks in
the road delayed him and he was *hors de combat* throughout all the events now described.

Hunter Escapes

After Hunter retreated beyond the mountains to the
Ohio River, General Early sent General Imboden with
a force of cavalry to destroy the Baltimore and Ohio Railroad above Martinsburg, and that officer had damaged
the road considerably as far west as Cherry Run, about
fifteen miles, and also slightly further up. This required
Hunter to disembark from the cars at Cherry Run and
to march from that place with his infantry on his return
several days later.

Hunter being thus removed from the Valley with his
army, there were no other Union forces to oppose Early's
march toward the Potomac, except two rather small
forces under Gens. Franz Sigel and Max Weber, operating about Harpers Ferry and Martinsburg; and these
Early promptly disposed of, as we shall see.

Hunter Is Driven From The Valley

In his *Memoirs* General Grant has this to say of the
situation about Petersburg and in the Valley of Virginia
at this time:

"After these events comparative quiet reigned about
Petersburg until late in July. The time, however, was

spent in strengthening the intrenchments and making our position generally more secure against a sudden attack. In the meantime, I had to look after other portions of my command, where things had not been going on so favorably, always, as I could have wished.

"General Hunter who had been appointed to succeed Sigel in Shenandoah Valley, immediately took up the offensive. He met the enemy on the 5th of June at Piedmont, and defeated him. On the 8th he formed a junction with Crook and Averell at Staunton, from which place he moved direct on Lynchburg, via Lexington, which he reached and invested on the 16th. Up to this time he was very successful; and but for the difficulty of taking with him sufficient ordnance stores over so long a march through hostile country, he would, no doubt, have captured Lynchburg. . . . . To meet this movement under General Hunter, General Lee sent Early and his corps, a part of which reached Lynchburg before Hunter. After some skirmishing on the 17th and 18th, General Hunter, owing to a want of ammunition to give battle, retired from before the place. Unfortunately this want of ammunition left him no choice of route for his return but by way of the Gauley and Kanawha rivers; thence up the Ohio River, returning to Harpers Ferry by way of the Baltimore and Ohio Railroad. A long time was consumed in making this movement. Meantime the valley was left open to Early's troops and others in that quarter; and Washington was uncovered. Early took advantage of this condition of affairs and moved on Washington. *Grant's Memoirs,* Volume 2, pages 303-4.

Early pursued Hunter for several days after the latter withdrew from before Lynchburg, but being unable to overtake him in force, and as he was all the time getting further and further away from his base of supplies, he finally gave up the chase and returned to the Valley, with Lee's suggestion about marching on Washington, and at the same time liberating the prisoners at Point Lookout still in mind.

On the morning of June 28, 1864, he moved down

the Shenandoah toward Harrisonburg, and passed through
that town, also through New Market, Mt. Jackson, Woodstock, Strasburg and Winchester, arriving at the latter
place on July 2. There General Early divided his corps
into two columns which marched from thence by two
different roads; Early himself, with part of his forces,
taking the road to Harpers Ferry by way of Charlestown.

Sigel And Weber Retreat

He took possession of Harpers Ferry from Gen. Max
Weber, who evactuated it, leaving behind him few valuable army stores. Weber took refuge on Maryland
Heights, an almost inaccessible mountain opposite the
Ferry, on the Maryland side of the river. Here he was
joined by General Sigel a few days later. Not being able
without great loss of time and men to capture the
Heights, Early left Sigel and Weber there in a manner
isolated on the mountain, and moved his forces across
the Potomac at Williamsport and Shepherdstown, the
latter crossing place being near the old Antietam battlefield.

General John B. Gordon was placed in command of
the other part of the corps, and moved by the highway
directly from Winchester to Martinsburg, West Virginia.
Winchester was noted for being distinctly Southern in
sentiment and sympathy, while Martinsburg, just 22
miles away, was just as distinctly and pronouncedly
Union.

Gorden arrived at Martinsburg on the evening of
July 3, and the next day drove the Union forces under
Gen. Franz Sigel off without much fighting, capturing
the town and a quantity of army stores, though Sigel

had succeeded in removing and destroying much of it before his departure. On the 4th Sigel retreated across the Potomac by way of Shepherdstown and took a position on Maryland Heights opposite Harpers Ferry, where General Weber had already gone the day before. Gordon then crossed the Potomac into Maryland. Five companies of the 38th Georgia Regiment were left at Martinsburg to guard army stores captured there. On July 6th Gordon's division drove the forces of the enemy more closely into their stronghold on Maryland Heights. Leaving a small Confederate force to hold Sigel and Weber in check, Early moved with his main force on the 8th of July over South Mountain, at Fox's Gap, Crampton's Gap and Boonsboro Gap into Middletown Valley, Maryland, about ten miles west of Frederick. Gen. Bradley T. Johnson's cavalry was in advance. Thus the greater part of Early's army was in Maryland, headed for Washington by way of Frederick, and yet so well were his numbers and his purposes concealed from the enemy that no one in the Federal cause knew how large or how small an army Early had, or whether Washington or Baltimore was his objective, or what his purpose was as to either.

UNEASINESS IN WASHINGTON

The following dispatches show how disturbing to the Federal officers and authorities this movement under Early was, the more so because the movement was clouded in mystery. Gen. Max Weber at Harpers Ferry sent the following to General Couch, commanding a small Union force at Chambersburg, Pennsylvania:

Headquarters,
Harpers Ferry, W. Va.,
July 3, 1864. 8 P. M.

Maj. Gen. D. N. Couch,
Chambersburg, Pa.

The enemy are reported 10,000 to 20,000 strong, with infantry, cavalry and artillery. Martinsburg is evacuated. . . . . . I have had no communication with General Sigel since 11 o'clock this morning. He is trying to reach Harpers Ferry. The enemy are reported to be moving toward the Potomac at Martinsburg.

MAX WEBER,
Brigadier General.

The following dispatch was received at Washington at noon on the 4th of July from John W. Garrett, the president of the Baltimore and Ohio Railroad, then at his office in Baltimore:

Baltimore, Md.,
July 4, 1864. 11.35 A. M.

Hon. Edwin M. Stanton,
Secretary of War, and
General H. W. Halleck,
Chief of Staff.

General Weber telegraphed me from Harpers Ferry, at 10.48 this morning that "the enemy are in sight. Two thousand cavalry and a force of infantry are in sight. . . . . If they press me I shall retire to the Heights." (Maryland Heights.)

At 11.05 our agent at Harpers Ferry telegraphs: "Great excitement here. All citizens are leaving. Harpers Ferry is being evacuated by the military. . . . ."

J. W. GARRETT,
President Baltimore and Ohio Railroad.

Later the same day Mr. Garrett sent another telegram to the Secretary of War at Washington:

Camden Station, Baltimore, Md.,
Hon. E. M. Stanton,   July 4, 1864. 3.50 P. M.
Secretary of War.

The telegraph operator at Point of Rocks reports that the enemy has crossed the river half a mile west of that point and is driving our men. We are unable to learn what force, the operator having left. Operator at Frederick advises that all wires west of that point have been cut.   JOHN W. GARRETT,
                                             President.

MR. JOHN W. GARRETT'S CONCERN

Mr. Garrett was evidently greatly concerned for the safety of the great railroad, of which he was president, and which indeed was an important factor in transporting troops and supplies for the Union Army from Baltimore to Harpers Ferry, Martinsburg, Cumberland and beyond. Late the same night he sent to the Secretary of War another dispatch from Baltimore, which was received near midnight:

Camden Station,
Baltimore, Md., July 4, 1864.
Hon. E. M. Stanton,   Received 11.50 P. M.
Secretary of War:

The force attacking Point of Rocks at 1 this P. M. consisted of about 150 cavalry. . . . . It is clear that if there is not a large rebel force they are being handled with great vigor and skill to make such numerous attacks at points so distant.   J. W. GARRETT,
                                             President.

At half-past four on the same date S. F. Adams, aide-de-camp to Brig.-Gen. Max Weber at Harpers Ferry, sent the following message to W. P. Smith, master of transportation of the Baltimore and Ohio Railroad at Baltimore:

Headquarters,
Harpers Ferry, W. Va., July 4, 1864.
W. P. Smith,   4.30 P. M.
Baltimore, Md.:

I have just received information from General Sigel
that he is with his troops from Leetown and Martinsburg,
at Shepherdstown. General Sigel will cross the river
tonight and march to Harpers Ferry. The enemy took
possession of Martinsburg at 1 P. M. yesterday. . . . .

S. F. ADAMS,
First Lieutenant and Aide-de-Camp.
By order of Brig.-Gen. Max Weber.

This 4th of July was a stirring time for all concerned.
A rebel army was invading Maryland, numbers unknown,
destination unknown, object unknown. Wherever the
wires in Maryland could be used, dispatches were flying
fast, to and fro. Located at Sandy Hook, a few miles
south of Harpers Ferry, was a regiment of Union soldiers,
the First Maryland Potomac Home Brigade, under command of Lieut.-Col. R. E. Cook. During the day the following dispatch from Colonel Cook was received at
Washington:

Headquarters First Maryland Regiment, P. H. B.,
Sandy Hook, Md., July 4, 1864.
Capt. H. M. Burleigh,
Assistant Adjutant-General:

Captain—The enemy is reported at Catoctin Switch,
four miles below Berlin (now Brunswick), destroying the
Baltimore and Ohio Railroad. Cannot reliably ascertain
their strength.

R. E. COOK,
Lieutenant-Colonel, Commanding Regiment.

News of Early's movement down the Shenandoah
Valley toward the Potomac River had been received at

Washington from time to time, ever since the 30th of June, but at first no one there seemed to take the movement seriously. It was thought that, except for a comparatively small force under Gen. John C. Breckinridge, operating in the Valley to oppose Gen. David Hunter's work of destruction, that General Lee was holding all the forces under his command at Petersburg to aid in the defense of that place, which, as we have seen, was being closely besieged by General Grant with all available Union troops.

Even after it became known that Hunter had been driven away from before Lynchburg, and had withdrawn his army for more than 150 miles into the mountains of West Virginia, it was not thought possible that General Lee would permit a large Confederate force to separate itself from the main body, undertake an invasion of Maryland, and attack the National Capital itself. It was believed that his whole thought and purpose was to use the Army of Northern Virginia to the best of his ability to defend the Capital of the Confederacy, and that he would not undertake so bold and far-reaching an enterprise as the capture of the Union Capital; the most feasible route to which, then open to the Confederates, being by way of Harrisonburg, Strasburg and Winchester, Virginia, fording the Potomac at Williamsport or Shepherdstown, and thence through Frederick, Maryland, a total distance of about 300 miles from the main Confederate Army, manning the defenses of Petersburg.

The first dispatches from Washington to General Grant at City Point, Virginia, were rather mild in tone and did not disturb him greatly. Here is one sent him on July 1 by the chief of staff:

Washington, D. C., July 1, 1864.
Lieutenant-General Grant,   1.30 P. M.
City Point, Va.:

There are conflicting reports about the rebel forces
in Shenandoah Valley.   H. W. HALLECK,
                    Major-General and Chief of Staff.

Grant replied to this telegram two days later, evidently after he had made inquiries on his own account, as to the probable size of the Confederate Army operating in the Valley, as follows:

City Point, Va., July 3, 1864.
Major-General H. W. Halleck,   5 P. M.
Chief of Staff,
Washington, D. C.:

There are no troops that can now be threatening Hunter's Department, except the remnant of the forces of W. E. Jones and possibly Breckinridge. *Early's corps is now here.*   U. S. GRANT,
                    Lieutenant-General.

The reference in the aforegoing dispatch to the remnant of the forces of W. E. Jones was to his army, which had been attacked by General Hunter at Piedmont on June 5, 1864, and badly defeated. Jones was a brigadier-general, but in the absence of Major-General Breckinridge was put in command of the Department of Southwestern Virginia temporarily. His forces were very much depleted at the battle of Piedmont, and he, himself, was killed.

GRANT AT CITY POINT

Two days after the aforegoing dispatch from Grant was sent to General Halleck at Washington, General

Meade, who was in immediate command of the besieging Union lines at Petersburg, fifteen miles away, obtained information that he deemed important from two Confederate deserters who were brought in and questioned by him, and he immediately sent the following dispatch to General Grant at his headquarters, City Point on the James River:

> Headquarters Army of Potomac,
> July 5, 1864, 1 P. M.
>
> Lieutenant-General Grant:
>
> *General*—Two deserters state that it is currently reported in Richmond and in Petersburg that Early, in command of two divisions of Ewell's corps, with Breckinridge in command, and other forces, was making an invasion of Maryland with a view of capturing Washington, supposed to be defenseless. It was understood that Early would reach Winchester by the 3rd inst.
>
> GEORGE G. MEADE,
> Major-General.

This message from General Meade had the effect of stirring Grant to action, but he was not yet alarmed, and deemed one division all that was necessary for the defense of Washington. He accordingly sent the following telegram to General Meade:

> City Point, Va., July 5, 1864.
>
> Major-General Meade,
> Commanding:
>
> Send in one good division of your troops and all the dismounted cavalry to be forwarded at once.
>
> U. S. GRANT,
> Lieutenant-General.

The next day he sent the following message to General Halleck, chief of staff, at Washington:

City Point, Va., July 6, 1864,
3 P. M.

Major-General Halleck,
Washington, D. C.:

A part of force directed by me to go north is already off and the whole will be in an hour or two.

U. S. GRANT,
Lieutenant-General.

The same evening Grant's chief quartermaster sent General Meigs, quartermaster-general at Washington, the following message:

Headquarters,
City Point, July 6, 1864.

M. C. Meigs
Quartermaster-General,
Washington, D. C.:

Ricketts' division of about 5,000 infantry are embarking here today for Harpers Ferry by way of Baltimore.

RUFUS INGALLS,
Brigadier-General, Chief of Staff

GEN. LEW WALLACE
Commander-in-Chief of the Federal forces at the
Battle of Monocacy.

CHAPTER IV

INTRODUCING MAJOR-GENERAL LEW WALLACE

On March 12, 1864, several months before General Early's army corps was detached from the defenses about Petersburg for the purposes already mentioned, Major-Gen. Lew Wallace had been assigned to the command of the Eighth Army Corps, U. S. A., of the Middle Department, with Baltimore as his headquarters.

General Wallace was born at Brookville, in Franklin County, Indiana, April 10, 1827. His father was David Wallace, a graduate of West Point. The younger Wallace was studying law when the Mexican War commenced, and, suspending his studies, he entered the service of the Government as a first lieutenant.

After this war he completed his studies and was practicing his profession at Crawfordsville when the Civil War began. He became adjutant-general of the State, and went to the front as colonel of the 11th Indiana Infantry. In June, 1861, as colonel of the 11th Indiana Zouave Regiment, he guarded the Baltimore and Ohio Railroad, the great line of communication with the West, between Cumberland, Maryland, and Romney, West Virginia, and for his bravery and vigilance in the discharge of this duty he was commended by General McClellan and others, and rewarded with a commission as brigadier-general.

As brigadier he led a division in the siege of Fort

Donelson, in February, 1862, and rendered conspicuous service. For his services here he was promoted to major-general. In the battle of Shiloh he was again conspicuous for his gallantry. In recognition of these distinguished services General Wallace was, in March, 1864, put in command of the Eighth Army Corps, as stated.

The troops under his command were not more than 2,500 men, and were largely raw and inexperienced in warfare. General Wallace's department included Delaware and Maryland as far west as the Monocacy River, which was the dividing line between his own department and that of Gen. David Hunter, who commanded in the Department of West Virginia.

These troops of the Middle Department, under Gen. Lew Wallace, were the only Federal forces east of the Monocacy River that could be immediately used to impede the progress of Early's march upon Washington.

As said by General Grant in his *Memoirs*, "Sigel was held at Maryland Heights by a small force from Early's command, and the only Union troops available to arrest or impede the progress of Early was the small body of raw troops commanded by Gen. Lew Wallace."

Mr. John W. Garrett Calls

The first intimation that General Wallace had of the oncoming of an army of Confederates threatening an invasion of Maryland was on July 2, when Mr. John W. Garrett, the president of the Baltimore and Ohio Railroad, called at his headquarters in Baltimore and spoke of the great importance of maintaining open for traffic the line of the railroad, and mentioned especially the railroad iron bridge over the Monocacy River at Frederick Junction. The only important information Mr. Garrett had, or at least then imparted to General Wallace, was that certain station agents along the line of the railroad between Harpers Ferry and Cumberland had notified him of the appearance near those stations of detachments of Confederate troops.

In that conversation Mr. Garrett reminded General Wallace that Gen. Christopher C. Augur, in command of the Department of Washington, had not under his command more than enough troops to keep the peace in that city.

Mr. Garrett suggested that General Wallace at Baltimore and General Augur at Washington unite in defending the line of the railroad, the operation of which was not only important to the railroad company, but to the Federal Government as well. General Wallace replied that there were objections to his going west of the Monocacy because there his department had its western boundary, but he promised to assume guardianship over the iron bridge at Frederick Junction, or Monocacy Junction, as it was frequently called. He stated to President Garrett that there was a block house on the eastern bank of the river, with two guns in it, and that these covered the bridge and would be used, if necessary, to protect it.

Mr. Garrett was a man of prominence, and as the head of a great railroad system his visit disquieted General Wallace no little. No information had yet been received by him of General Hunter's withdrawal from before Lynchburg on June 18, or of his further withdrawal from the Valley of Virginia, leaving that valley open to the enemy. Although the adjutant-general's office at Washington had been notified of Hunter's retreat by the 28th of June, yet no such information had been communicated to General Wallace. The next day, July 3, he consulted his adjutant-general, Samuel B. Lawrence, at headquarters in Baltimore, and was told by him that according to the newspapers, General Hunter had crossed the mountains into the Kanawha Valley. He was therefore several hundred miles from strategic points in the great Valley of Virginia.

General Wallace then spread out a map on his desk and at a glance took in the dangerous situation. Said he to General Lawrence:

"What is to prevent General Lee from sending a large detachment from Petersburg and seriously attempting the capture of Washington."

General Lawrence answered, "Nothing, if he sees the opportunity." To which Wallace replied, "He is reckoned among the great soldiers, and it will not do to count upon his not seeing the opportunity."

Later the same day, that is on July 3, the following dispatch was received at the headquarters of the Middle Department at Baltimore:

Martinsburg, July 3, 1864.
Gen. Lew Wallace
Baltimore, Md.:

I have reports of an advance of the enemy in force down the Shenandoah Valley. His advance is now at Winchester.

F. SIGEL,
Major-General.

Acting upon this information, General Wallace immediately ordered Gen. E. B. Tyler, who was then at the Relay House, near Baltimore, in command of the

First Separate Brigade of Wallace's Corps, to proceed to Monocacy Junction with his command to reinforce the two companies of infantry already occupying the block house at that place. And also to send out scouts to ascertain, if possible, the location and numbers of the enemy.

General Tyler took train over the Baltimore and Ohio Railroad from the Relay for Monocacy Junction that night, and upon arrival there assumed charge of the block house protecting the railroad bridge over the Monocacy River. The next day he sent General Wallace at Baltimore this telegram:

Monocacy, Md., July 4, 1864.

Major-General Lew Wallace,
Commanding Middle Department,
Baltimore, Md.:

General Weber reports that the rebel cavalry under Major-General Ransom is said to be marching on Williamsport. . . . . The enemy's strength is extravagantly estimated. It would be folly to give figures.

E. B. TYLER,
Brigadier-General

This telegram was forwarded by General Wallace to Major-Gen. Henry W. Halleck, chief of staff at Washington, and by him forwarded to General Grant at City Point, Virginia.

Still General Grant was not convinced of any emergency arising at Washington requiring any greater force for the defense of that city than was available there under General Augur. Indeed, as already stated, he seemed to believe it impossible that General Lee would detach any considerable force from the defenses of Petersburg for such an hazardous undertaking.

General Lew Wallace At Baltimore

Consequently the commander of the Middle Department felt obliged to rely entirely upon the small forces
of his own command to defend the railroad bridge at
Monocacy, so important to be maintained, and at the
same time to stop, if possible, the march of the Confederates toward the Capital City. These forces, as we have
seen, numbered not more than 2,500 men, mostly of short
experience and training.

The situation placed a weighty responsibility on the
shoulders of the commander of the Middle Department.

Later the same day General Wallace received from
General Tyler at Monocacy Junction, saying:

"Operator at Point of Rocks says the enemy have
crossed the Potomac, one-half mile west of that point.

General Lew Wallace At Monocacy

What was his duty in the circumstances? How many
of the enemy were there? What was their real purpose?
As commander of the Middle Department, what should
he do in the circumstances?

He resolved to leave his headquarters in Baltimore
and go at once to Monocacy Junction. Accordingly, he
sent a request to President Garrett for a locomotive to
be ready at midnight to take him to that place, and to
arrange the movement of trains so that this engine should
have the right of way. Because he considered General
Halleck, the chief of staff at Washington, to be not
entirely friendly toward him, he kept his departure from
Baltimore a secret, as far as possible, for the time being,
at least. He feared he might be censured for leaving his
headquarters in Baltimore without permission of his

superior, and yet he consoled himself with the thought that the east bank of the Monocacy was in his department, and he was merely going to the western limit of his department to perform to the best of his ability whatever duty circumstances might require of him.

So a little after midnight of July 4 he climbed into the cab of the locomotive standing in readiness for him on an outer track of the railroad near Camden Street Station. One of his staff officers accompanied him, Lieutenant-Colonel Ross.

The engine made a fast run, and when it stopped just east of the bridge over the Monocacy, darkness still covered the earth, except for the stars shining overhead. Saying good-bye to the engineer, he stepped down from the cabin of the locomotive and was met by an officer from the block house, who led him and Colonel Ross to bunks within, and later, after a short rest, they were given a soldier's breakfast. It was now early in the morning of the 5th of July, 1864.

Immediately after breakfast General Wallace sent for Gen. E. B. Tyler and inquired of him what information he had concerning the enemy. The general replied that it was all guesswork as to the strength, but that it was put at from 5,000 to 30,000 men, with Early, Gordon, Breckinridge, Ransom and Bradley T. Johnson in command, and nobody seemed to know the position of the invading army.

All this shows how well the Confederate general in charge of the invading forces had been able to conceal his strength, his numbers and his purpose.

Late at night on the fifth several local citizens whom General Wallace had requested to go as private citizens, westerly from Frederick, over the mountains to ascertain, if possible, the strength and character of the rebel force, returned bringing him the news that by whichever road they separately sought to go over Catoctin Mountain, they were halted and turned back by squads of Confederate horsemen.

This indicated cavalry pickets on the several roads leading into Frederick, probably curtaining an army in motion not far behind. That army, it was clear, was moving toward Washington and possibly toward Baltimore. But only Washington as an objective seemed to justify the risks of the undertaking.

General Wallace, in his *Autobiography*, says that he knew Washington to be defenseless, as well as Baltimore, and that he felt it to be his duty, with his small force, to undertake to stand at the Monocacy and impede as far as possible the progress of the invading army.

Concerning the situation within the Capital City, he has this to say:

"At the Navy Yard there were ships making and repairing, which, with the yard itself, would be given over to flames. In the Treasury Department there were millions of bonds printed, and other millions signed ready for issuance. . . . . There were storehouses in the city filled with property of all kinds, medical ordnance, commissary, quartermaster, the accumulation of years, without which the war must halt, if not stop for good and all.

"Then I thought of the city, the library, the beautiful Capitol, all under menace—of prestige lost, of the faith that had so sublimely sustained the loyal people through years crowded with sacrifices unexampled in history, now struck dead—of Louis Napoleon and Gladstone hastening to recognize the Confederacy as a nation. Certainly these were calamities, everyone of them, in the category of what would happen if Washington fell; yet, strange to say, not one or all of them projected itself in the swarming of my thoughts, with such instantaneous hardening of purpose as an apparition of President Lincoln, cloaked and hooded, stealing like a malefactor from the back door of the White House just as some gray-garbed Confederate brigadier burst in the front door."

Accordingly, he says, he determined to stand at Monocacy and fight. In this determination he says he had three objects in view:

1. To make the enemy disclose his strength.
2. To make him disclose where he was going.
3. If to Washington, to stay him long enough to enable General Grant at City Point to forward his troops for the defense of the city.

No higher authority or superior officer directed him as to what he should do. He had to decide for himself, on his own initiative, the momentous question. It meant standing his own small, ill-trained, hastily-gathered force in the way of an experienced army of as intrepid soldiers as ever faced a cannon, marching upon the Capital of the Nation, bent upon its capture.

In his *Autobiography* General Wallace says that the fight which he made at Monocacy was the most trying and most important incident in his life. Especially trying because it was undertaken upon his own judgment and responsibility, without an order from any of his superiors, and without their knowledge.

After the war General Wallace devoted himself to literary pursuits and became famous as an author. His most famous literary production being *Ben Hur—A Story of the Christ*. But the difficult position he was placed in at Monocacy, of deciding whether to imperil the lives of his small, ill-trained army in the effort to stay Early's march upon Washington, with a larger and more experienced military force, or to retreat, was "the most trying and most important incident of his life." To retreat was to abandon his guardianship of the most important railroad iron bridge over the Monocacy, and leave open the way for Early's unhindered advance upon Washington. To stay and fight meant the loss of many human lives, and much human suffering. The only object to be gained thereby being the delay of an invading army. He had no expectation of being able to defeat Early or to turn him back, but merely to impede his progress toward the National Capital long enough to give time for reinforcements to be sent to the defense of that city, the capture of which would be fraught with such fearful consequences to the cause of the Union, for which so much blood had already been shed and so great treasure already expended.

CHAPTER V.

THE BATTLE GROUND

Before proceeding with an account of what further transpired between the two hostile forces daily getting nearer to each other, it may be well to describe the region where, within a few days, a short, sharp, and bloody battle is to be fought.

THE MONOCACY RIVER

The Monocacy River has its source in southern Pennsylvania, its headwaters flowing through the battlefield of Gettysburg and its several branches uniting about the Mason and Dixon Line to form the river. Its course is in a general southerly direction, through Frederick County, with many bends and curves, as its Indian name implies. It finally empties its waters into the Potomac River about ten miles below the railroad iron bridge at Frederick Junction. This winding river drains a large and fertile valley known as the Frederick Valley.

FREDERICK CITY

Located in the middle of this extensive valley, about three miles west of the river, is Frederick City, the county seat of Frederick County, and at the time of the war, a city of some 10,000 inhabitants. Five miles west of Frederick is the Catoctin Mountain, beyond which, west, six miles across the Middletown Valley, is South Mountain, where was fought September 14, 1862, another battle of the Civil War.

Frederick is an historical city, famed as the home of Francis Scott Key, Thomas Johnson, Revolutionary patriot and first Governor; Roger Brooke Taney, Chief Justice of the United States; Winfield Scott Schley, hero of Santiago during the Spanish-American War, and of Barbara Fritchie, heroine of Whittier's poem. All of these heroes and the heroine, except the hero of Santiago and Taney, lie buried in beautiful Mount Olivet, where fine monuments have been erected to the author of the national anthem, and to the heroine of Whittier's poem.

FREDERICK CITY IS A GREAT HIGHWAY CENTER

Frederick City is a great highway center. Indeed, it would be difficult for persons travelling by highways from the Shenandoah Valley across the Potomac on the way to Washington or Baltimore, to avoid passing through Frederick, for all roads from the West and Southwest lead to Frederick, and thence on to those big cities.

The Monocacy River is east of Frederick, and the two great highways leading by divergent courses, out of the city, eastwardly, one to Baltimore and one to Washington, cross the Monocacy on bridges about three miles east of the city, and two and a half miles apart.

THE JUG BRIDGE

The Baltimore turnpike road crosses on a fine stone bridge built about 1815, when the national highway from Baltimore to Cumberland, and on to Wheeling, was constructed. At the eastern end of the bridge is a vase-shaped structure, about eight feet higher than the bridge itself, built of stone and cement, from which peculiarly shaped structure, the bridge is known to everyone in the community as the "Jug Bridge." By this road, the distance from Frederick to Baltimore is about 46 miles, the road passing through New Market, Ridgeville, Lisbon, and Ellicott City, Maryland.

THE WOODEN BRIDGE

The Washington highway crosses the Monocacy, as stated, about two and one-half miles south, or down stream from the stone bridge, and about three miles from the city. At the time of the battle of Monocacy, the bridge carrying the Washington highway across the stream was an old, wooden affair, but strong and substantial, weatherboarded and covered with a shingle roof. The bridge was perhaps 250 feet long, 50 feet wide, and 16 feet high, with heavy arched timbers on each side and in the middle and a line of heavy supporting timbers running through the middle its entire length and thus dividing the bridge into two driveways, one for eastbound and the other for westbound traffic.

This bridge was located down stream about 300 yards from the railroad iron bridge, the safety of which was of so much concern to President Garrett of the Baltimore and Ohio Railroad.

THE RAILROAD BRIDGE

The railroad bridge over the Monocacy was a well-proportioned structure with a double track on the top and heavy iron supports, props and struts under the cross ties, on which the tracks were laid. There were no side rails for protection of pedestrians, and one in walking across, would have to walk on the cross ties, except that there was a narrow footway of boards through the middle. It was against the rules of the company for any pedestrian to cross the bridge, except employees. This was because of the danger of meeting trains on the bridge, which would oblige the pedestrian to leave the narrow footway and to use only the cross-ties of the other track, with no protection whatsoever at the side, and the ties far enough apart to make walking unsafe. The top of the bridge was about forty-five feet from the water below.

Besides the three bridges mentioned, there were several fords across the Monocacy, one a short distance upstream from the Jug Bridge was known as Hughes' Ford, another, about three-fourths of a mile down stream, or south from Jug Bridge was known as Reich's Ford. A little farther down the river was still another, known as Crum's Ford. The next crossing south, about a mile distant, was the railroad iron bridge, already mentioned, and below that, in plain view, about three hundred yards distant, was the wooden bridge, on the Washington Road. There was also a ford a hundred yards below the wooden bridge, that was very much used after the bridge was burned.

THE WORTHINGTON-McKINNEY FORD

About a mile below the wooden bridge was still another ford. This may be called the Worthington-McKinney Ford. It was here that the main Confederate Army crossed, on that hot summer day, July 9, 1864, just before the short, sharp and bloody encounter which took place between the two contending forces in the afternoon of that memorable day. There were other shallow places in the stream, which were fordable, but those named were the ones that had been used as fords, previously, and were then readily accessible.

THE EASTERN BANK OF MONOCACY

Along the eastern bank of the Monocacy, above the railroad bridge, there is a steep bluff or hill extending northward toward the stone bridge, a greater part of the distance. This bluff is so bold, at many places, as to be impassable to a climber, and from it, looking toward Frederick, one can view a large area of the fertile valley lying between him and the city, and beyond, even to the Catoctin Mountain. South of the railroad, on the east side of the Monocacy, is a small valley through which runs, in a northwesterly direction, Bush Creek, which empties into the Monocacy midway between the iron bridge and the wooden bridge. In this little valley was located Gambrill's flour mill which, in its palmy days, was operated regularly by the water power derived from Bush Creek.

The Gambrill property abutted on the Monocacy at the mouth of Bush Creek, just south of the Baltimore and Ohio Railroad, and extended from thence to the Georgetown road. Across the road, south, lay the hill field of the Thomas farm, and next south, on the same side of the river, lay another field on same farm, then came the Worthington farm, which was separated from the Thomas farm by a long straight dividing line, along which was erected a good post and rail fence. This fence ran obliquely from the river in a southwesterly direction from a point a short distance below the wooden bridge; and along this fence, and on the east side of it, was posted a part of Ricketts' Division of the Union Army on the morning of the day of the battle. This division fence represented in a general way, the front line of the Federal forces at the beginning of the battle, and it was here that the first attacks by the Confederates were made. Later in the day Ricketts' left was driven away from this fence. Even after being driven away at the left of the line, the right of Ricketts' line clung to it as a sort of barrier to the enemy, until finally driven back, late in the afternoon. The mansion house on the Worthington farm is located about three hundred yards east from the river and further over, eastward, about a half-mile distant, is the mansion house on the Thomas farm. Both these dwellings are of brick, with a large cellar under each. In the Worthington house, the cellar windows are above ground about three feet.

The Baltimore and Ohio Railroad

The Baltimore and Ohio Railroad crosses the Monocacy westerly on the iron bridge, then turns in a southerly direction and runs along about a quarter of a mile west of the river, for a distance of several miles, then bears away in a southwesterly direction and runs on to Point of Rocks, thence up the northern bank of the Potomac nearly to Harpers Ferry where it crosses into West Virginia.

The Battle Ground—The Y

At Frederick Junction there is a branch road leading from the main line, northerly, into Frederick, three miles away. For the convenient use of this branch, there is a railroad Y at the junction; there is also a railroad station-house, two stories high, the downstairs being then used for railroad and telegraph offices, while the upstairs rooms were used as dwelling apartments for the family of Mr. Frank Mantz, the railroad manager stationed there.

THE TRIANGULAR FIELD

At the west end of the iron bridge, there is a high railroad fill for a distance of a hundred yards or more, to raise the flat land on that side of the river, to a level with the tracks on the bridge; then as the railroad line passes on west, it runs through the end of a small hill, and here is rather a deep cut. The fill and cut, in continuation of each other, form an excellent breastwork, probably three hundred yards long, extending from the west end of the iron bridge to a small wooden bridge, carry the Georgetown Road over the railroad, which may be called the over-pass bridge. Near this bridge, close to the Georgetown Road and about one hundred yards north of the western end of the long wooden bridge over the Monocacy, had been erected by the Federal Government, a substantial blockhouse for defense purposes. In and around this blockhouse, and behind the embankment made by the fill and cut above mentioned, a small force of Federals, under Captain George Davis, was able to hold off, during the day, a much larger force of Confederates under General Ramseur, who sought to make a way for the passage of the invading army across the wooden bridge. But of that later on.

A BLOCKHOUSE

It might be well to explain here that a blockhouse is a square structure built of heavy timbers with loopholes in the sides for rifle fire. The one mentioned as standing on the west side of the river was also surrounded by a circular palisade of upright poles, planted in the ground and about twelve feet high, for its better protection.

RIFLE PITS

Because of the railroad bridge over the Monocacy, a most important span in the line of the Baltimore and Ohio Railroad, and because of the wooden bridge nearby carrying the main highway to Washington over the river at that place, Frederick Junction was deemed a strategic point during the Civil War, or War between the States, as it is more appropriately called. Two block-houses had been constructed there by the Federal Government, and rifle pits had been made along the east bank of the Monocacy River for a considerable distance above the railroad bridge, on the steep bluff that runs along that side of the river, and also both above and below the wooden bridge. These were all close to the river bank and were designed to protect the defenders of these bridges. Traces of these rifle pits or intrenchments are still discernible after sixty years and more. The block-houses have been completely destroyed. One was burned the day of the battle and the other on the east side of the river was sold to Mr. Gambrill after the war and removed.

CHAPTER VI.

WEDNESDAY, JULY 6, 1864

WALLACE CONCENTRATES HIS FORCES

Having resolved to stand and fight, General Wallace began to concentrate his whole corps at and near the east end of the railroad iron bridge over the Monocacy. About noon on July 6, a train arrived from Baltimore bringing Colonel Landstreet and his regiment, the Eleventh Maryland. They encamped near Gambrill's Mill. The same train also brought Lieut.-Col. Lynde Catlin, Lieut.-Col. Alexander Bliss, and Capt. Maxwell Z. Woodhull, all of the general's staff. Col. James R. Ross, of his staff, was already with him.

GENERAL WALLACE'S HEADQUARTERS

At first General Wallace's headquarters were in the blockhouse at the east end of the iron bridge but they were soon after transferred to a small dwelling house just across the railroad, it being the second house on the south side of the railroad tracks, east of the bridge.

A MESSAGE FROM SANDY HOOK

About noon of July 6, the telegraph operator at Frederick Junction, just across the railroad bridge, brought to headquarters the following telegram from Gen. Franz Sigel, at Sandy Hook, Maryland:

Sandy Hook, Md.,
July 6, 1864.

Major-General Lew Wallace,
Monocacy Junction, Md.

The enemy appears to be moving in strong force toward Frederick: size of numbers not yet ascertained. . . . . F. SIGEL,
Major-General.

Sandy Hook is a small town on the Baltimore and Ohio Railroad about one mile below Harpers Ferry. At this point the railroad approaches close to the Chesapeake and Ohio Canal and Potomac River, and except for the one highway passing through from Harpers Ferry to Knoxville, and the railroad, whose trains seldom stop there, it is a rather inaccessible place, because of the steep hill sides to the north of it, and the canal and river to the south. No Confederates, on this invasion appear to have passed that way.

THE CONFEDERATES REACH THE POTOMAC

The Confederates had chosen to cross the river into Maryland by the fords at Shepherdstown and Williamsport. These fords are about eight and twenty miles, respectively, up stream from Harpers Ferry.

"MARYLAND, MY MARYLAND!"

It is related that, as they waded across the stream, some one with a bass voice, raised the song of "Maryland, My Maryland," and one by one, the weary, perspiring soldiers, worn by their long marches along the dusty roads, in a sweltering heat, but refreshed by contact with the waters of the river, joined their voices to those of their comrades, until the whole army was singing as it crossed, the words of that stirring song.

The appeal was to Maryland to join the Confederacy. As her northern boundary touched along its entire length the strong Union State of Pennsylvania, and its southern boundary was along the south bank of the Potomac in the equally strong Southern State of Virginia, the people of Maryland were very much divided in sentiment. Maryland did not secede but she furnished many soldiers for the South as well as for the North, during the four years struggle, and it was still hoped by some that she would yet join the Confederacy.

Here are some of the stanzas of the hymn:

Come, for thy shield is bright and strong,
 Maryland, My Maryland!
Come, for thy dalliance does thee wrong,
 Maryland, My Maryland!
Come to thine own heroic throng,
That walks with liberty along,
And Give a new *Key* to thy song,
 Maryland, My Maryland!

Dear Mother! burst the Giant's chains;
 Maryland, My Maryland!
Virginia should not call in vain,
 Maryland, My Maryland!
She meets her sisters on the plain,
"Sic Semper" 'tis the loud refrain
That baffles minions back amain,
 Maryland, My Maryland!

I see the blush upon thy cheek,
 Maryland, My Maryland!
But thou wast ever bravely meek,
 Maryland, My Maryland!
But lo there surges forth a shriek
From hill to hill, from creek to creek,
Potomac calls to Chesapeake,
 Maryland, My Maryland!

I hear the distant thunder hum,
    Maryland, My Maryland!
The Old Line bugle, fife and drum,
    Maryland, My Maryland!
She is not dead nor deaf nor dumb,
Hurrah! She spurns the Northern call,
She breathes! She burns! She'll come, She'll come.
    Maryland, My Maryland!

THE CONFEDERATES CROSS THE POTOMAC

The Confederate Army appears, from the most available data, to have forded the Potomac on the 4th and 5th of July. It was probably the 6th before they were all across.

In the van was Gen. Bradley T. Johnson of Baltimore, with a brigade of Confederate cavalry and also Gen. John McCausland, with another brigade of cavalry. These were several miles in advance of the infantry and artillery.

COLONEL CLENDENIN

On the 6th of July, the intelligence reached Wallace's headquarters at Monocacy that Col. David R. Clendenin, with five squadrons of Union Cavalry, was scouting in the neighborhood of the mouth of Monocacy. This cavalry was part of General Augur's command, but not withstanding, General Wallace sent a messenger to request Colonel Clendenin to report at his headquarters. At the same time, he sent a request by telegraph to General Halleck, chief of staff at Washington, for permission to use this cavalry.

CHAPTER VII.

THURSDAY, JULY 7, 1864

However, Colonel Clendenin responded immediately to General Wallace's request, and appeared at his headquarters early on the morning of the 7th, before daylight. He had ridden with his men, 230 in number, through the night, knowing that in warfare, time is of the essence.

Clendenin was a tall, fine looking man, and quick of discernment. He commanded the Eighth Illinois Cavalry, and acceded at once to the request that he go to Frederick and beyond, to Catoctin Mountain to ascertain what he could, concerning the enemy.

TRYING TO ASCERTAIN THE CONFEDERATE NUMBERS

A part of General Wallace's defensive weapons consisted of six Parrott three-inch rifles, finely horsed and equipped, known at the "Baltimore Battery," and commanded by Capt. Frederic W. Alexander.

Two of these guns Colonel Clendenin was told he might take with him on his reconnoissance.

Of course, the colonel might have refused the mission assigned him because he and his forces belonged to another department. But he did not hesitate. He simply asked when the guns would be ready. Later on he received a telegram from General Halleck directing him to report to General Wallace, and to obey his orders, but he did not wait for that. He saw the necessity of immediate action, and responded to the mere request.

General Wallace sought to impress upon the Colonel the importance of the mission upon which he was going, and told him that no one yet knew how strong the enemy was, or what his object, but that the salvation of the Capital depended on troops being sent up from City Point by General Grant. The colonel stated that he would be ready to start out as soon as his horses were fed, and the men had a bit of breakfast. This was the morning of the 7th of July. The two Parrott rifles were got ready, the horses were fed, the men ate an early breakfast, and at daylight, Colonel Clendenin set out. He had with him 230 mounted men and the two pieces of artillery, horsed and manned.

THE FIRST GUN

On the bench by the blockhouse, on the bluff at the iron bridge overlooking the beautiful Frederick Valley, General Wallace waited. In his autobiography, he says:

"All under a cloudless sky lay in a shimmer of sunshine. The wheatfields, the houses, the barns, the visible church spires—everything, describable and indescribable, entering into the composition of the scene, lent it a homelike sweetness peculiarly attractive; and it was having its effect on me when I heard the report of a distant gun, muffled to be sure, but from the right direction, and distinctive in that it seemed dropped from the sky, high up, as I fancied it would come, if at all.

"I started to my feet and listened. Then another gun! An interval—and then the third gun, echo like and fainter, because farther down the mountain side! There could be no mistake. Clendenin had found the enemy! The occupants of the blockhouse rushed out and lined the bluff. There was shouting from the men in bivouac in the low grounds back of the wooden bridge. My officers joined me; and presently we were all silently intent upon the exchange of shots going on in the west.

"The difference in sound became more noticeable, and we knew in a short time that those plainest to the ear were Clendenin's. Now he was on the summit—now he was on the hither side. I took to the bench again. There was nothing to do but wait."

The shots which were heard at the blockhouse at Monocacy Junction were being fired on Catoctin Mountain, eight miles distant, and beyond Frederick City several miles. It was then 10 o'clock A. M., July 7.

General Wallace further says:

"An hour passed and then a courier from Frederick galloped thunderously across the wooden bridge, and with a stoppage or two to make inquiry brought up in front of me. The dispatch he delivered was on a pocket scratch-book leaf, in pencil—'. . . .' It was dated, 'Catoctin Pass, July 7, 1864, 10.15 A. M. . . .' Half an hour later another courier brought a second dispatch, which was as follows:

"I have abandoned the pass. Am falling back towards Frederick. A strong skirmish line of two hundred and fifty men advanced on my skirmishers, which I could not spare force to meet, and protect my flanks at the same time. A mounted force of at least a squadron moved to the left and an equal force has gone through on Harpers Ferry pike. I will be in Frederick in two hours."

Besides the "Baltimore Battery" under Captain Alexander, there was already at the block house a big brass howitzer, brought there for the protection of the iron bridge some time previously. This was now mounted in a hastily constructed demi-lunette on the very brow of the bluff, where, through its broad embrasure, the howitzer possessed lines of fire commanding every possible approach from the west.

Thus preparations went forward for the struggle which was impending and could not be long delayed.

Until this moment General Wallace had no forces at his command except the 2,500 men composing the Eighth Army Corps, and Colonel Clendenin's Cavalry, and he had no intimation that any reinforcements were to be sent him from anywhere. Yet, with his small force of inexperienced men, he resolved to resist the onward march of the rebel host; numbers unknown, destination unknown, purpose unknown.

Brig.-Gen. E. B. Tyler was sent to the stone bridge on the Baltimore pike to take charge of the forces guarding that road. Col. Charles Gilpin, commanding the Third Maryland Regiment, and Captain Alexander, with three of his guns, were sent forward to Frederick to take position west of the town and support Colonel Clendenin's Cavalry, which was falling back slowly.

These reinforcements to Colonel Clendenin were shipped by a special train over the three-mile branch railroad from the Junction to Frederick.

ANOTHER DETACHMENT OF CAVALRY

About noon a body of horsemen, two hundred and fifty strong, fragments of the First New York Veteran Cavalry, and also an organization called the Independent Loudoun County Rangers, reported to General Wallace, and were all sent to Frederick by the highway to support Colonel Clendenin, who had fallen back before the cavalry advance-guard of Early's army, to a position just west of Frederick, where he had been joined by

Colonel Gilpin and Captain Alexander.   At this place a stand was made.

At four o'clock on the afternoon of the 7th the rebel cavalry with several pieces of artillery advanced close enough to open with its artillery, and a right furious cannonading went on between the opposing forces for several hours.   Finally the small arms were brought into use, and quite a hot skirmish continued until eight o'clock, when Gilpin and Clendenin charged the enemy and drove him back toward the foot of Catoctin Mountain, or at least he retired under fire.

Thus closed the contest on July 7 at nightfall.

CHAPTER VIII

REINFORCEMENTS SENT

Let us now turn our thoughts for a short while upon what is transpiring at City Point on the James River, in Virginia. As already stated, General Wallace was wholly unaware that General Grant had taken any action toward sending reinforcements from the besieging army before Petersburg to aid him in repelling the invasion.

But, as a matter of fact, General Grant had already been moved by the message from General Meade to order one division sent in from the lines before Petersburg to City Point for shipment north, as shown by his telegram to General Halleck, dated July 6, 1864, already quoted. The division sent was the Third of the Sixth Army Corps, under command of Gen. James B. Ricketts.[1]

Grant was still of opinion that the Confederates were not in formidable numbers, and that these were then in the neighborhood of Harpers Ferry, and so he ordered the transports to Baltimore, where the troops were to debark, and take the cars of the Baltimore and Ohio Railroad to Harpers Ferry, which is perhaps seventy miles from Baltimore and twenty miles or more west of Monocacy Junction. But at that time, before the so-called "Metropolitan Branch" of the railroad had been built, all westbound trains from Baltimore to Harpers Ferry were obliged to pass over the main line and over the iron bridge at Monocacy.

The Ride Up The Bay

Several transports were required to carry this division of 5,000 men from City Point to Baltimore. Some of these transports appear to have left City Point loaded with troops on the evening of the 6th of July. Some on the morning of the 7th.

Moreover some of the boats were faster than others, and the faster ones passed the slower ones on the way up the Bay, consequently their arrival at Baltimore was at different hours and at varying intervals.

In a *History of the 87th Pennsylvania Volunteers,* which regiment was a part of Ricketts' Division, and one of the regiments "sent in" to go to Harpers Ferry by way of Baltimore, at page 174, the marching in from the lines before Petersburg, and the progress on the water is thus described:

"Early on the morning of July 6, just as the sun was rising, this division (that is Ricketts' Division) with two days' rations began the march. The roads were dusty, the sun was hot, and before they had reached City Point, a distance of twelve miles, the blue uniforms of the soldiers were thickly covered with the dust of old Virginia. At City Point they embarked for Baltimore. The 14th New Jersey and part of the Eighth Pennsylvania, with Col. W. S. Truex and his staff, boarded the steamer Columbia at noon, and sailing down the James River they reached Fortress Monroe at 9 P. M. While passing through Hampton Roads, where the Monitor defeated the Merrimac, two years before, the Columbia anchored for half an hour. The ride up the Chesapeake was delightful, for the weather was cool and bracing and the air invigorating. The military band of the Eighth played its best selections, including 'Maryland, My Maryland,' and the men of both regiments applauded.

"Some of the men fell into a deep, sound sleep early in the evening, while others sat on deck and watched the soft rays of the moon shed a liquid light over the placid waters of the Bay. . . . .

"The Columbia anchored at Locust Point at 12 o'clock noon, July 7, after a trip of 250 miles down the James River and up the Chesapeake to Baltimore. Orders were given to remain on board until the transports came up, bringing the balance of the division. One of them arrived at 6 P. M. (the 7th). . . . . The Star, one of the later transports to leave City Point, arrived at Fortress Monroe at midnight of July 6, remaining there till early dawn the next day, and reached Baltimore at 1 A. M. of the 8th."

A WATER TRIP

Another interesting account of the movement from the trenches before Petersburg to Baltimore is given in *The Ninth New York Heavy Artillery* by its author, Alfred Seelye Roe, beginning at page 120:

"On the 6th come orders to pack up and start for City Point; at 9 P. M. the boys were on their way, and they marched nearly all night through indescribable dust. Every face in the morning looked like it wore a mask.

"They board the steamer Thomas Powell at 9 P. M. and are delighted to be free from the dust for a short time. Few know or care about the object of the change from land to water; but they are grateful for a little vacation.

"The ride down the James on the 7th of July was an oasis in the campaign's desert. To be sure, much of interest along the river's banks was passed in the night, but we touched at Fortress Monroe; we saw the tip of a ship's mast, flag surrounded, above the water of Hampton Roads, and we were told that it was that of the Cumberland, destroyed by the Merrimac, March 8, 1862. . . . . The vessels bearing the division do not keep together; indeed some troops, including the division commander, are distanced, and the Scriptures are again vindicated, for the last has become the first.

"This trip up the Bay could not have been more pleasant, though our boat had been a stock transport, and still bore unmistakable traces of the stable. As we passed the mouth of the Potomac it became evident that Washington was not our destination. . . . . Many letters were written, and it was not an infrequent sight to see a score of lines trailing along behind the boat. To each was attached at least one soldier's shirt; we were not fishing, though some did suggest live bait for the sharks. It was an opportunity to give one's garments a good soaking and their denizens a pickling, and we felt cleaner for the operation.

"Night shut down upon us while we were still steaming southward (down the James River), and we gave ourselves to dustless sleep. Early on the morning of the 8th of July we were docked somewhere, but no one seemed to know just the place. The rising sun soon disclosed such an abundance of chimneys and steeples that we were sure Baltimore was the name, and our impressions were soon confirmed."

The Columbia, bearing the 14th New Jersey and part of the 87th Pennsylvania, was the first to arrive at Baltimore. As soon as the arrival of this transport was known to President Garrett he telegraphed General Wallace at Monocacy as follows:

Camden Station, Maryland,
July 7, 1864.

Major-General Lew Wallace,
Monocacy Junction.

A large force of veterans arrived by water and will be sent immediately. Our arrangements are made to forward them with the greatest possible dispatch.

JOHN W. GARRETT.

Mr. Garrett was evidently not aware that the reinforcements were destined for Harpers Ferry. Their arrival at Baltimore was not, however, generally known in that city, so when General Wallace telegraphed his adjutant to "Rush the veterans just arrived forward," he replied:

"I don't know what you mean by the veterans just arrived."
Wallace replied: "See President Garrett."

How welcome was this news to the commanding general at Monocacy, who had already resolved to stand and fight with only 2,500 men, may well be imagined.

This telegram from Mr. Garrett was received during the afternoon of July 7, but night came without the arrival of any veterans. The skirmish west of Frederick was ended, and so the commanding officer betook himself to his headquarters for rest, and sleep, if possible to be had.

(1) James Brewerton Ricketts was born in New York City, June 21, 1817; he graduated at West Point in 1839; served in the war against Mexico; and when the War Between the States began was placed in command of the first battery of rifled guns. He distinguished himself in the battle of Bull Run, where he was severely wounded, taken prisoner, and confined eight months in Richmond, when he was exchanged. He was then made brigadier-general of volunteers; was in the second battle of Bull Run, in which he commanded a division of the Army of Virginia, and was again wounded; in the battle of Antietam he commanded General Hooker's corps after that officer was wounded. He was engaged in the campaign against Richmond in March, 1864, and after Monocacy in the Shenandoah campaign until October of that year. He was breveted brigadier-general, United States Army, for gallantry at Cedar Creek, and major-general for meritorious service through the war, and was retired because of wounds in 1867. He died in Washington, D. C. September 22, 1887. (From *Harpers Encyclopedia of United States History*.)

BRIG.-GEN JAMES B. RICKETTS,
Commanding Third Division, Sixth Army Corps,
U. S. A., at the Battle of Monocacy. This divi-
sion bore the brunt of the fighting on the
Federal side.

CHAPTER IX.

THE TENTH VERMONT ARRIVES

The small house along the railroad near the iron bridge taken over for General Wallace's headquarters was bare of furniture. There were no chairs or camp stools, no cots, and but one table. There were blankets, and the general and the members of his staff would lie down from time to time, in the hope of getting sleep, but the anxiety concerning the coming of a train from Baltimore, carrying some portion of the expected reinforcements from City Point, made it impossible for any to sleep.

Several times the general walked to the bluff, but in the moonlit expanse around him, discovered nothing indicative of war or armies. "Everywhere was a deep and all-pervading hush."

Finally he went back into his headquarters, lay down on his pallet of boards and blankets, and fell asleep. Not long, however, was he allowed to repose. An orderly presently waked him and said:

"I hear a train in the direction of Baltimore."

As the instructions from General Grant at City Point, were that troops sent by him should proceed to Harpers Ferry by way of Baltimore, it was doubtful if the train would stop at the iron bridge over the Monocacy. So Col. James R. Ross of the general's staff was instructed to flag any train approaching from Baltimore, and bring it to a stand near the headquarters.

The coming train was flagged and stopped, and Col. William H. Henry of the Tenth Vermont, alighted.

"By what authority do you stop me?" he asked. To which Wallace replied, "Have you no orders to stop here?" "None!"

Then Colonel Henry was told of the near approach of a Confederate Army under Gen. Jubal Early. This information changed his attitude immediately, and he expressed willingness to take orders.

CHAPTER X.

FRIDAY, JULY 8, 1864

It was then early in the morning of July 8th. The men of the Tenth Vermont were ordered out of the cars for breakfast.

Very quickly, they were off. In a few minutes a hundred little fires could be seen, each with a black pot in the blaze, or hanging from a cross-stick, and each surrounded by a group of hungry soldiers, whose handiness with coffee-pot and skillet betokened the veteran.

Within an hour, the men had partaken of their soldier's breakfast and were back in the cars. The regiment was ordered to Frederick to reinforce Colonels Catlin and Clendenin, the whole force being placed in command of Gen. E. B. Tyler; its position being just west of Frederick across the Hagerstown Road, almost the same position held by the smaller force the day before.

The Confederates could be seen a mile and a half away toward Catoctin Mountain. They were at a halt, apparently awaiting reinforcements. Small clouds of dust on the mountain side, five miles beyond, indicated the coming of these reinforcements.

Now and then could be heard by the waiting Federals, the sound of bugles, and the sharp yelp of many voices.

The rebel yell.

About 10 o'clock in the morning, July 8, a squadron

of cavalry left the main body and advanced along the highway toward Frederick.

Reaching a hollow place in the road, the horsemen disappeared, and when they reappeared they were dismounted and advancing as skirmishers.

Then the larger body, halted in the distance, began to move forward. Then a Confederate gun broke the quiet pervading all the field, and a shell came hurtling over the Yankees' heads.

SKIRMISHING WEST OF FREDERICK

Almost immediately a rifle from Alexander's battery replied. Then another from the Confederates, and another from the Parrott gun.

The Federal videttes rode in and soon the skirmishers had gotten near enough to each other to fire. Neither side made any energetic advance and the firing was desultory. Evidently the rebels were not intending to make an attack. Still it was no play, for men on both sides could be seen limping to the rear. Cannon and rifle fire went languidly on for several hours.

Once during the day, the advance guard of the rebel army went forward to closer range, and firing was more brisk, but they soon retired, and there was another lull in the operations. Indeed, while a real attack seemed probable in the morning, as the day wore away, it became evident that these dismounted rebel skirmishers were merely engaging the Federals' attention while the larger movement beyond the mountain was in progress.

Beyond the mountain was Middletown Valley and concealed from view, the whole Confederate invading army was moving toward Frederick.

There are three principal roads from Middletown

Valley over Catoctin Mountain into Frederick Valley. One, the main road from Hagerstown; another, a road toward the south, through Jefferson and one north of the Hagerstown Road through Shookstown.

General Wallace in his *Autobiography*, states at page 142, that he was with his forces west of Frederick during the skirmishing just narrated, and says:

"Meantime I kept my glass busy searching the purpling face of the mountain, and about 4 o'clock, was rewarded by catching sight of three long, continuous, yellow cloud lines, apparently on as many roads, crawling serpent-like down toward the (Frederick) Valley. Watching first one and then the other, I fancied I could now and then see a flag gleaming faintly through the dust. There could no longer be room for doubt; what I saw were columns of infantry, with trains of artillery. Good strong columns they were, too, of thousands and thousands. I called to Tyler: 'Look yonder! That is what the fellows in our front have been waiting for. They think we will stay to be taken in. We will disappoint them. Tonight, we will go back to the junction. Only keep your counsel. I will give you the word.'"

FREDERICK RESIDENTS UNDISMAYED

That the skirmishing of July 8 was not alarming to the inhabitants of Frederick may be gathered from the following incident related by General Wallace:

"In the midst of the flurry, someone called my attention to people perched on a fence back of the line toward town. There were women and children in the crowd.

" 'Good heavens!' I cried out. 'Those people are in the range of the bullets. Ride, some of you, and order them away.'

"Someone spoke up: 'It is useless. They were here all day yesterday. We tried driving them off, but they would not go.'

" 'They must go. Some of them will be hit.'

"Several officers thus urged, hurried off, and riding up and down, exerted themselves to disperse the assemblage. But persuasion and threats were in vain.

"I could think of but one explanation of the very remarkable indifference to danger thus displayed. Frederick City and the region around it had been a playground for the game of war from its first year and the people had grown so used to it in all its forms that even battle had ceased to have terrors for them."

Finally the sun went down and the Confederates, who had carried on the desultory firing, having retired, all skirmishing ceased. A noticeable quiet settled over the valley, the more noticeable because of the distracting noises of shot, and shell, and shout, that had rent the air during the day.

CHAPTER XI.

WALLACE POSTS HIS FORCES

In his memoirs already referred to, General Wallace says:

"Then I sent for General Tyler and we talked over the situation. I said, 'The enemy is moving on our left. It is evident to me that he wants the pike from Frederick to Washington, which means Washington; and he will get it unless we can hold him back long enough for General Grant to send a corps or two from City Point. The enemy outnumbers us, that is plain, but because we don't know how much, we must fight. At all hazards, we must fight'."

Gen. E. B. Tyler was then ordered to take command of the 2,500 men belonging to the Eighth Army Corps, and to post them on the east side of the Monocacy River, facing west, on the hills and bluffs on that side, extending from the railroad iron bridge northwardly to the Jug Bridge and beyond, a distance of about two and one-half miles, thus guarding the fords and bridge above the iron bridge as far as Hughes' Ford. This army under General Tyler thus would defend Crum's Ford, Reich's Ford, the Jug Bridge and Hughes' Ford. The most important of these crossings being the Jug Bridge on the great highway from Frederick to Baltimore.

This bridge General Tyler was told to hold against all attacks, for if a crossing should be effected there, the enemy would cut off retreat by that route, and might envelop the whole army.

During the night of July 8 all the Union forces were withdrawn from Frederick by way of the Baltimore pike to the east side of the Monocacy, and there at the Jug Bridge was posted a part of the force for the defense of that crossing, while other detachments moved down the river on the east side to the fords, and still others to the neighborhood of Wallace's headquarters at the east end of the railroad iron bridge and near the wooden bridge on the Georgetown Road.

General Wallace thus describes his retirement from Frederick:

"The town undoubtedly had its disloyal faction, bitter to vituperation; in counter balance, however, it had its legion, devoted soul and purse to the Union. And it was hard abandoning them. In fact, I remember few circumstances in my life more trying."

"Our way was along the Baltimore pike. Crossing the river at the stone bridge we turned to the right, and with some stumbling through the dark, deepened by the trees overhanging the road, at last regained headquarters at the junction."

It was near midnight when headquarters were reached, and inquiry was made of Col. Lynde Catlin, of the general's staff, as to what arrivals in the way of reinforcements had already come from Baltimore.

Here is a list of the arrivals during the day of the eighth:

106th New York—Capt. Edward Paine, commanding.
151st New York—Col. William Emerson, commanding.
14th New Jersey—Lieut.-Col. C. K. Hall, commanding.
87th Pennsylvania—Lieut.-Col. J. A. Stahle, commanding.

This constituted the First Brigade of the Third Division of the Sixth Army Corps, under Col. William S.

Truex, except the Tenth Vermont Colonel Henry, which had arrived early in the morning, and was then moving from Frederick to bivouac with the other regiments.

It was estimated that these five regiments made up a force of 2,500 men or about one-half the whole force sent from City Point.

Wallace then lay down in his meagerly furnished headquarters and tried to sleep. But the impending events were too weighty to permit sleep.

About one o'clock in the morning of the 9th, a train from Baltimore arrived, bringing Gen. James B. Ricketts, the commander of the Third Division of the famous Sixth Army Corps.

He was a man slightly above the average height, a little inclined to be corpulent, quick and bluff in manner and speech; Celtic in feature and complexion.

After a handshake with General Wallace, the two began to talk at once of the business before them.

General Ricketts: "Is Gen. Jubal Early here?"
General Wallace: "Yes, at Frederick, three miles from here."
"How many men has he?"
"His numbers are variously estimated from twenty- to thirty thousand."
"What are you going to do?"
"Fight."
"How many men have you?"
"Twenty-five hundred of my own department. How many have you?"
"About five thousand."
"That's first rate. Seven thousand five hundred against thirty thousand."
General Ricketts: "What are your objects in fighting here?"
General Wallace: "I have three. First, I want to know for sure whether he is on his way to Washington or

to Baltimore. Second, I want to push aside the curtain
of mystery as to his numbers. Here he has marched all
the way from Lynchburg, and no one knows what his
forces consist of. Third, if Early's objective is Washington, I want to detain him here thirty-six or forty hours.
That will give General Grant ample time to get a corps
or two into Washington and make it safe. General Grant
is the only hope and we must give him notice and time."

General Ricketts: "We will stay here. Give me your
orders."

The aforegoing is substantially the conversation between the two officers, as narrated in the *Autobiography,*
page 752, *et seq.*

The conversation then turned to the placing of the
troops, that were to combat the approaching army of
invaders under General Early. As the principal attack
of the enemy was expected against the wooden bridge on
the Georgetown Road or against the fords below the
bridge, in the effort to reach the National Capital, it was
deemed important that General Ricketts' veterans should
occupy that part of the defense line where the brunt of
the battle was likely to fall. So he was instructed to
place his brigades on the ridge or hill extending from
the wooden bridge obliquely from the river in a southwesterly direction towards Brooks' Hill and the Thomas
house.

His right was to form a liaison with the left of
Gen. E. B. Tyler's command, which as we have seen had
been posted, as directed by the commanding general,
north of the railroad along the bluffs of the river all the
way to the Jug Bridge on the Baltimore turnpike and
beyond. Thus the whole Eighth Corps constituted the
right wing of the defending army while General Ricketts'
seasoned fighters from the intrenchments around Peters-

burg, consisting of the Third Division of the Sixth Corps, were to constitute the left wing.

The plain road to Washington was over the Georgetown highway which crossed the river on the wooden bridge and to prevent the Confederates from using this easy means of advance toward their goal, the defense of this bridge was deemed of prime importance. To this end rifle pits had been dug along the river on the east side extending at right angles with the highway a considerable distance both above and below the bridge.

During the night of July 8 several more regiments from the army besieging Petersburg arrived at Monocacy and joined the forces already on the ground. These were the residue of the Third Division, Sixth Army Corps, commanded by Gen. James B. Ricketts, except that by some misunderstanding or from a want of proper information, the 67th Pennsylvania, part of the 122nd Ohio, and the Sixth Maryland Regiments were held at Monrovia eight miles away from the Monocacy, and they did not therefore participate in the battle. Just why they did not reach the battlefield has not been very satisfactorily explained. They came all the way from before Petersburg by dusty roads, by water and by rail and reached within a few miles of the place where the fight occurred and yet were not in it. The railroad train bearing them stopped at Monrovia and they got no further.

The regiments actually arriving during the night at Frederick Junction were as follows:

9th New York Heavy Artillery—Col. William H. Seward, Jr.
110th Ohio—Lieut.-Col. Otho H. Binkley.
122nd Ohio (detachment)—Lieut. Charles J. Gibson.
126th Ohio—Lieut.-Col. Aaron W. Ebright.
138th Pennsylvania—Major Lewis A. May.

This constituted the Second Brigade of Ricketts'
Division and was under the immediate command of Col.
Matthew R. McClennan.

The First Brigade had arrived the day before and
its composition has been given a few pages back.   Col.
William S. Truex commanded this brigade.

Before it was yet broad daylight, Ricketts' men had
partaken of a hasty breakfast which they themselves
prepare at their hundreds of little camp fires; and under
the direction of Col. James R. Ross, of General Wallace's
staff, were being posted on that part of the field assigned
them by the commander-in-chief.

Col. William S. Truex, commanding the First Bri-
gade, was placed on the left of Ricketts' line, near the
Thomas house and at the intersection of the Georgetown
Road with the Baker Valley Road.

Col. Matthew R. McClennan, commanding the Second
Brigade, was placed on the right of the line.   His men
occupying the hill field on the Thomas farm, just southeast of the Monocacy, and near to the southeastern end
of the wooden bridge.

Several of his regiments were in the valley behind
the ridge near Gambrill's Mill, and some were further
west at the turn in the old Georgetown Road and behind
the fence running up over the hill at that place.

Later a skirmish line was thrown out in front extend-
ing from the hill field at the fence all the way to the
Baker Valley Road.   This line faced west toward the
Worthington house on the next farm.

Besides these brigades Colonel Clendenin was scouting on both sides of the river with his 230 cavalrymen
and sending information of the movements of the enemy
to General Wallace at headquarters.   When the fighting

was going on, a little later, Colonel Clendenin's force was placed at the left of Ricketts' line near the junction of the Baker Valley Road with the old Georgetown Road.

The Triangular Field

In order to defend the wooden bridge at its northwesterly approach, and to prevent the Confederates from crossing there, several companies were sent across the river to occupy the triangular field on that side, lying between the Georgetown highway on the west, the Monocacy River on the southeast, and the Baltimore and Ohio Railroad on the north. It should be remembered that there was a good, strong block house in this field near the highway, and that the heavy fill west of the railroad bridge, and the cut in the ground a little further west, together with the block house, afforded excellent protection to a defending force from an attack on the north and west, and it was from the north and west that the attacking force must come, that is from the direction of Frederick City.

The companies sent across the wooden bridge over the Monocacy and posted chiefly in this triangle, though some were in the field west of the highway, were the following:

Companies C and K of the First Maryland Regiment, Potomac Home Brigade, under the command of Capt. Charles J. Brown.

Seventy-five picked men from the Tenth Vermont Regiment of Volunteers under command of Lieut. George E. Davis, of Company D.

Company M, Ninth New York Heavy Artilley, under command of Capt. Anson S. Wood.

There were also for part of the day two companies from the 106th New York under Captain Parker.

Captain Brown's men occupied the blockhouse on that side of the river. This was so located as to enable its garrison to defend the small wooden bridge over the railroad tracks, that might be called the over-pass bridge, as well as the wooden bridge over the river. It was between the two bridges and close to the highway. This defensive body of about 350 men constituted the whole federal fighting force on the west side of the river at that place. Their backs were toward the stream and their faces toward Frederick. The most ready way to retreat in case retreat became necessary, was by way of the wooden bridge over the Monocacy.

Of the six pieces of artillery in Alexander's battery, three were with General Tyler's command above the rail road, and three with General Ricketts'.

Besides the guns of Alexander's battery it must not be overlooked that there was also a brass howitzer mounted on the bluff just east of the railroad iron bridge. This howitzer was in a position to cover with its fire, the fields and highway over and along which the Confederates must pass on their way from Frederick to the wooden bridge over the Monocacy, on the road to Washington.

Such was the arrangement and disposition of the Union forces at the Monocacy, near Frederick Junction, on the morning of July 9, 1864.

CHAPTER XII

EARLY'S OWN ACCOUNT

Meanwhile the cavalry, the infantry the wagon trains and the artillery constituting the Confederate Army under General Early were making their way southeastward by several roads all converging at Frederick. General Sigel was temporarily isolated at Maryland Heights; his generalship being deemed so poor by those above him that on July 7 he was superseded in command by Brig.-Gen. Albion P. Howe.

It seems desirable at this point to introduce General Early's own account of his movements. In his account of his operations in the Valley of Virginia and in Maryland to be found in *Battles and Leaders of the Civil War,* Volume 4, page 492, etc. published by the Century Company in 1888, General Early says:

"On July 2nd we reached Winchester. On the 3rd we reached Martinsburg which Sigel evacuated. Sigel retreated to Maryland Heights and on the night of the 4th the enemy evacuated Harpers Ferry. Breckinridge crossed the Potomac at Shepherdstown. Rodes and Ramseur crossed on the 6th. On the 7th Rodes moved through Rohrsville and Crampton's Gap to Jefferson. McCausland occupied Hagerstown and levied $20,000 on it. An effort to release the prisoners at Point Lookout and unite them with my command, was to be made.

"Breckinridge moved over South Mountain through Fox's Gap and Ramseur with trains through Boonsboro Gap, followed by Lewis Brigade of North Carolinians.

"Early on morning of July 9th, 1864, Gen. Bradley T.

Johnson in command of cavalry was directed to move northeast by way of Libertytown, strike the railroads, burn the bridges and also to cut the railroad between Washington and Baltimore. Then to move to Point Lookout for the purpose of releasing the prisoners, if we should succeed in getting into Washington.

"The other troops moved toward Monocacy Junction. General Wallace was found strongly posted on the east bank of the Monocacy near the Junction, with earthworks and two blockhouses commanding both the railroad bridge and the bridge on the Georgetown pike. Rodes was directed to demonstrate against the bridge over the Monocacy on the Baltimore pike. Ramseur was to try the strength of the enemy at the wooden bridge on Georgetown road. The enemy's position here was too strong and the difficulties of crossing the river at this bridge, under fire, too great to attack in front without greater loss than I was willing to incur. I therefore made an examination in person to find a place or ford which could be crossed so as to take the enemy in the flank.

"While thus engaged I discovered McCausland in act of crossing the river with his brigade of cavalry. As soon as he crossed, he dismounted his men and advanced rapidly against the enemy's left flank which he threw in confusion. . . . . . but the enemy concentrated on him and he was forced back. . . . .

"McCausland's move, which was bravely executed, solved the problem for me, and as soon as I discovered it, orders were sent to Breckinridge to move up rapidly with Gordon's division to McCausland's assistance. This division crossed . . . . and Gordon was ordered to move forward and strike the enemy on his left flank and drive him from his position covering the crossing in Ramseur's front, so as to enable him and the whole army to cross.

"This movement was executed under the personal supervision of General Breckinridge and while Rodes and Ramseur were skirmishing in front, with the enemy, General Gordon in gallant style and with the aid of several pieces of King's artillery which had crossed over, and Nelson's from the opposite side, threw the enemy into confusion and forced him from his position."

GORDON'S ACCOUNT

This is the account of the commander of the expeditionary force. It is very general and gives few details of the important battle, the real battle, which was fought on the east side of the Monocacy on the afternoon of July 9, 1864.

Gen. John B. Gordon, in his account and report says:

"About 2.30 P. M. I was ordered by Major-General Breckinridge, commanding corps, to move my division to the right and cross the Monocacy about a mile below the bridge and ford on the Georgetown Pike, which was then held by the enemy. On reaching the river I directed my brigade commanders to cross as rapidly as possible, and then to file to the left in the direction of the enemy's line, and I rode to the front in order to reconnoiter the enemy's position. I found that Brigadier-General McCausland's cavalry (dismounted) had been driven back by superior numbers, and that the enemy was posted along the line of a fence on the crest of a ridge running obliquely to the left from the river. In his front lay an open field which was commanded by his artillery and small arms to the extent of their range, while in his rear ran a valley nearly parallel with the general direction of his line of battle. In this valley I discovered, from a wooded eminence in front of his left, another line of battle in support of the first. Both these lines were in advance of the Georgetown road. The enemy's line of skirmishers covered the front of his line and stretched far beyond it to the left.

"Having been ordered to attack this force, I had the division skirmishers under Captain Keller, of Evan's Brigade deployed, and directed one brigade (Evan's), under the protection of a dense woodland about 700 yards in front of the enemy's left, to move by the right flank and form, so as to overlap the enemy's left.

"The two brigades (Hayes' and Stafford's), united under command of Brig.-Gen. Zebulon York, were ordered to form on the left of Brigadier-General Evans, and Brig.-Gen. William T. Terry's brigade to move in support of the left of my line. These dispositions having been made,

I ordered the command to advance in echelon by brigades from the right."

This force under Gordon was soon to meet in a bloody contest the veterans under Ricketts, who had been waiting in the fields of the Thomas and Worthington farms, the oncoming of the invading army since the early morning of that hot July day.

CHAPTER XIII

ALARM IN WASHINGTON

Meanwhile the officials at Washington were in a state of great alarm. Telegrams received by the Secretary of War, Mr. Edwin M. Stanton; by the Chief-of-Staff, Major-Gen. Henry W. Halleck; and by the Adj.-Gen. E. D. Townsend, telling of the onward march of a large Confederate army toward the National Capital caused the greatest anxiety there.

General Lew Wallace on the 4th had sent the following to the Adjutant-General's office:

Baltimore, Md., July 4, 1864.
Colonel E. D. Townsend,   3.30 P.M.
Assistant Adjutant-General.

Telegram just received from Gettysburg:—Rebels are in Hagerstown in force coming down the valley.

LEW WALLACE,
Major-General Commanding.

The President himself was greatly distressed. He held a conference with Secretary of War and others, after which the following telegrams were sent to the Governors of several Northern States:

71/74   War Department, July 5, 1854.
Governor Curtin,   3.20 P. M.
Harrisburg, Pa.

The President directs me to call on you for 12,000 militia or volunteers to serve at Washington and vicinity for 100 days unless sooner discharged.

EDWIN M. STANTON,
Secretary of War.

War Department, July 5, 1864.
4.20 P. M.

Hon. Horatio Seymour,
Governor,
Albany, New York.

The President directs me to inform you that a rebel force, variously estimated at from 15,000 to 20,000 men, have invaded Maryland and that the public safety requires him to call upon the state executives for a militia force to repel the invasion. He therefore directs me to call upon you for a militia force of 12,000 men from your state to serve for 100 days and that you will with the utmost dispatch forward the troops to Washington by rail or steamboat, as may be the most expeditious.

EDWIN M. STANTON,
71/75   Secretary of War.

Governor Curtin replied to the telegram received by him as follows:

Harrisburg, Pa., July 5, 1864.
5.10 P. M.

Hon. E. M. Stanton,
Secretary of War.

I have made proclamation for 12,000 men as requested in your dispatch of this afternoon, and will do all in my power to enlist the men in the shortest possible time.
71/75   A. G. CURTIN,
Governor.

To the telegram received by him, Governor Seymour sent the following reply:

Albany, N. Y., July 5, 1864.

Hon. E. M. Stanton,
Secretary of War:

Your dispatch received. I will do all I can. Orders sent to the commanders of the State National Guard.
71/78   HORATIO SEYMOUR.

Besides the urgent appeals to the governors of New York and Pennsylvania, telegrams were sent to General Grant at City Point for succor.

Grant was not easily excited and was slow to respond. Indeed his information was to the effect that Early's corps was still behind the fortifications at Petersburg.

In a paper read by First-Lieut. Edgar S. Dudley, of the Second U. S. Artillery, before the Ohio Commandery of the Military Order of the Loyal Legion, he has this to say of the state of mind of official Washington where he was stationed at the time:

"There is no doubt that he (Grant) was entreated, implored, almost commanded by frightened officials, to come to Washington, for the demoralization at that time was extensive." At another place, he says: "The alarm in the city was intense."

Two days before, Grant had telegraphed from City Point to General Halleck: "Early's Corps is now here." meaning behind the fortifications at Petersburg. It was his information that Early, after chasing Hunter out of the valley from before Lynchburg, had returned to Petersburg with his corps, to join Lee in the defense of that beleaguered city. But on the same day these urgent dispatches for help were sent to the governors for succor, General Grant ordered in one division of the Sixth Army Corps to go to Baltimore by boat and thence to Harpers Ferry by rail. He evidently deemed this force sufficient to repel any probable invasion of Maryland at that time. This division was on its way up the bay on the 6th and 7th as we have already seen. But though Grant was not

Washington was greatly perturbed. Though it had no definite information as to the character or numbers of the invading army, it correctly sensed the danger and correctly surmised that Early's army was no inconsiderable one, and that the capture of the Federal city was his object and purpose.

It was not until the very day that the sanguinary delaying battle was being fought at Monocacy, within less than forty miles of Washington, that two other hard fighting divisions of the 6th Corps were being loaded on transports at City Point, 250 miles away, for shipment to the capital for its defense.

Without this delaying battle, Washington must have fallen, as shown by the records quoted herein.

After the danger of its capture had passed and the alarm subsided some writers sought to make it appear that there was no alarm or apprehension in the city, but the records of the day prove that there was. And it was not without reason for danger was real as we shall see.

CHAPTER XIV

JUST BEFORE THE BATTLE

On the morning of July 9, 1864, the sun rose in fiery splendor over the "Hills of Linganore" which lie east from the scene of the stirring events to be narrated. The crop of wheat which had ripened under the summer skies, on the Worthington and Thomas farms, as well as elsewhere in the community had been reaped and was standing in shocks over the wheat fields, ready to be gathered into the barns or put in stacks.

On both farms, notwithstanding the proximity of an armed force, and the ominous sounds of cannon firing in the distance, the work of "hauling in" went nervously on. On each farm could be seen a four-horse wagon and team with wide and long "carriages" on which sheaves of wheat were being thrown from the shocks standing on the ground, by strong men with pitch forks, and loaded on the wagons by other men with their hands. Those wagons moved from shock to shock, and the shocks disappeared off the ground as the sheaves were loaded neat and straight on the wagons until the load was complete. Then the loaded wagons were drawn to the barns, where the sheaves were lifted, one by one, by pitch fork, into the mow or thrown on a rick or stack already started on the ground near the barn, and raised by layers of sheaves to a height even above the loaded wagon.

John T. Worthington owned a few slaves which he

inherited from his ancestors. These were still loyal to home and master, and were hauling in the sheaves of grain and stacking them.

John Ephraim Tyler Butler, one of the colored men, said to Thomas Palm, another of them, as they loaded the wagon in the field:

"See 'dem buzzards flying around in a circle? Deres gwine to be trouble here today, sure." To which the one addressed replied:

"Dere sure is kwine to be trouble here today. Dats so, Ephraim."

This was early in the morning, which means about 6 or 7 o'clock. Two or three loads were hauled in, and stacked. It is now 8.30 o'clock in the morning. The booming of cannon in the distance could be heard at intervals, towards Frederick, three miles away, and from near the Junction, one mile distant. At 9 o'clock Mr. Worthington said to his men as they came to the stack with a load: "Boys, fill up the middle of the stack high so as to turn the rain that may fall, then unhitch your horses from the wagon, unharness them, and take them all, including those in the stable, to the Sugar Loaf Mountain, and tie them by their halters in the darkest and loneliest place you can find." The wheat was unloaded in haste, the horses unhitched and unharnessed, and led away. All save old Davy, the carriage horse, and an old mule of small value, these were left in their stalls in the stable.

At Mr. Keefer Thomas's place, the same thing was done. Mr. Thomas's men were unloading his wheat into his barn, but about 9 o'clock, the wheat garnering was stopped and the horses led away to be hidden in Sugar Loaf Mountain, a rugged isolated mountain, about five miles from these farms. It was thought by the owners that there their horses would be safe from discovery and seizure by either army. It was well known that soldiers were no respecters of private property when their needs were pressing. Many other horses of farmers were secreted in the recesses of the mountain, but the sharp eyes and ears of the Confederate "Foot Cavalry" discovered them and they were all taken and led or ridden away, nearly two hundred of them, including nine belonging to Mr. Worthington and about as many to Mr. Thomas. This was quite a heavy loss to many farmers, horses being worth about $200 apiece; for which no remuneration was ever had.

But this is anticipating.

After the horses were taken away to the mountain, Mr. Worthington had heavy two-inch oak boards put across the cellar windows, which were above ground about three feet; also he had several tubs and a barrel filled with water, placed in the cellar. As the hours wore away, the blue-clad Union soldiers could be seen taking position in the fields on the Thomas farm adjoining, squadrons of blue-clad cavalrymen rode past the Worthington house towards the river, and musketry firing as well as the boom of cannon could be heard from near the Junction. There was every indication that a battle between the armed forces of the Union and of the Confederacy was about to take place not far away, and preparations were made to retreat to the cellar with the family and the slaves, should the battle come near the dwelling house.

The Mantzes Family Come

About 11 o'clock, Mrs. Frank Mantz with her children, Miller, Clarke, Lillie and William, came from the house at Frederick Junction in which they lived, and which was then in the midst of hot skirmishing, and asked to be permitted to go into the cellar with the Worthington family and slaves.

Of course this request was instantly granted and as an armed force of Confederate cavalry was seen about this time, crossing the Monocacy, five hundred yards to the westward, it was deemed prudent then to seek the protection from shot and shell, offered by the spacious cellars under the dwelling house. These cellars extended under the whole house, and were well lighted by half windows above ground. The Worthington place was known as "Clifton", or more appropriately, "Riverside Drive and Farm."

At the Thomas house was the family, consisting of these: Mr. and Mrs. Thomas, their two daughters, Alice and Virginia, and one son, Frank. These also sought the protection of their cellar. Mrs. James Gambrill, with her sons, Richard and Staley, came from her home at the mill to the Thomas house, known as "Araby", and went into the cellar there, with the family. Mr. Gambrill remained at his mill, which was constructed of stone, and was therefore a tolerably safe place to be.

EARLY LEVIES $200,000 ON FREDERICK CITY

About 8 o'clock in the morning, General Early at Frederick, entered the dwelling house of Dr. Richard Hammond, at the northwest corner of Market and Second streets, and one of his staff asked for the use of a pen and ink. This was accorded him, and he sat down at a small table, and at the direction of his chief, wrote an order to be delivered to the mayor of the city, as follows:

Fredericktown, Md., July 9, 1864.
By order of the Lieut.-Gen. Comdg:
We require of the mayor and town authorities $200,000 in current money for the use of this army.

The general said he did this in retaliation for the destruction wrought by General Hunter in the Valley of Virginia.

The money was raised by the mayor through the five banks of the town, to-wit: The Farmers and Mechanics Bank, now the Farmers and Mechanics National Bank; The Frederick County Bank, now the Frederick County National Bank; The Central Bank, now the Central Trust Company of Maryland; The Fredericktown Savings Institution, and The Franklin Savings Bank, the latter now merged with the Commercial Bank.

Years after an imaginative colored man of Frederick, named John Murdock, used to boast, untruly, that he carried the money in a hand-satchel from the banks to General Early whose headquarters were then in a tent near where the baseball park is now located. In telling the story John stated that at General Early's direction he emptied the money from the satchel on to a blanket which General Early caused to be spread on the ground near his tent. "Jubal" and several officers then knelt on the ground around the blanket and the money was counted. The amount was found to be $2.35 short of full sum demanded. John stated that thereupon "Jubal" told him to go back and get the $2.35 or else he would blow the town to hell. Whereupon, according to John's story, he went back into the town and told a man whom he met on the street the predicament. The man gave him the needed balance which he took to "Jubal" who then said: "Now John, your town is safe." There was not a word of truth in John's story. The money was never entrusted to him, but he told the story so often that he began to believe it himself; some times he created wonderment in his hearers but more often, amusement.

CHAPTER XV

SKIRMISHING AT JUG BRIDGE

Meanwhile orders had been given Gen. Robert E. Rodes, commanding a Confederate division, to demonstrate against the Union forces guarding the stone bridge on the Baltimore turnpike. The force defending this bridge was under the immediate command of Col. Allison L. Brown, who directed the operations of the 144th and 149th Ohio National Guard, and other troops. Some brisk skirmishing occurred here on the morning of the 9th, lasting intermittently until near 5 o'clock in the afternoon. Several men on both sides were killed and a larger number wounded during the day, in the charges and counter charges of the opposing skirmish "lines."

DEFENDING THE BRIDGES

While Rodes was demonstrating against the stone bridge, General Ramseur was sent to "try out" the defense of the wooden bridge on the road to Washington. A shell from one of the guns of Nelson's battery in Ramseur's command, was fired about 8.30 o'clock in the morning, from Cronise's farm, and mortally wounded two men of the 151st New York, and soon after, several more were wounded in the 87th Pennsylvania by shell fire from the same battery. Ramseur then advanced his brigade down the public road leading from Frederick toward the wooden bridge and on to Washington, and met the strong skirmish line or advance guard of the enemy, posted chiefly in the triangle near the Junction, though some of the skirmishers were in the field along the west bank of the Monocacy, southwest of the public road. This skirmish line, as already stated, was under the command of Capt. George E. Davis, Company D, Tenth Vermont Volunteers.

The fire of the 350 skirmishers who had the advantage of position behind the embankment, and in the blockhouse, aided by the brass howitzer, was so effective that Ramseur would not press the attack. Then he tried to gain entrance to the triangle by sending some men close to the river above the railroad bridge, where they were, in a measure, hidden from view of the enemy, by the undergrowth, and these tried crawling forward toward the embankment at the west end of the iron bridge, but they were discovered by the scouts of Captain Davis, and driven back. Ramseur still persisted, however, and sharpshooters were sent to occupy Best's barn a short distance west of the small wooden bridge over the railroad. These sharpshooters, though three hundred yards or more away, were able to make the situation very uncomfortable for Davis and his men. The bullets from their rifles hit the ground all around these defenders of the bridges, killed one or two, and wounded several.

Three guns of Alexander's battery on the hill in the Thomas field near the wooden bridge, now directed their fire at this barn. In a short while, a shell from a well-aimed gun of this battery hit the barn and set it on fire, thus scattering the rebel sharpshooters and relieving the skirmishers of this very galling and nerve-racking rifle fire. The skirmishers held their ground well after this, and at times went forward along the turnpike and in the adjoining fields, toward Frederick a short distance, but were driven back by Ramseur's men to the triangle behind the railroad cut and embankments. Once General Ricketts rode across the bridge to this advance guard or line of skirmishers and surveyed the situation, but the Confederates further up the pike recognized the rank of the horseman, and paid their compliments by a fusillade which caused the General to retire, and recross the bridge to the east side.

CAPTAIN BROWN'S REPORT

Captain Charles J. Brown in his report of his part in the Battle of Monocacy, says:

"My two companies, C and K, First Maryland, Potomac Home Brigade, were occupying, at the commencement of the fight, the blockhouse on the west side of the Monocacy, which I, in obedience to orders from the general commanding, evacuated and burned. I was then ordered to hold the bridge over the railroad on the Georgetown pike, one company of the Tenth Vermont Infantry and one company of the Ninth New York Heavy Artillery, being added to my command. This position I held until the left of our army fell back, when, having received a discretionary order to fall back while I could do so with safety, I left my position and fell back across the railroad bridge and occupied the rifle pits on the east side of the Monocacy, covering the retreat of our army for a short time, and then followed the line of march," etc.

It will be seen that Captain Brown's report is very meagre of what occurred around and near "the bridge over the railroad on the Georgetown pike," on the west side of the Monocacy. According to the best information obtainable, the blockhouse was burned about 3.30 or 4.00 o'clock in the afternoon.

Captain Wood's Account

In an account (not official) written by Captain Wood, Company M, 9th New York, he says, among other things, that he was directed to take his own company and enough men from Company E, to make his company 100 men, for picket duty. He was shown his position by an orderly of General Wallace's staff:

"I crossed the bridge, and marched up the pike toward Frederick, anticipating a pleasant day on picket, when suddenly a rebel skirmish line opened fire upon us. . . . I soon discovered a Union captain, and learned from him that he had some sort of a skirmish line on the left of the pike looking toward Frederick, and that he outranked me. I told him that I reported for orders and awaited his instructions. He said he thought I had better move up and reinforce his line. I did so, and within five minutes the captain and the few men he had there disappeared from my sight, and hearing forever. . . . I had been upon the skirmish line but short time when I received a visit from General Ricketts accompanied by two or three men of his staff. . . . . Just at that moment the rebel skirmishers gave the general a salute, and he turned and rode away. I immediately deployed the larger number of my men to the east side of the pike. (That is, to the right looking toward Frederick.)

"About this time Captain Parker of the 106th New York, with one or two companies, moved forward on my left. . . . .

"In falling back to the railroad, my skirmish-line displayed about as good soldierly qualities as the most strict disciplinarian could desire. They maintained an excellent line, loading and firing rapidly, and keeping the rebel advance in check until they reached the cover of the railroad cut. I recall particularly one soldier, a tall, stern man, formerly a schoolteacher in one of the western counties of the State (New York) (I think his name was Wellon), who stopped and fired each time with great deliberation and excellent effect. After reaching the line of the railroad, a few of the Maryland 100-day men made their appearance and helped to hold the line."

Burning The Bridge

About noon, while this skirmishing was going on, a still larger Confederate force was seen coming down the pike from toward Frederick, and fearing the skirmishers defending the bridge might be routed, and the bridge captured, General Wallace ordered the bridge burned.

Roe's Account

In a very interesting account of the battle by Alfred Seelye Roe, a member of the "Ninth New York Heavy Artillery," and author of the book by that name, published by the author at Worcester, Mass., in 1889, he says, beginning at page 128:

"Colonel William H. Seward, Jr., received orders from General Wallace about 9.00 A. M. to detach two companies from his regiment for perilous duty. Colonel Seward immediately detached Company B, by the following order: 'Lieutenant Fish, order your company in line and move down to that bridge, and hold it at all hazards.' . . . The company arranged to stubbornly defend the passage of the bridge. The rebels tried to dislodge the company by directing shells on the bridge, which raked the structure with terrific force, but failed in their design. 'Hold it at all hazards' was the order." . . .

"About 12.30 P. M. Lieutenant Fish received an order from Colonel Seward to burn the bridge, which was promptly executed. Members of the company procured sheaves of wheat from a nearby field, and placed them under the southeast corner of the roof of the structure. Privates Alven N. Sova, Samuel R. Mack and Sergeant Albert L. Smith participated in setting the fire, which wrapped the roof in flames like magic."

The dry shingled roof and the long seasoned pine weather-boarding burned like tinder, and quickly the flames were mounting skyward. A great smoke began to fill the sky and blot out the sun. But the roaring flames did their work rapidly, and soon the large timbers began to fall into the water. It was a great fire and the whole superstructure was consumed in a very short time. The burning of the bridge left the defenders on the west side of the river without any easy means of retreat. Their only way now was either to wade through the water or to cross on the railroad iron bridge, which was not a safe or convenient means of crossing. It was built to carry trains of cars, not men afoot.

General Wallace, in his account of the burning of the bridge, says that just as the bridge was being fired, he thought of the skirmishers on the other side. "My God, what will become of them?" Then immediately his staff officer, Ross, rode through the bridge to the other end to notify them what was about to be done. But they were too far away to be reached, and when Ross returned and made his report, it was deemed prudent to fire the bridge, although doing so looked like willful desertion of the men on the other side of the river.

Old wooden bridge over the the Monocacy at Frederick Junction, on the road leading from Frederick to Washington. Burned by order of Gen. Lew Wallace July 9, 1864. This is the bridge that General Ramseur's Division tried repeatedly, but vainly, to possess, being held back by Lieut. George E. Davis and his skirmish line of 350 Federals.

CHAPTER XVI

CAPTAIN DAVIS' ACCOUNT

Capt. George E. Davis, of Company D, Tenth Vermont Volunteers, made no official report of his part in this brave defense of the wooden bridge and iron bridge, but in a letter dated Burlington, Vt., May 10, 1893, he says:

"Early in the morning of July 9th, with Second-Lieutenant . . . and seventy-five men of our regiment, I was ordered to report as skirmishers, to Capt. Charles J. Brown, commanding Companies C and K, First Maryland Regiment, Potomac Home Brigade, near the block house, on the west bank of the Monocacy River. He and his two hundred men had just entered the service for one hundred days, to repel this invasion, and knew nothing of actual service. I was sent to General Wallace's headquarters on the hill east, for orders, which were to hold the two bridges across the river, the wooden bridge and the railroad bridge, at all hazards, and to prevent the enemy from crossing. No intimation was made that the wooden bridge might be burned. General Ricketts' division was in two lines of battle in our rear on the east bank of the Monocacy. Some of the Ninth New York Heavy Artillery pickets were at our left, near the northwest end of the wooden bridge, making something over three hundred men in all, on the west bank, and we were the only Union troops on that side of the stream, confronted with Ramseur's division of Confederate troops. We faced north and west to cover a triangle, the north line of which was three hundred and fifty yards from the railroad bridge to the turnpike over the railroad. . . .

"When the enemy advanced, about 8.30 A. M. along the pike from Frederick, ... Captain Brown turned to me in disgust and insisted upon my taking command. I assumed command instantly, brought up my Tenth Vermonters to this point, and after a severe fight of about one hour, the enemy retired. I knew nothing of the situation or of the plan of battle, except as apparent to the eye. The natural advantages of cover and position were in our favor. . . .

"About 11.00 A. M. a second and much severer attack was made upon our right and rear, by which they intended to cut us out, take us prisoners, cross the railroad bridge and turn Ricketts' position. . . .

"I had, on assuming command, sent pickets up and down the river, who warned me of this (flank) movement, that was entirely hidden from my view, so that I drew back my men to the west end of the railroad bridge, faced north, repelled the attack, then assumed my former position on the pike, which we held until the retreat about 5 o'clock. In the early part of the noon attack, the wooden bridge over the Monocacy was burned, without notice to me. At the same time the Ninth New York pickets were all withdrawn, also without notice.

"The third and last attack began about 3.30 P. M. The situation was critical; the enemy came upon us with such overwhelming numbers and desperation, it seemed that we must be swept into the river. The place of the Ninth New York pickets at my left had not been filled for want of men. The hundred-day men at my right were melting away and went over the iron bridge to the rifle pits on the east bank of the river. Nevertheless, we fought for over an hour and kept back a much larger force than ours. Apprehending an advance on my left, I sent Corp. John G. Wright, Company E, Tenth Vermont, through the cornfield to examine and report. He was killed at once. . . .

"Immediately the enemy was seen passing around my right to cut off my retreat by the iron bridge. . . . We must leave now or never. Our noble band of Vermonters stood by me till I gave the order to retreat, when we kept together and crossed the railroad bridge, stepping upon ties, there being no floor."

The stand made by Captain Davis and his Vermonters was truly a trying affair, displaying alertness, courage, judgment and self control worthy of high commendation. And his retreat across the bridge was conducted
in a manner equally commendable.

General Wallace, from an elevation near his headquarters, was an eyewitness to this withdrawal, and his
own words best describe it. He says:

"A cheering and an outbrust of musketry arose
beyond the railroad bridge; and looking thither, a sight
broke upon me in the stress of which all interest, else,
was for the moment smothered.

"I looked, as did my officers, and we were all astonished,—I never more so.

"In the allusion to the skirmishers in the direction
of Frederick, a page or so back, I described them as
shifting from their original position by crawling back
toward the river, with what hopeful purpose I could not
make out. Hours had come and gone, hours of painful
retirement, during which the good men, undiscouraged,
undaunted by the abandonment so discernible after the
burning of the wooden bridge, literally wormed themselves off the field, stopping at intervals to fight the enemy off, and keeping the railroad bridge always in mind.
Now they had reached the bridge. By what signal I do
not know, not unlikely by spontaneous impulse, they
sprang up, and unmindful of exposure, made a dash for
liberty. And when I saw them, they were on the bridge
coming.

"To judge of this feat, and what courage there was
involved in it, the reader should keep in thought that
the great steel structure was of goodly length, sixty or
sixty-five yards at least, and unfloored, leaving passage
over it afoot along cross ties and girders. Nor should
one's fancy stop here. Quite forty-five feet below the
adventurers ran the water swiftly enough to make the
head swim, and only too ready to catch a sufferer falling,
and hide him in its remorseless, dark-brown current.
Danger upon danger—and yet another. Every step was
taken under fire of antagonists pressing forward furious

at the sight of possible escape. Such the spectacle presented to us spellbound on the hill!

"We saw two or three hundred reach the bridge—we saw them on the ties stepping short and carefully, as they needs must — we saw them from habit form in column order, not crowding or pushing, or struggling to pass one another, or yelling. Now and then we could see one stop short, let go his musket, throw up his hands, and with a splash disappear in the stream beneath. . . . . How many were thus overtaken may never be known. *Missing* was the simple record written on the next muster roll over against their names.

"Fortunately, though holding the moving files in plain view, the artillerymen mercifully refrained from firing. We watched the coming breathlessly; and when the crossing became assured, I was the first of by party to speak.

"Hurry down," I said to Colonel Catlin, "and meet those men. The man in command is brave. I should like to know his name.

"Catlin went running.

"Upon our shore the fugitives halted, and while some of them turned for a last shot at the enemy, the others swung their caps and cheered, then reformed and in perfect order marched away as I supposed, to their commands. I have not words to express my admiration. Enough that I cannot now recall an incident or occurrence under my eyes, more desperate in the undertaking, yet more successful in the outcome. From every point of view it was heroism."

Captain Davis Gets Congressional Medal

Colonel Catlin brought the name of the gallant leader. It was Lieutenant, afterwards Capt. George E. Davis, of the Tenth Vermont Infantry. Congress rewarded Captain Davis with a medal engraved thus: "The Congress to Captain George E. Davis, Co. D, Tenth Vermont Vols. for distinguished conduct in the battle of Monocacy, Md., July 9, 1864."

ARTILLERY REFRAINED FROM FIRING

One statement in General Wallace's narrative is especially noteworthy. He says that although the moving mass of Federals on the bridge were in plain view of the Confederate artillerists, they mercifully refrained from firing.

Thus even in the heat of battle the chivalrous spirit of American manhood asserted itself, and Southern artillerists refused to commit needless slaughter even of their enemies. To their praise be it said.

CHAPTER XVII

McCAUSLAND'S FIRST ATTACK AND REPULSE

While these events just narrated were transpiring at Frederick Junction, Gen. John McCausland, commanding a body of about 400 or 500 Confederate cavalry, proceeded from his position near Frederick City to a place on the west side of the Monocacy about a quarter of a mile above the mouth of Ballenger Creek, almost due west of the Worthington house and about 500 yards therefrom. Here his troops were hidden from the view of the enemy by the thick foliage of the trees and bushes growing along the banks of the river. Having crossed over unperceived three-fourths of the men dismounted and one-fourth held the horses of the dismounted ones. The horses were then led back across the river and held in position concealed by the trees.

The dismounted cavalrymen, perhaps 350 of them, armed and accoutered after the fashion of Southern troopers, led by officers on horse back, moved up the incline toward the Worthington house, and climbing the fence running from the house straight to the Monocacy, formed in line of battle in the front field of the Worthington farm and moved forward toward the front line of the enemy who was in large part concealed behind the division fence between the Worthington and Thomas farms, near several walnut trees and a locust tree still standing along the fence. The Worthington front field was then in growing corn about waist high over the field. Lying down behind the division fence on the Thomas side, and hidden from view by the fence and growing corn, lay two battalions of Ricketts' seasoned soldiers. The only man on horseback being General Ricketts, himself, sitting quietly and soldierly on his horse, at the left of the line. His staff officers having dismounted, were standing by their horses. Toward these horsemen, and toward the clump of walnut trees, McCausland advanced his line through the cornfield with banners and guidons waving and a general feeling of an easy victory prevailing. Onward they went through the growing corn, drawing nearer and nearer to the enemy, neither side firing a shot until the Confederate line had reached a small elevation in the ground, within 125 yards of the division fence. Then at a word of command, the whole Federal line of infantry rose to its feet and resting their guns on the upper rails of the fence, took aim and fired a volley, a murderous volley into the ranks of the approaching foe. Watched from a distance the whole rebel line disappeared as if swallowed up in the earth. Save and except several riderless horses galloping about, and a few mounted officers bravely facing the storm, the attacking force had vanished. As a matter of fact, not a few lay motionless and silent amidst the broken and trodden corn, never to march, or ride, or charge again. Many others lay sweltering and helpless under the burning sun, from gunshot wounds inflicted by their countrymen, then enemies in a horrible civil war. Still others, unhurt, had fallen to the ground to escape the deadly rifle fire and were crawling along, under cover of the remaining stalks of broken corn, to and over a rise in the ground and into a depression out of range of the enemy's guns.

There was more firing and more empty saddles, and more riderless horses galloping about, and more men killed and wounded. But once over the small elevation in the field and into the depression out of sight for a moment, the unwounded foot cavalry rose to their feet and ran. Back to the Worthington house they fled and beyond, now pursued by the blue-clad Federals.

Mr. John T. Worthington who witnessed the attack and retreat from an upstairs window of his home, stated that he could not understand why the Confederates went forward as if on parade, for from his position he could see the blue-clad fighters lying in wait. The attacking force consisted of brave and experienced soldiers, but for the moment they were panic stricken by the deadly ambush into which they were unwittingly led. The officers tried in vain to rally the men. They swore at them and threatened them with sword and pistol, but for a while they would give no heed. After retreating past the house for a few hundred yards they were halted and formed into ranks again. The curses of the officers in their efforts to stop the men and their threats to kill the fugitives unless they turned could be plainly heard by the occupants of the cellar, as the retreating force passed the house. Mrs. Worthington was moved to exclaim: "Poor creatures, it means death to them either way."

The noise of the retreating rebels passed and then could be seen through the cracks between the heavy boards at one of the cellar half-windows, the blue pants of the pursuing Yankees. The noise of the clamor and straining as of men in mortal combat could be distinctly heard as they passed. After a brief space they could be heard going back again past the house to their position

WORTHINGTON HOUSE AND PREMISES

at the division fence, and glimpses of blue could be seen as they again passed the windows. This time the noise and clamor and straining was like that of men fleeing from a deadly peril, panting aloud mingled with exclamations of pain and terror. More than one received his death wound close to the house and fell there to die, in the Worthington yard. Others were wounded thereabout and their moans could be heard by the family in the cellar, of whom the writer was one. The rebels had recovered themselves and were fighting now. It is no disparagement of the valor of the attacking force that the men fled when fired upon at close range in so deadly and unexpected a manner. In the first place they were more accustomed to fighting on horseback than on foot. In the next place they were unaware that so many blue-coated men were confronting them. Then they had been informed that the only foe they would have to meet would be raw and inexperienced troops of the 8th Corps. But they came close up to an experienced body of men who wrought havoc among them in an instant. That they had the true metal of experienced fighters is shown by the fact that they rallied and turned on their pursuers, and drove them.

McCausland's men were very much incensed that they had been led into what proved to be a deadly ambush and they complained bitterly of it. Gen. Lew Wallace who witnessed the attack and retreat from a distance through his field glass states in his *Autobiography* that after the war he met General Gordon in Washington while the latter was serving as United States Senator from Georgia, and that the two sat on a sofa in the Senate chamber and discussed the Monocacy battle. He (Wallace) states that he asked General Gordon if he knew why General McCausland had marched his men so deliberately across the Worthington front field in so unwary a manner. General Gordon replied that McCausland was not aware that any veterans from the 6th Corps were around and expected the undisciplined troops which, as he was told, were the only ones he would meet there, would run when the Confederates approached in menacing line of battle.

It was a sad mistake as the Confederate loss was considerable and no one was hurt on the Federal side at the fence. Their task was merely to rest their guns on the rails of the fence, take aim and fire.

However it must not be overlooked that this was merely a skirmish fight, and the numbers engaged were not large.

While this skirmish was going on the greater part of Ricketts' brigades was waiting in the positions assigned them, a half mile or more to the eastward. McCausland's cavalry footmen were the only Confederates then on the east side of the Monocacy and these remained at the place they had been halted in the Worthington barn field. Rodes was demonstrating against the Federal force at the Jug Bridge and Ramseur was trying to get possession of the wooden bridge over the Monocacy, but the main body of Confederates was stationed near Frederick awaiting orders from the commander-in-chief of the invading forces.

CHAPTER XVIII.

McCAUSLAND GOES IN AGAIN

It was two o'clock when complete order was again brought out of panic and confusion. Then the surviving troopers were ordered forward for a second attack. It may appear almost incredible to one uninformed that soldiers who have just a few hours before been through a hell of deadly gunfire, who have suffered severe losses, and who have, moreover, become panic-stricken, can be so soon rallied and again made to charge a foe superior in numbers, and now known not to be novices on the battlefield, in the game of war. Yet that is what was done with these troopers of McCausland, on that hot July day.

This time they went forward several hundred yards to the right of the first line of attack, that is directly from the Worthington barn toward the Thomas house. Consequently Ricketts' men along the division fence, had to shift their position quickly to their left to meet this second attack. The contour of the ground is such that the Confederates in their second attack were concealed from the view of the brigades at the fence by a small hill and by the growing corn, until they had almost reached the division fence, several hundred yards beyond the left of Ricketts' line. This caused Ricketts' men to run toward their left flank, but in doing so they were pushed back by the advancing Confederates.

THE CONFEDERATE BATTERIES DO THEIR PART

The Confederate batteries on the other side of the river were active, and shells were flying over the river and across the fields toward the Federal line, from several directions. Actually shells seemed to be in flight from every direction, and the horrible hissing and screeching they made in going were perhaps more dreadful to the imagination than were the shells themselves in their effect. These shells swept over the Union line, from flank to flank, and the noise they made in passing and in their explosions, was terrible. But the execution done was slight. The trees growing along the river, which were then thick with foliage, prevented the gunners, though good ones, from getting an accurate range.

Now and then, as the din of the shells subsided, could be heard the firing of small arms. The dismounted troopers were advancing to the combat again, but this time they indulged in no foolishness. They were firing as they went forward, and they were all in a mood to avenge the loss of their many comrades who had fallen in the first charge.

In that first attack, the force went by the Worthington farmhouse on the north side; this time they were going forward on the south side of the house, between the house and the end of Brooks' Hill. As they advanced, the enemy was to their left, along the fence, in other words, this time they advanced toward that part of the fence where no enemy was stationed, and nearly outflanked the line. By a quick movement Ricketts' front line sought to intercept the troopers, but, as stated, were pushed back in the effort toward the Thomas house. Both sides were loading and firing. It was load and fire, load and fire: Kill, kill, kill, and they were brothers, too; all American citizens, now strangely divided and arrayed against each other in deadly combat. Oh, the pity of it all! The Federal line is driven back. The division fence is reached by the troopers. They climb over. Firing goes on, men are killed on both sides, others are wounded. The sun is very hot. The shocks of wheat in the Thomas field are overthrown, and the sheaves scattered.

It is said that a horse spoils a good soldier and that dismounted cavalry are not good fighters. But not so with McCausland's men. They climbed the fence into the Thomas wheat field. Ricketts' first line falls back toward the Thomas house, passes it by and joins the reserves behind the embankments of the Georgetown and Baker Valley Roads. McCausland's men follow fighting. Now the rebels have reached the Thomas house, they surround it and have taken possession. But their line is very thin. They hold the house and surrounding premises for a short time under the fire of a larger force of the enemy at the Georgetown Road. Then realizing that they are in close proximity to a much superior Federal force, and that they are unsupported, to prevent being surrounded, they falter—some fall back.

Now General Wallace, from his elevated position near headquarters, through his field glasses, sees the faltering troopers. A courier is dispatched to Ricketts, whose place during the battle is near the entrance gate to the Thomas driveway, to suggest to him a charge by the men held in reserve along the cuts in the Georgetown Road, near its intersection with the Baker Valley Road.

The courier, Colonel Ross, meeting Capt. William H. Lanius, then serving as an aide to Col. William S. Truex, commanding the First Brigade, gives the message to him to be delivered to the general.

Captain Lanius, without delivering the message, knowing the importance of prompt action, himself ordered the 87th Pennsylvania and the 14th New Jersey, to charge upon the Thomas house, drive the rebels back and establish a Federal line there. The two regiments went forward in gallant style, driving the rebels before them, occupying the Thomas house and establishing their lines in accordance with instructions. The rebels were driven back again to the Worthington farm, past the barn and on toward the fording place on the river. This repulse ended the skirmishing between McCausland's men and the enemy.

In the posts of the front porch of the Thomas house may still be seen "the marks of the battle." Also in the shutters to the front windows and in the door frame and brick wall. These were caused by the Federal bullet fire and shell fire in the effort to drive out McCausland's men, who temporarily occupied the house from about 2.25 to 2.45 o'clock. The bullet wounds in the Thomas house, that is those in the posts to the front porch and in the front of the house, came from gun fire from the Georgetown Road at the intersection of the Baker Valley Road, and the shell wounds from the shells fired by a piece of artillery planted east of where the Pennsylvania monument now stands, near the Yaste house.

The occupancy of the house and grounds by the rebels had been made very uncomfortable and when the charge was made on them they promptly retired to the Worthington farm, where they awaited the coming of reinforcements under Gen. John B. Gordon, who was at that time in command of one of Breckinridge's Divisions of Early's army of invasion. The main part of this army was located near Frederick with Rodes demonstrating

against the Jug Bridge, and Ramseur feeling out the
strength of the opposition at the wooden bridge on the
road to Washington. Breckinridge's Divisions were held
in readiness south and west of Mt. Olivet Cemetery from
which position a broad highway led southwardly to the
wooden bridge at Frederick Junction, and one mile out
a branch road led toward Buckeystown past the McGill,
now the McKinney house, and in its course it crossed
Ballenger's Creek and drew close to the Worthington-
McKinney Ford over the Monocacy. Near this ford
McCausland had crossed over in the morning at 11 o'clock
when he led the first attack against Ricketts' strong
advance guard posted along the division fence between
the Worthington and Thomas farms, which resulted so
disastrously. McCausland's dismounted cavalry, having
now been repulsed a second time, retreat past the Worthington barn toward the Worthington-McKinney Ford on
the Monocacy, and halt until succor should arrive.

CHAPTER XIX.

THE BATTLE

GORDON LEADS ATTACK

General Early had remained at Frederick until past noon. During the morning hours while McCausland was skirmishing so hotly with the enemy, and Rodes was demonstrating against the Jug Bridge, Ramseur had been contending with the Federal forces defending the bridges at Frederick Junction, and he has reported to the general commanding, that the enemy's position at the wooden bridge over the Monocacy had proven too strong to be vigorously attacked in front without a loss of men greater than it was thought wise to incur; and now that the wooden bridge has been burned an attempt to ford the river under fire of the enemy was not to be thought of. General Early therefore made an examination in person to find a place on the river where it could be crossed without such strong opposition.

While he was thus engaged he ascertained where McCausland had crossed with his cavalry for the purpose of locating the enemy's position and developing his strength, as already narrated. Having learned the result of McCausland's first encounter and that his men were still on that side of the river, he resolved to go to McCausland's assistance and to make the principal attack of the day against Ricketts' command, that is against Wallace's left wing.

In pursuance of this plan Early sent orders to General Breckinridge, who seems to have been in command of two divisions, Gordon's and Echols', to move from near Frederick with Gordon's Division to reinforce McCausland who was about to make his second attack unaided. It was considerably after the noon hour when these orders were sent by Early to Breckinridge, it was 2.30 o'clock before the start was made, and it was 3 o'clock when Gordon's Division, consisting of three brigades, under command of Generals Evans, York and Terry, respectively, had marched from Frederick out the Georgetown Road one mile to the Buckeystown Road, and thence by that road three miles more to Ballenger's Creek. After crossing Ballenger's Creek on the Buckeystown highway, Gordon's column turned abruptly to the left on McGill's, now McKinney's, land, crossed the railroad, which runs nearly parallel with the Buckeystown Road, and came to the Monocacy. Here the men stopped to remove their shoes before wading into the water, but the order was given to jump in and not stop to remove shoes. Reaching the opposite bank, the men came up out of the water into a meadow on the Worthington farm. Their feet were sodden, but that made little matter considering the serious nature of the work before them. Gordon's place of crossing the river was below the mouth of Ballenger's Creek.

The Worthington meadow lies along the east bank of the Monocacy, and afforded a fine field in which to manoeuvre the men into position. The meadow there is quite extensive and level, and was also well protected from the view of the enemy by the higher ground that lay between this meadow and the upper fields of the Thomas and Worthington farms, where the enemy's forces were posted, as well as in the cuts of the Georgetown Road, beyond.

Having gotten his forces across to this meadow, General Gordon disposed of his several brigades in order to make the principal and decisive attack of the day. Gen. Clement A. Evans, in command of the Georgia Brigade of seven regiments, was directed to go by the right flank. Gen. Zebulon York, in command of two brigades (Hays' and Stafford's) was ordered to form on the left of Brigadier-General Evans.

Hays' Brigade had consisted of five Louisiana regiments, and Stafford's of four regiments from the same State, but these regiments had been so depleted by the fights at the Wilderness, Spottsylvania Court House, and Cold Harbor, that whole regiments were not more than full companies. Because of the depleted condition of these two brigades, they had been combined under one command, that of Gen. Zebulon York.

Brig.-Gen. William T. Terry was directed to move with his brigades, consisting of the fragmentary remains of fourteen Virginia regiments, in support of the left of the Confederate line.

Gordon Makes A Reconnaissance

While the brigades were crossing the river and being arranged in order, according to General Gordon's instructions, he, himself, made a reconnaissance to discover the position of the enemy's lines. Riding with certain members of his staff across the lower fields of the Worthington farm, all while concealed from the view of the Federals by a long, high hill, known as Brooks' Hill, he ascended the wooded side of the hill, by an old road to the top, and there before him lay a perfect panoramic view of all the valley below, including the Thomas farm, mansion and barn; the Baker Valley Road, the Georgetown Road, Gambrill's Mill, and including also a complete survey of the position of the enemy. (See map.)

He says in his report:

"I found that Brigadier-General McCausland's cavalry brigade (dismounted) had been driven back by superior numbers, and that the enemy was posted along the line of a fence on the crest of the ridge running obliquely to the left from the river. In his front lay an open field, which was commanded by his artillery and small arms to the extent of their range, while in his rear ran a valley, nearly parallel with the general direction of his line of battle. In this valley I discovered, from a wooded eminence in front of his left, another line of battle in support of his first. Both of these lines were in advance of the Georgetown road. The enemy's line of skirmishers covered the front of his first line, and extended far beyond it to the left."

EVANS' BRIGADE ATTACKS FIRST

Having been ordered to attack the Federal forces, and to drive them, and all the dispositions having been made in accordance with instructions, the whole command was ordered to advance in echelon by brigades from the right. General Evans advanced across the lower fields of the Worthington farm first southerly, then southeasterly, then in a northeasterly direction toward the left of the Federal line, all the while keeping Brooks' Hill between him and the enemy. General York advanced by the same circuitous route toward the centre of the line, while General Terry, after following General York for a considerable distance, then bore to the left and passed north and south of the Worthington house, his general direction being toward the northern end of the division fence between the Worthington and Thomas farms, across the cornfield where McCausland had met disaster in the morning about 11.30 o'clock.

Evans' Brigade was the first to come in contact with the enemy. It came from the Worthington lower fields up the narrow meadow just west of Brooks' Hill to a knoll at the north end of that Hill, wooded on the west or Worthington side, but cleared and cultivated on the east, or Thomas side.

This cleared hillside on the Thomas farm was part of a large field of 40 acres, more or less. The whole field was in wheat and the ripened grain had been reaped and bound in sheaves, and was then standing in rows of shocks all over the field.

Evans' Brigade marched from the narrow meadow up the wooded side of this hill and mounting the fence, came out in the open in full view of Ricketts' left wing, under command of Col. W. S. Truex, and within 250 yards of his skirmish line.

As the gray-clad boys climbed the post and rail fence, running along the top of the hill, and dividing the Thomas and Worthington farms, they gave the rebel yell and moved resolutely forward.

But as they proceeded down the slope of the hill, between the shock-rows of wheat, they were met by a tempest of bullets and shell which sent many to the ground, some never to rise again, and others to lie wounded, bleeding and suffering until the storm of battle had passed and the stretcher-bearers could come to their rescue. Once down at the bottom of the hill, they were in a ravine along which runs a spring branch, and here they are somewhat protected by the rising ground in front of them, from the fire of the enemy, whose skirmish line had fallen back, but whose left wing was located about the Thomas house and in the fields, some concealed behind the shocks of wheat, others partly concealed and protected by the small embankment at the bottom of a lane fence running west from the Thomas premises, by the outbuildings on the Thomas premises, and by the contour of the ground. A number of sharpshooters occupied the Thomas mansion and as the Confederate line went forward, the roll of dead and wounded rose rapidly. Not only scores of unknown and unnamed privates fell, but also officers of rank; Col. John H. Lamar and Lieut-Col. James D. Van Valkinburg, both of the 61st Georgia Regiment of Evans' Brigade, and both meritorious officers, were killed; and General Evans himself was severely wounded, at first it was thought mortally, and fell from his horse. The leaden bullet struck him in the side, but its course was stayed by a folded paper of pins which he carried in his coat pocket. The pins were driven into his body by the force of the bullet and were not all extracted until several years later. General Gordon's horse was killed under him as he rode forward.

Private George W. Nichols in his *"Soldier's Story of His Regiment,"* the 61st Georgia, says in his account of the Battle of Monocacy:

"Our beloved commander, Col. J. H. Lamar and Lieut.-Col. J. D. Van Valkinburg (the hero of the Wilderness) were both killed on the field. We truly mourned the loss of these good men and noble Christian commanders."

Colonel Lamar was quite a young man and a military graduate with a promising career ahead of him. He was shot from his horse riding at the head of his regiment. General Evans recovered of his wounds, and afterwards wrote a *"Military History of Georgia"* and *"Confederate Military History"*. When he died in his home in Atlanta, July 2, 1911, the whole town mourned

The loss in Evans' Brigade was so great, including the wounding of the brigade commander himself, to whom instructions had been given, that it threw his brigade into no little confusion which was added to by the difficulty of advancing through a field covered with wheat shocks.

In the meantime, however, the Louisiana brigades, under command of Brigadier-General York became engaged, just to the left of Evans' Brigade, with the centre of Ricketts' line. The Louisianians moved forward with great gallantry past the Worthington house, routing the pickets from the garden and yard, and driving Ricketts' men from their first line at the division fence, back upon his second. General York's men halted a moment at the fence from which the enemy had been driven. Being ordered to climb over and charge, this was done promptly, and the enemy moved further back toward the Thomas mansion.

It was now discovered that the strongest lines of defense were yet to be overcome. General Ricketts had posted his second brigade, under command of Col. Matthew R. McClennan, not far from Gambrill's Mill, behind the crest of the hill in the Thomas fields, in the cuts of the Georgetown Road, behind fences and in depressions left by an abandoned road.

SHARPSHOOTERS IN THOMAS HOUSE

And we have seen that the Federal forces constituting the left wing of Ricketts' command, under Col. W.

S. Truex, were firmly established in and about the Thomas house about 2.45 P. M. This position was maintained until the coming of Gordon's Division one hour later, that is about 3.45, and the sharpshooters from the 87th Pennsylvania and 14th New Jersey occupying the Thomas house and premises kept up a galling fire upon the advancing Confederates, doing terrible execution among them. To the well-directed aim of these sharpshooters was attributed the killing of the officers and many men of the 61st Georgia, as well as of the other regiments of Evans' command.

The resistance about the Thomas house, lane, lawn and premises was so stubborn, and Confederate casualties so great, that Evans' advance was halted, and General Terry, who had not been yet engaged, was ordered to attack the right of Ricketts' line, part of which had moved forward from the hill field on the Thomas farm to the northern end of the division fence to meet Terry's attack. Terry advanced his brigade through the Worthington corn field over which McCausland had fought in the morning, toward the fence, and drove the enemy back to the hill field near the burned wooden bridge, and here another sanguinary engagement took place. The Federal brigades constituting Ricketts' right wing, commanded by Colonel McClennan, were in part concealed from view over the crest of the hill and in depressions in the ground made by an old abandoned road, and behind fences. As the Confederates went forward along the high ground near the crest of the hill, they were met by a decimating fire from these half-concealed and protected troops. In a moment numbers of the Confederates fell, killed outright, or mortally or seriously wounded. The loss here was severe on both sides. The Confederates pressed the

attack, however, and finally the Federals abandoned some
of their positions and fell back to others, but they were
not yet defeated, and the fighting went hotly on. General
Gordon, seeing the stubborn resistance made by the enemy at every point and the great loss suffered in his own
ranks, sent a courier to General Breckinridge, whose
other division under General Echols, was on the west side
of the river near the McGill residence, for reinforcements.

SHELLING THE THOMAS HOUSE

But while the courier was carrying the message, a
piece of Confederate artillery from King's battery was
brought up and planted in the Worthington yard, at the
South end of the house next to the quarter, and shell fire
directed against the Thomas house to dislodge the Federal sharpshooters who hung on there with great determination. The Confederate gunners were experienced
artillerists, and it required only a few shots to get the
range. About the second or third shell struck the side
of the house at the dining room, crashed through the brick
wall, fell on the table where a number of knives and forks
lay, and exploding, scattered them in every direction.
Spangler Welsh, of Company F, 87th Pennsylvania, was
one of those in the house at the time, shooting out of the
windows. He and his comrades departed at once, but
were taken prisoners by the Confederates, who had
pressed forward. Other shells were fired against the
house from the cannon in the Worthington yard, and
tore great holes in its brick walls, drove out the last of
the sharpshooters and cleared the way for an advance of
all that part of the Confederate line.

Meanwhile, before the message for reinforcements
could be delivered and the reinforcements sent, General

Gordon ordered General Terry, whose advance had been checked, to change his front to the right and renew the attack. Whereupon General Terry sent forward by way of the Worthington entrance road to the farm, Col. J. H. S. Funk in command of five fragmentary companies of Virginians, remnants of the old Stonewall Brigade, toward the hollow where the Worthington spring runs unceasingly at the river's edge. Concealed by the bank on their right these Confederate veterans reached the hollow almost unperceived, when they suddenly opened fire upon the Federal line occupying the old sunken road in the Thomas hill field, which runs toward the spring near the river. By this manoeuvre the Confederates obtained a position opposite the right flank of Ricketts' line in the old abandoned road, and their fire enfiladed the Federal line. After a few minutes fighting here the Federals retreated eastwardly over the hill pursued by the Virginians. It had not been an easy task to dislodge the Federals from their position in the sunken road for on both sides were veteran fighters, and courage strengthened by experience animated the attacked as well as the attackers. But an enfilading fire is destructive and presently the Federals gave way and retreated over the crest of the hill toward the Georgetown Road. This being accomplished, and the sharpshooters having been driven from the Thomas house, a combined attack was made all along the line, and after very hot fighting, during which the losses on both sides were heavy, the Federals were at last dislodged and routed.

In these later attacks, the Federal loss became the greater. In the earlier attacks, the Confederates suffered most. When McCausland made his first attack in the morning about 11.30 o'clock and lost so heavily, not a

man at the division fence on the Federal side was killed
or wounded, for not a shot was fired then from the Confederate line. When the Federals had pursued the retreating Confederates a short distance beyond the Worthington house, the latter recovered themselves sufficiently to
open fire and some Federals fell in the Worthington yard,
but none were hurt at the fence. McCausland's second
attack at 2.00 o'clock, was more cautiously made, and
though he suffered loss, he inflicted loss on the enemy.

Evans' Brigade suffered terribly in its first contact
with the foe, especially on the hill side at the end of
Brooks' Hill, and in the onward push toward the Thomas
house, and beyond, to the Georgetown Road. York's
Brigade lost men about the Worthington house, fields and
premises, as did also, to a lesser degree Terry's Brigade.

Federal And Confederates Losses

McCausland's first loss was in the Worthington front
field about one hundred yards west of the clump of walnut trees standing along the division fence where his
ill-starred attack was made at 11.30 in the morning.
Terry's Brigade advanced later through this same field
further north and here not a few men were lost, and Col.
Randolph Barton's horse was killed under him, but how
many of Terry's men were killed or wounded in the field
has not been ascertained. After the battle, numerous
wounded were brought in out of the front field to the
Worthington front yard in the shade made by the house,
to be treated of their wounds, but to whose brigade they
belonged is not known.

The Federals and Confederates, both, lost severely
in the hill field near the bridge on the Thomas farm,
many meeting their death messengers in the old sunken

and abandoned road, and along the fence running directly north over the hill, and also in the field just northwest of the hedge fence along the west side of the
entrance-way to the Thomas house, through a corner of
which runs a spring branch, and about the Thomas
garden, yard, lawn and premises. The total loss in
killed and wounded was approximately about as follows:

Killed, Federal.........	130	Confederate	250
Wounded, Federal....	560	Confederate	650
Total, Federal...........	690	Total, Confederate...	900

Total casualties, 1,590

Besides the killed and wounded, the Federals lost
about 700 prisoners.

To show the sanguinary nature of the battle, General Gordon reported that a small stream of water, running through the battlefield, probably the one flowing
across the Thomas lawn down toward Gambrill's Mill
and Bush Creek, was reddened for one hundred yards
with the blood of soldiers, from both sides, who fell
along its banks killed, or wounded and bleeding.

A soldier of the 61st Georgia, George W. Nichols,
who fought in this battle, in an interesting story of his
regiment, says:

"The Sixty-first Georgia Regiment went into battle
with nearly one hundred and fifty men, and after the
battle was over we could stack but fifty-two guns by
actual count."

The fact that Nichols had stated that there were
only "one hundred and fifty men" in his regiment at
the beginning of the battle, was called to the attention of Mr. I. G. Bradwell, who was also a member of

Evans' Brigade and fought in the Battle of Monocacy, and he replied that Nichols' statement of numbers was correct.

He said that at the Wilderness and at Spottsylvania Court House two months previously, the brigade had suffered severely and that companies were reduced to from 15 to 20 men to a company. Hence, he says Gordon's whole division did not comprise more than 2,500 men. But they were all veterans, the survivors of many a hard fought battle. Mr. Bradwell is still living (1932) with memory and faculties clear at 88 years. His address is Brantley, Alabama.

Gordon's Own Account

In his *"Reminiscences of the Civil War,"* General Gordon has this to say of the battle at Monocacy, and especially of the attack by the command of Evans after crossing the Worthington farm and going up through the wooded knoll at the end of Brooks' Hill:

"The battle of Monocacy which ensued was short, decisive and bloody. While the two armies, under command respectively of Lew Wallace and Jubal Early, were contemplating each other from the opposite banks, my division was selected, not to prevent Wallace from driving us out of Maryland, but to drive him from our front and thus re-open the highway for our march upon the Capital. My movement was down the right bank of the Monocacy to a fording-place below, the object being to cross the river and then turn upon the Federal stronghold. My hope and effort were to conceal the movement from Wallace's watchful eye until my troops were over, and then apprise him of my presence on his side of the river by a sudden rush upon his left flank; but General McCausland's brigade of Confederate cavalry had already gallantly attacked a portion of his troops, and he discovered the maneuver of my division before it could

GEN. JOHN B. GORDON,
Who led a division of Confederate veterans
against Ricketts' Division of Federal veterans at
the Battle of Monocacy, and won after a bloody
encounter.

drag itself through the water and up the Monocacy's muddy and slippery banks. He at once changed front and drew up his lines in strong position to meet the assault.

"This movement presented new difficulties. Instead of realizing my hope of finding the Federal forces still facing Early's other divisions beyond the river, giving my isolated command the immense advantage of the proposed flank attack, I found myself separated from all other Confederate infantry, with the bristling front of Wallace's army before me. In addition to this trouble, I found difficulties before unknown which strongly militated against the probable success of my movement. Across the intervening fields through which we were to advance there were strong farm fences, which my men must climb while under fire. Worse still, those fields were thickly studded with huge grain-stacks which the harvesters had recently piled. They were so broad and high and close together that no line of battle could possibly be maintained while advancing through them. Every intelligent private in my command, as he looked over the field, must have known before we started that my battle-line would become tangled and confused in the attempt to charge through these obstructions.

"With an able commander in my front, and his compact ranks so placed as to rake every foot of the field with their fire, with the certainty of having my lines broken and tangled by fences and grain-stacks at every rod of advance, it is not difficult to understand the responsibility of hazarding battle without supporting Confederate infantry in reach. The nerve of the best-trained and bravest troops is sorely taxed, even under most favorable conditions, when assaulting an enemy well posted, and pouring an incessant well-directed fire into their advancing ranks. To how much severer test of nerve were my troops to be subjected in this attempt to charge where the conditions forced them while under fire to break into column, halt and reform, and make another start, only to be broken again by the immovable stacks all over the field, I knew, however, that if any troops in the world could win victory against such

adverse conditions, those high-mettled Southern boys
would achieve it there.

"En échelon by brigades from the right the movement began. As we reached the first line of strong and
high fencing and my men began to climb over it, they
were met with a tempest of bullets, and many of the brave
fellows fell at the first volley. But over they climbed
or tumbled, and rushed forward, some of them halting
to break down gaps in the fence, so that the mounted
officers might ride through. Then came the grain-stacks.
Around them and between them they pressed on, with
no possibility of maintaining orderly alignment or of
returning effective fire. Deadly missiles from Wallace's
ranks were cutting down the line and company officers,
with their words of cheer to the men but half spoken. It
was one of those fights where success depends largely
upon the prowess of the individual soldier. The men
were deprived of that support and strength imparted by
a compact line, where the elbow touch of comrade with
comrade gives confidence to each and sends the electric
thrill of enthusiasm through all. But nothing could
deter them. Neither the obstructions nor the leaden
blast in their front could check them. The supreme test
of their marvelous nerve and self-control now came.
They had passed the forest of malign wheat-stacks; they
had climbed the second fence and were in close proximity
to Wallace's first line of battle, which stood firmly and
was little hurt. The remaining officers, on horseback
and on foot, rapidly adjusted their commands, and I
ordered 'Forward!' and forward they went. I recall no
charge of the war, except of the 12th of May against
Hancock, in which my brave fellows seemed so swayed
by an enthusiasm which amounted almost to a martial
delirium; and the swell of the Southern yell rose high
above the din of battle as they rushed upon the resolute
Federals and hurled them back upon the second line.

"The Union lines stood firmly in this second position,
bravely defending the railroad and the highway to Washington. Between the two hostile lines there was a narrow
ravine down which ran a small stream of limpid water.
In this ravine the fighting was desperate and at close
quarters. To and fro the battle swayed across the little

stream, the dead and wounded of both sides mingling their blood in its waters. Nearly one-half of my men and large numbers of Federals fell there. Many of my officers went down, and Gen. Clement A. Evans, the trusted leader of my largest brigade, was severely wounded. A Minié ball struck him in his left side, passing through a pocket of his coat and carrying with it a number of pins which were so deeply imbedded that they were not all extracted for a number of years. But the execution of his orders was superintended by his staff officer, Maj. Eugene C. Gordon, who was himself severely wounded.

"In that vortex of fire my favorite battle horse, presented to me by my generous comrades, which had never hitherto been wounded, was struck by a Minie ball, and plunged and fell in the midst of my men, carrying me down with him. Ordinarily the killing of a horse in battle, though ridden by the commander, would scarcely be worth noting; but in this case it was serious. By his death I had been unhorsed in the very crisis of the battle. Many of my leading officers were killed or disabled. The chances for victory or defeat were at the moment so evenly balanced that a temporary halt or slight blunder might turn the scales. My staff were bearing orders to different portions of the field. But some thoughtful officer sent me a horse and I was again mounted.

"Wallace's army, after the most stubborn resistance and with heavy loss, was driven from railroad and pike in the direction of Baltimore. The Confederate victory was won at fearful cost and by practically a single division, but it was complete, and the way to Washington was opened for General Early's march."

CAPTAIN BOATRIGHT OF GEORGIA

A Confederate captain, Captain Boatright of Georgia, visited the battlefield in 1910 and pointed out the place in the Thomas lawn where one of his young men was lying down on his belly in the grass trying to catch sight of the head of an enemy in the cut in the Georgetown

Road near the Thomas gate, when a bullet from an enemy musket came through the grass and hit the young man in the top of the head, killing him instantly. He merely stretched himself and died, said Captain Boatright. "I covered him with his blanket and left him there." A fine promising black-haired boy, only nineteen years old. Captain Boatright also stated that he and four others went further toward the gate when suddenly there came a volley from behind the embankment of the Georgetown Road, resulting in the killing of two and the wounding of two of the little squad, he only escaped unhurt, and that narrowly; a bullet passing through the sleeve of his coat. The next moment Terry's attack had dislodged Ricketts' right in the Thomas hill field and the whole Federal line retreated in haste, so that no further shots were fired. The battle was over. But what a terrible toll of human life and human wholeness in so brief a space of time! Besides the dead, more than one thousand men suffered from wounds received in that struggle; and 700 suffered the terrible privations and hardships of prison life at a Confederate prison at Danville until the end of the war, almost a year later.

The Federal line of retreat was past Gambrill's Mill and over the hills, across the Baltimore and Ohio Railroad, toward the Baltimore turnpike, which passes through New Market and Ridgeville.

CONFEDERATE ARTILLERY

Throughout the hot fight, the artillery of the Confederates continued to do its part as well as it could without doing injury to the men in gray. Some pieces were brought across the river at the Worthington-McKinney Ford, one of which was operated from the Worthington yard, and others from vantage points on the Worthington farm, while other batteries continued to be operated from across the river.

In every sense it was a real battle and its sanguinary character is shown by all the official and unofficial accounts of it. The losses by regiments may be estimated from the few accounts that have come to notice from persons who participated and who observed the loss sustained at the time. For instance, Private Nichols says that his regiment, the 61st Georgia, went into battle with about 150 men and the next morning it could stack but 52 muskets by actual count.

In his address at the unveiling of the monument to the 14th New Jersey Regiment, on the battlefield in 1908, Major John C. Patterson said that his regiment went into the fight with about 256 rifles, the next morning only 92 men answered to their names. That out of 15 officers, four were killed and eight wounded, and that out of seven men of the color guard, two were killed and three wounded, the color sergeant himself being killed. Nichols also relates that five men in succession were shot down in Evans' Brigade, bearing the colors.

The importance of a battle is not shown merely by the number killed and wounded, but these show whether or not there was a real fight. On the Federal side six captains of companies and eight lieutenants were either killed outright or mortally wounded.

SOME OF THE OFFICERS KILLED OR MORTALLY WOUNDED

FEDERAL

Capt. John V. Morris, Eighth Cavalry—Illinois.
Capt. Henry J. Conine, 14th Infantry—New Jersey.

Capt. Henry W. Stults, 14th Infantry—New Jersey.
Lieut. James H. Ellis, Ninth Heavy Artillery—New York.
Capt. Alfred J. Hooker, 106th Infantry—New York.
Capt. Martin J. Chamberlain, 106th Infantry—New York.
Lieut. John Kingston, 106th Infantry—New York.
Capt. William A. Hathaway, 110th Infantry—Ohio.
Lieut. George O. McMillen, 110th Infantry—Ohio.
Lieut. Jefferson O. McMillen, 122nd Infantry—Ohio.
Lieut. Anthony M. Martin, 87th Infantry—Pennsylvania.
Lieut. Charles F. Haack, 87th Infantry—Pennsylvania.
Lieut. Daniel D. Dietrich, 87th Infantry—Pennsylvania.
Lieut. John F. Spangler, 87th Infantry—Pennsylvania.

The above list is not complete but it shows in a measure the heavy mortality among the officers and the severity of the fighting.

Other officers dangerously wounded were:

Lieut.-Col. E. P. Taft, Heavy Artillery—Ninth New York.
Capt. G. W. Guss, 138th Infantry—Pennsylvania.
Capt. Luther Brown, 110th Infantry—Ohio.

CONFEDERATES

The names of the officers in the Confederate Army killed or mortally wounded at Monocacy could not be ascertained, except as to a few. As already narrated two were killed in the charge on the Thomas house:

Col. John H. Lamar, 61st Infantry—Georgia.
Lieut.-Col. James D. Van Valkinburg, 61st Infantry—Georgia.

Brid.-Gen. Clement A. Evans, First Brigade, Gordon's Division—Georgia.

Col. John Hodges, Ninth Infantry, Hays' Brigade—Louisiana.

There is little doubt but that as many or more Confederate officers were killed or wounded as Federal, but the Confederate records are apparently not preserved.

(Note)—The Confederate losses at Monocacy have been placed elsewhere in this chapter at 250 killed and 650 wounded. These figures are obtained from the records in part and are mere estimates in part.

On a tablet erected over a mound in Mt. Olivet Cemetery, some years after the war, there is the following inscription:

"THIS STONE MARKS THE LAST RESTING PLACE OF

408 CONFEDERATE SOLDIERS

WHO GAVE THEIR LIVES IN THE BATTLE OF MONOCACY

JULY 9, 1864. HONOR THE BRAVE."

Besides this marker there are 87 individual graves with headstones and in most instances the names of the deceased engraved thereon, all of whom are said to have died at Monocacy, wearers of the gray. Thus making a total of 495 Confederates killed or mortally wounded in that battle.

It is not known from what source the number of dead in the mound was obtained, but it is known that some years after the battle the Ladies' Confederate Memorial Association of Frederick raised money and employed men to go over the Monocacy battlefield and gather all the bones of the Confederates who lay buried there in trenches and in scattered graves, and to bring them to Mt. Olivet Cemetery, at Frederick, where many of them were reburied in one mound because their indentity could not be determined, due to the fact that a large number had no headboards when originally interred, or the headboards had been destroyed. General Gordon in his official report of the battle gave the loss in his division as 698, but no official report of General Rodes, or of General Ramseur, or of General McCausland, as to their losses was found in the *Official War Records*. General Gordon says the victory was won "at fearful cost," and though actual numbers are uncertain, it was, indeed, without question a most sanguinary battle. Some one has said that, considering the numbers actually engaged, it may well be termed "one of the bloodiest fields of the war." Here the veteran forces from Georgia, Virginia, North Carolina, Louisiana and Alabama met the equally veteran forces from New Jersey, Pennsylvania, New York, Ohio, Illinois, Vermont and Maryland, and it was like Greek meeting Greek.

On the one side a martial spirit animated the Southerners to "do or die." And on the other a similar spirit animated the Northerners to "hold the ground or die."

And the ground over which was fought this terrible tug of war is hallowed by the blood shed there by brave and consecrated Americans, unafraid even in the face of death.

CHAPTER XX.

FEDERAL ACCOUNTS OF THE BATTLE

WALLACE'S ACCOUNT OF THE MAIN BATTLE

In his account of the battle, General Wallace says that when McCausland's second attack was repulsed at the Thomas farm about 2.45 o'clock, he sent for General Ricketts to come to his headquarters; that the general came promptly and they discussed the advisability of retreating then, as they saw a long line of gray moving down the Buckeystown Road toward Ballenger Creek and the lower ford on the Monocacy; that General Ricketts was not yet ready to quit and that he was of the same mind. So they resolved to stay and fight it out with Gordon's Division then about to cross the river at the Worthington-McKinney Ford. After this conference, General Ricketts went back to his position near the gate at the entrance to the Thomas driveway. Of what occurred between Gordon's and Ricketts' divisions, General Wallace does not appear to have had a clear view. He says little in his book about the details of this part of the battle, which took place between 3.30 and 5 o'clock.

Wallace does say, however, that:

"The men of the Sixth Corps retreated reluctantly under my orders. They bore the brunt of the battle with a coolness and firmness which, I venture to say, has never been exceeded in any battle of the war.

"It would be difficult for me to say too much in praise of these veterans who made this fight.

"Although the appearance of the enemy's fourth line of battle made their ultimate defeat certain, they were not whipped. On the contrary, they were fighting steadily in an unbroken front when I ordered their retirement. The fact speaks for itself: 'Monocacy' on their battle-flags is a word of honor. . . . Too much credit cannot be given General Ricketts for his skill and courage. In this battle we did not lose a flag or a gun."

In concluding his report of the battle General Wallace said, "Orders have been given to collect the bodies of our dead in one burial ground on the battle-field, suitable for a monument, on which I propose to write:

" 'These men died to save the National Capital and they did save it'."

Col. Matthew R. McClennan, commanding Second Brigade, says in his report:

"The battle of Monocacy was one of great spirit and importance, and in my belief saved the city of Washington from the ravages of the enemy."

This report was dated September 10, 1864, after he had time to consider the consequences of the delay of Early's march upon the National Capital.

ALFRED S. ROE'S ACCOUNT

No report from General Ricketts has been found and the official reports of the commanders or regiments are very general, giving few details. Alfred Seelye Roe, a private of the Ninth New York Heavy Artillery, has narrated much of interest as to what he saw during the engagement and what follows is largely drawn from

his book.   Near the bottom of page 131 of his book,
he says:

"It was well along in the afternoon when we, who
had been lying so long on the brow of the hill, were
ordered in.   We were very near the river, only one regiment, the 110th Ohio, at our right, intervening.   Colonel
Seward sat on his horse as erect as a centaur; Lieutenant-
Colonel Taft was also in his place and mounted with
Adjutant Pringle.   Our alignment is excellent and the
colors stream along as we advance over the space sepa-
rating us from a standing field of corn.   Here is another
strong fence whose rails afford us excellent rests for
our guns as we rapidly fire into the field through which
the enemy is making his way and firing as he comes.   We
are finding no fault with our part of the game, and our
Harpers Ferry muskets are doing such execution that
we think ourselves able to hold the place indefinitely.
But there is trouble at the extreme left, where we are
flanked.   Soon the order comes to fall back, which we
obey slowly, keeping up a desultory fusillade at the
rebels who climb our fence in a suprisingly brief time
after our leaving it.   A halt is made near the point where
we had thrown down the fence.   Lieutenant Harmon of
Company H unconsciously used the refrain of Root's
battle hymn as he exclaimed, 'Rally 'round your flag,
boys,' for the colors were there.   Further along towards
the left and under the hill Colonel Seward, who had been
injured by his wounded horse falling upon him and who
was supported by two men, was directing an officer and
guard to advance to a tree some rods nearer the enemy
to secure Lieutenant-Colonel Taft, who was lying there
wounded.   This order Lieutenant Colvin of Company H
essayed to obey, but before the officer could be reached,
the rebel line had swept by and the effort was futile."

Our lieutenant-colonel thus wrote later of his injury:

" 'I was withdrawing from the field when a numbness
seized my left leg and I dropped to the ground. . . . .
He was afterwards carried to Frederick, but it was not
till September 10 that Lyons accorded him a handsome
welcome home, the Reverend L. W. Brown speaking for
the people and Col. A. D. Adams for the wounded officer.

"By this time our own lines were thrown into great confusion. The flank movement on the left had driven down towards Gambrill's Mill portions of the First Brigade and our own Second was mingled with them. Col. M. R. McClennan of the 138th Pennsylvania was in temporary command of the Second Brigade and, possibly, he was the officer who was shouting, 'Elevate your pieces, men; elevate your pieces'; this, in regard to the advancing Confederates who, in great numbers, are bearing down upon us. From some source comes the order to shift for ourselves, and the Monocacy field is left behind us. One private recalls hearing the color-sergeant of the Ninth say, 'I don't see any use in staying here any longer,' and said private thought his record safe in that he left the field behind the colors. Colonel Seward got away, riding on a bridleless mule, which he directed by means of a silk handkerchief inserted in its mouth. The day had ended disastrously, so far as we are concerned, but for nine hours a handful of men has held Early's thousands, thus permitting the remainder of our corps to reach Washington and so prevent the consummation of the rebels' audacious plan to capture the Capital."

In a *History of the 87th Pennsylvania Volunteers,* it is said (bottom of page 183):

"At 3.30 P. M. the Confederates emerged again from the woods, a strong skirmish line appearing first. Then two battle lines followed, both of which overlapped the Federal line on the right and left flanks. They came charging down the hill giving the "rebel yell." Ricketts' men stood their ground with determination, repulsing the skirmish line and holding the third charge in check until their ammunition had nearly given out. The enemy now came in on their flanks and captured some prisoners.

"At this juncture, about 4.30 P. M., General Wallace gave the order to fall back. It was during the afternoon that the 87th Regiment had most of its casualties, losing in killed, wounded and captured, 74 men."

There was one incident of the battle that gave General Wallace no small concern. That was the non-arrival at the battlefield of the 67th Pennsylvania, the Sixth Maryland and part of the 122nd Ohio regiments. These came from Baltimore as far as Monrovia on the Baltimore and Ohio Railroad and there, for some reason, debarked and waited. They did not reach the battlefield eight miles distant, but they joined the other Federal forces in their retreat and served a good purpose in warding off pursuit. Just why they did not push for the place of battle more promptly seems not to be satisfactorily explained.

CHAPTER XXI.

INCIDENTS OF THE BATTLE

1. A WHEAT SHOCK A POOR FORTRESS

During the advance of Evans' Brigade across the wheat field from the end of Brooks' Hill to the Thomas house, a Federal soldier fired at the advancing enemy from behind a wheat shock. The man himself was not visible, but the smoke of his rifle was. Immediately the guns of many Confederates were turned upon that particular wheat shock, and when the Confederates in their onward go, came to the shock of wheat, the Federal soldier lay there dead with a dozen bullet wounds in his body.

2. A MAN'S BRAINS SHOT OUT

Thomas Nichols of Company A, 61st Georgia Regiment, was badly wounded in the head. He was able to sit up and was seen wiping his brains from his temple with his hand. A bullet had just grazed the man's temple and broken the skull enough to allow the brain tissue to ooze out. He lived twelve hours before death came to his relief.

3. THE COLOR BEARER

Lieut. James Mincy of Company D, 12th Georgia Regiment, picked up the battle flag after five other men had been shot down in succession carrying the flag in this battle. Mincy, himself, was immediately shot down, the bullet going through his left lung, and he was left for dead. He afterwards said: "A Yankee doctor drew a silk handkerchief through me and treated me very kindly." He finally recovered.

4. A QUESTION OF SECONDS

The truth of the following cannot be vouched for with certainty, but it is believed to be an incident that actually happened:

A captain of one of the Confederate companies was standing by his men at the fence, just across one field, west from the Thomas house. Firing was going on from both sides. The captain, whose name was given but cannot be recalled, saw a Union soldier standing down by the small stream that flows through the Thomas lawn, aim at him and fire. The bullet whizzed by close. A reloading and a re-aiming and a refiring. This time the bullet tipped a piece of the captain's ear. With his sword he touched a man of his company who was known to be an expert marksman. The Union soldier, again reloading his gun, was pointed out to this marksman, and the result of the two preceding shots briefly told to him. It was now a question of seconds. The expert rested his gun on a fence rail, aimed carefully and fired. The rifleman by the rivulet dropped his gun, threw up his hands and fell, but how seriously wounded he was is not known.

5. COLONEL BARTON GETS A HORSE

Just before the battle, as already related, the horses from the Worthington farm were, all except one horse and a mule, taken to Sugar Loaf Mountain and hidden in the dark recesses there. The one horse that remained in the stable was "Old Davy," the carriage horse. During the engagement Col. Randolph Barton of Terry's Brigade, had his horse shot under him in the front cornfield. His orderly, in looking around for another horse, discovered "Old Davy" in the stable and took him to the colonel.

The saddle and bridle from the wounded animal were transferred to "Old Davy," and the colonel mounted his new charger. In a few minutes "Old Davy," too, was hit by a musket ball and went down, never to rise again.

Finally another horse was obtained from somewhere and again the doughty colonel was in the saddle. After the war, Colonel Barton was a prominent Baltimore lawyer; he was a gentleman of the old school in every way and a fearless soldier as well.[1]

6. COLONEL WILLIAM H. SEWARD, JR.

Among the prominent figures in the battle on the Union side was Col. William H. Seward, Jr., son of Lincoln's great Secretary of State. Colonel Seward was a native of Auburn, New York, where his family have resided for several generations. He was conspicious in the battle of Monocacy for his gallantry in command of the Ninth New York Heavy Artillery, an infantry regiment. During the battle his horse was wounded under him and falling, injured him severely. He was being supported by two men under the hill in the Thomas field and at the same time he was endeavoring to direct an officer to go to the rescue of Lieut.-Col. E. P. Taft, who was lying wounded under a tree further up the hill, toward the advancing foe. Before Colonel Taft could be rescued, the rebel line swept by and the effort to save him from capture was futile. Colonel Seward himself got away, when the final break came, on a bridleless mule, guided by a silk handkerchief in his mouth. Colonel Taft was shot in the leg and severely wounded; his black horse galloped riderless to the rear. Later his leg was amputated at Frederick. Colonel Taft never fully recovered of his wound and died a little more than two years later at his home in Lyon, New York. He was less than thirty-five years of age at the time and a most meritorious officer.

7. A LUCKY STRIKE

During the fight a tall young fellow of Company D, Ninth New York Heavy Artillery, was hit by a bullet, striking the eagle-plate of his cartridge box straps. The bullet was half spent and penetrated just far enough to stick in the eagle-plate. There it stuck fast. When this company reached Washington several days later, President Lincoln came out to congratulate the officers and men on their gallant services at Monocacy. The young fellow with the rebel bullet in his equipment stepped forward to the President's carriage and showed him the trophy of his salvation, saying, "See, Mr. Lincoln, this saved my life at Monocacy, the force of the bullet knocked me down."

The President took the relic in his hand, looked at it carefully, commented on the lucky escape of the soldier, and handing it back, said, "Young man, keep that for your children and grandchildren, for future generations will prize that as the greatest heirloom you could possibly leave them."

8. THE CHANTICLEER

An interesting fact of the battle is that when the Worthington family went into the cellar for protection from flying missiles, the chickens and other domestic fowls, of which there were quite a number, were left running at large in the backyard of the farmhouse. Among them was a big rooster with a flaming comb and throttle, and withal, a big voice. The Confederate cannon planted in the yard to dislodge the sharpshooters from the Thomas house was being operated, and every time the cannon was fired, the chanticleer would lift up his voice and crow most lustily. This was repeated as often as the cannon was discharged. After every report, it was crow, Chapman, crow. It was premature as a crow for victory, but encouraging to the gunners.

9. COLONEL HODGES WOUNDED

During the engagement Lieut.-Col. John Hodges of the Ninth Louisiana Regiment, Hays' Brigade, was severely and painfully wounded by a leaden bullet striking him in the upper right arm and shattering the large bone, called the "humerus." When the firing had ceased, the aid and sympathy of every member of the Worthington household was given to the wounded and suffering. Among those near the Worthington house to receive attention was Colonel Hodges. He was standing at the time in the rear of the house, but evidently suffering great pain. Mr. Worthington went to him and speaking to him, led him to a place beside a post and rail fence running from the house to the Monocacy. Mr. Worthington's two small sons, Glenn and Harry, were told by their father to go into the wheat field nearby and get several sheaves of wheat, and to make a pallet beside the fence, on the east side of it. The sheaves were gotten, the pallet made and Colonel Hodges was assisted to lie down on it. Then the boys were told to get more sheaves to put up against the fence to keep off the warm rays of the sun, then slowly sinking in the west. This also was done and Colonel Hodges made as comfortable as circumstances would allow. But so great was his suffering, so oppressively warm the weather that he fainted away just as he was being placed on his improvised bed. Mr. Worthington had a barrel of good whiskey in his cellar, and a tablespoonful of this was given the wounded man, whereupon he soon revived. Later in the evening the colonel was taken to Frederick in an ambulance. Whether his arm was amputated or not is not known, but it is understood that he survived many years.

10.   A Bullet Enters The Worthington House

Although a Confederate cannon was fired a number of times from the Worthington yard near the house, at the Thomas house, no Federal shell struck the Worthington house. A number of leaden bullets hit the walls of the house and the slate roof and broke off bits of brick and slate, but only one bullet entered. Two Confederate officers came during the battle and asked permission to survey the battle-line of the enemy from an upstairs front window. Permission could not be refused and the two officers went up stairs, threw open the shutters which had been closed, and with their field-glasses surveyed the enemy's lines.

They had just finished their survey and closed the shutters when instantly a ball came through one shutter and hit the opposite wall in the room, breaking the plaster. The shutter is still there with the bullet-hole in it. The officers escaped injury. No other bullet entered the house during the battle and the damage to the outside was slight.

11.   The Thomas House Torn With Shot And Shell

The Thomas house was badly damaged. Not only were the brick walls toward the Worthington house torn in great gaps and holes by Confederate shell fire, but the front of the house, including the fine piazza, was hit by bullets and shells fired by the Federals.

When the Confederates of McCausland's Regiment seized the house and held it for a short while, they were

fired on by the men of the 14th New Jersey, 87th Pennsylvania, 10th Vermont and other regiments occupying
the Georgetown Road near the intersection of the Baker
Valley Road, and also by one or more of Alexander's
pieces located further east near the Yaste house. The
Confederates had only a slim force at the time and when
finally the regiments above named charged, McCausland's
men retreated from the house and premises back toward
the Worthington barn, but marks of the fusillade against
the house from the Federal guns may still be seen in the
shot-scarred pillars to the front porch, and bullet wounds
in front wall and shutters. Marks of the battle are
plainly visible there after more than sixty-seven years.

12. The Harvest Of Death

After the battle the dead and many wounded lay
over the fields where, as soldiers militant, they fought
and fell. There were dead and wounded on the Worthington farm, in the cornfield, in the pasture-field, in the
wheatfield and in the yard and garden; and on the
Thomas farm in almost every field as well as about his
house, yard and premises; and down by Gambrill's Mill
there were others who gave their lives or suffered grievous
wounds, fighting for the cause they deemed to be just.

Where the peaceful harvesters had, but a few days
before, cut and gathered into stacks, the ripened grain,
there on this day was the harvest of death and the blood
of heroes on both sides stained the stubble and the straw
of the bound grain, and the bodies of the dead and
wounded were mingled with the scattered sheaves.

13. The Stubble Burns

In some fields the dry wheat stubble caught fire and
burned over wide areas, threatening to envelop the help-

less wounded who lay there, but friendly hands with blankets beat out the spreading flames. One wounded rebel stated that a Yankee beat out the flames close to him and thus saved him from the torture of being burned to death. A wounded and helpless foeman is no longer an enemy. Such deeds of mercy and humanity are not infrequent in war, it is said, thanks to our better nature and Christian nurture.

14. INDIVIDUAL CASES

One who was in the battle thus writes:

"I pass a comrade sitting by the roadside. Blood is trickling from a wound just below the heart. . . . I say, "Goodbye,' to him; there is no regret or fear in his tone as he replies. A brave country boy he had lived and death has no terrors for him. He could not have smiled more sweetly had he been lying down to pleasant dreams."

"Hours afterward I carry a canteen full of water to another comrade lying on a pile of grain in the storehouse by the railroad, and he too had no complaints or repinings. He only said, 'I have my death wound,' and with the dew of youth yet fresh upon him, with all the prospects of a long life ended, he closed his eyes in dreamless sleep."

After the battle, dead and wounded lay around and about the Worthington house, some wounded screaming with pain, some groaning in agony, others enduring silently. One large Confederate lay bleeding in the backyard, in the angle made by the wings of the house. He was shot several times and was mortally wounded. He died within the hour. Mrs. Worthington spoke to him shortly before his death and inquired, and he replied saying that he had a wife and children at home.

Another, a soldier in blue, had a bullet wound in his body that caused him to bleed internally. His abdomen was discolored from the internal hemorrhage.

He was propped against a tree in the front yard of the Worthington house, and his groans were pitiable. A Confederate surgeon at Mr. Worthington's request gave him morphia to deaden his pain. He died during the night. Many others were brought in on stretchers. Some to be treated, some to be buried. Hospitals were also established at the McKinney home, at the Thomas house, at Gambrill's Mill and along the highway near the Yaste house. And so they died, the young and the old, on the field amidst the roar of cannon and musketry, in the hospitals of wounds, on the picket line, anywhere, those who wore the blue and those who wore the gray. They deemed the cause worthy the sacrifice. God give them rest and a rich reward.

15.   A ROMANCE

Growing out of the battle the following romance and marriage occurred.

During the engagement Capt. Chauncey Harris, Company C, 14th New Jersey Volunteers, was wounded severely twice, once in the shoulder and while lying in an ambulance ready to be moved, he was hit in the knee by a flying bullet which made an ugly and painful wound. Because of his suffering he was removed to the farmhouse of Mr. Edward Baker, in Baker's Valley, about one mile south from the scene of the conflict.

Here he was put to bed and carefully nursed by Miss Clementine Baker, a daughter of the landowner. After weeks of attentive nursing Captain Harris was able to be out again and to resume a peaceful occupation, though his knee was always stiff afterwards.

The lady's sympathy and careful nursing won the captain's heart completely, and her pity was akin to love from the beginning. They were married shortly after and lived happily together for many years at Elizabeth, New Jersey, the captain's home. For his gallant services at Monocacy, Captain Harris was brevetted colonel. He served as postmaster of Elizabeth for a long time after the close of the war.

16. A Half Romance

Another romance or half romance also resulting in marriage, grew out of the battle.

Lieut. John F. Spangler, of Company A, 87th Pennsylvania Volunteers, was mortally wounded when the rebels made their last charge down past the Thomas house. The ball penetrated his breast and taking a downward course, lodged in his stomach.

Late in the evening he was taken to the home of Mrs. Ruth Doffler, widow of John Doffler, living at Frederick.

Lieutenant Spangler lived six days and while he was being nursed by the widow, Doffler, his father came from York to see him. The young man died on the 15th of July and his body was carried to York, Pa., and buried there in Union Cemetery, North Penn Street. The father afterwards came to Frederick and was married to the motherly woman who had so tenderly nursed his son.

17. The Coveted Bayonet

After the battle, while the stretcher-bearers and surgeons were busy about the front yard of the Worthington farmhouse, gathering the dead and caring for the wounded, other men were sent out to gather up muskets thrown away by the Federals in their retreat from the field. In order to destroy them, these muskets were placed in a pile in the Worthington backyard with the muzzles all pointing one way toward 'Brooks' Hill. Then an armful of straw was thrown over the pile and set on fire. The dry stocks burned freely and soon there was left only a collection of stockless gun barrels and a few loose bayonets. One of these bayonets, Glenn H. (the writer of these pages), a son of Mr. John T. Worthington, aged six, desired for his own purposes. So he procured a stick, the half of a barrel-hoop, and undertook to pull the coveted bayonet out of the coals and embers of the then smouldering fire. Slowly the bayonet was pulled to the rim of the circle made by the fire. There, all unknown to the youthful bayonet-seeker, just outside the rim of the circle, lay a paper cartridge, dropped by some soldier during the fight. The bayonet brought with it a coal of fire. The coal of fire touched the side of the paper cartridge. Just as the acquisitive small boy stooped to pull the bayonet out of the circle of fire, the cartridge exploded and the boy's face was terribly powder-burned. Skin seared, eyebrows burned away, ends of eyelashes crisped.

Then there was a yell, akin to the rebel yell, and some pitying Confederate picked the boy up in his arms and carried him, blinded and yelling, to the house. There it was thought he had lost the sight of both eyes. Cream cloths were applied, and after a time, the boy was asked to open his eyes. But he would not or could not. In bed, on his back, cream cloths over his face, he lay the night through. The next day, the boy was again asked to open his eyes, and open them he did and his sight was not impaired. Another day in bed with cream cloths on his face and then up and about. The skin healed in time, the eyebrows grew and the disfigurement was not noticeable at the end of a year. But to the boy the incident blended with the other events of the day and became a part of the memorable battle of Monocacy.

18. AN INTERESTING ACCOUNT

Private George W. Nichols of the 61st Georgia, who served in Evans' Brigade, says in his interesting account of his experiences in the battle:

"Evans' Brigade crossed the river, formed in line and advanced on their position about three-quarters of a mile through an open field. Wallace's men were well posted in a road that was washed out and graded until it was as fine breastworks as I ever saw. Here our brigade suffered as bad as it ever did in battle for the amount of men and length of time engaged, especially the 61st Georgia Regiment and the 12th Georgia Battalion.

"We advanced to within thirty yards of the line, but we would have to fall back, for our men were killed and wounded until we had but a mere skirmish line. . . . .

"It made our hearts ache to look over the battlefield and see so many of our dear comrades, friends and beloved officers killed and wounded. Our loss was terrible while the Yankees lost but few. . . . . It was called our victory but it was a costly one, for it cost Evans' Brigade over five hundred men, in wounded and killed. It was said that it was raw troops we were fighting, but I never saw old soldiers shoot better."

This tribute from a rebel soldier in the ranks proves pretty conclusively that Ricketts' men fought valiantly and tends to corroborate the statement by Gen. Lew Wallace in his report of the battle that these men were not whipped when he ordered their withdrawal. In his report General Wallace also says that "too much credit cannot be given General Ricketts for his skill and courage." According to all information this praise was well deserved.

James Brewerton Ricketts was born in New York City, June 21, 1817, and died of wounds in Washington, D. C., September 22, 1887. Before his death he was brevetted major-general for meritorious services through the war.

19. A Minor Detached Incident

Another incident of the battle, though insignificant in itself, seems worth relating:

During the engagement, Gen. John C. Breckinridge, who was in command of two divisions of the Confederate Army, that of Gordon and Echols, and who gave orders to Gordon to take his division across the river and drive the Federals, also crossed the Monocacy and went forward as far as the Worthington house to watch the progress of the fighting and to be near enough to give counsel and advice in case it should be needed. After a very determined resistance the Federals were finally dislodged from their positions and routed. As the firing subsided Mr. John T. Worthington (a non-combatant), who had been, during the heat of the engagement, in the cellar of his house with his family and a few slaves, went outside in the backyard where he saw General Breckinridge; a very distinguished person in his day and generation, for he had been Vice-President of the United States, a candidate for the Presidency, and a United States Senator from Kentucky. Now a famous general in the Confederate Army. Mr. Worthington went forward to greet the general, who dismounted from his horse and extended his hand. As the two stood there facing each other shaking hands, a cane which Mr. Worthington carried in his left hand, at the moment, the end of which rested on the ground between them, was struck by a flying bullet and knocked out of his hand.

Whereupon General Breckinridge said: "Mr. Worthington, it is not safe for you to be here, bullets are still flying and you might be seriously hurt."

MAJOR-GENERAL JOHN C. BRECKINRIDGE

To which Mr. Worthington replied: "It is just as dangerous for you, General."

"Yes, I know," replied the famous man, "but it is my duty to be here and not yours."

Whereupon Mr. Worthington retreated to the cellar and remained until the firing had entirely ceased. Mr. Worthington often told the story of the little incident, always with manifest respect and admiration for the distinguished and dignified Southern statesman and soldier.

---

[1]Many years after the war the writer became pleasantly acquainted with Col. Randolph Barton and in his law office in Baltimore jocosely referred to the taking of the horse on the day of the battle. To which the colonel banteringly replied: "I suppose you came to collect." Being answered laughingly in the affirmative, he replied: "I plead *inter arma silent leges.*"

Afterwards Colonel Barton came to the Court of Appeals of Maryland as counsel in a case and appeared before the court of which the writer was then a member for the purpose of arguing the appeal. Before starting the argument he said to a friend close by, but not loud enough for the court to hear: "I do not know what chance I have to win this case before this court because I understand that one of the judges of the court charges that my orderly stole his father's horse at the battle of Monocacy, and that I received him; and he wants payment of me for it."

The writer had previously mentioned the circumstance of the taking to the other members of the court. Just as the argument was about to begin, Judge Burke in a spirit of fun passed a note by the hands of the judges behind the bench to the writer, on which was written: "Now is the time to collect for "Old Davy." To which was made reply in the same fashion: "Would be glad to place the claim in your hands. Two hundred and fifty dollars and interest for 44 years."

Neither the court nor the counsel knew of these little jests on the part of the other and the case was argued in perfect decorum. It happned, too, that the chief judge assigned the writer of these pages to prepare the opinion in the case which wholly sustained the colonel's legal propositions, and all the judges concurred. For years the pleasantry was carried on and the taking of "Old Davy," made the subject of much jest and merriment. The case argued will be found reported in 108 Md. Rep., at page 620.

As long as he lived Colonel Barton was greatly esteemed and beloved by all who knew him. His son, Randolph Barton, Jr., still carries on as a member of the Baltimore bar and maintains the high standard of the legal profession so scrupulously maintained by his venerated father.

CHAPTER XXII.

THE THREE CIVILIAN SOLDIERS

An Episode Of The Battle

The following rather amusing episode of the battle occurred. It is amusing in retrospect, though at the time, it was too full of hazard to the young men who participated in it to be laughable, and there was no laughter in their hearts as they performed the part assigned them and endured the dangers of actual battle and other perils.

To certain young ladies it was no laughing matter either at the time. The Thomas house, so often mentioned in the course of the narrative, is a fine brick mansion with a wide-roofed porch or piazza in front, looking down a shaded lawn or driveway leading to the Georgetown Road. Two tall, venerable pine trees stand just in front of the porch and furnish shade from the morning sun. The porch floor is about eighteen inches from the ground and the porch itself extends across the whole front of the house, a distance of perhaps forty feet.

The porch was ever a favorite place for the family to sit in summertime. There is a fine view from the porch of Frederick Valley, including the Worthington house, Monocacy Junction, Gambrill's Mill and the railroad from Baltimore, near the iron bridge, where General Wallace had established his headquarters.

The farm and house have long been known as

"Araby." The owner, Col. C. Keefer Thomas, was rather proud of his possessions, as well he might be. The colonel's family consisted of himself, his wife, two daughters and two sons. His daughter, Alice, was then a young woman not out of her teens and comely. She was fair complected with blue eyes and rosy cheeks, but dark hair. With the freshness of youth upon her, she was beautiful, gay, and most chaming in every way. At Baltimore lived her fiancé, Julius H. Anderson, a young man just past his majority.

Visiting at the Thomas mansion was a friend of Miss Alice, a Miss Mamie Tyler, also a beautiful and attractive young lady. Her fiancé was Hugh M. Gatchell, whose residence was also in Baltimore. At the time of the battle and before, Miss Alice's brother, Samuel S. Thomas, was also located at Baltimore, having some business connection in that city.

The 4th of July everywhere in this Union is recognized as a national holiday and the three young men at Baltimore arranged to spend the 4th of July, 1864, at "Araby," the hospitable home of Col. C. Keefer Thomas. It was father's house to Samuel S. Thomas, and as to the other two young men, it contained two expectant young ladies.

So on the morning of the 4th these three young men took the cars of the Baltimore and Ohio Railroad at Camden Station for Frederick Junction. Arriving, they were met by the horse-drawn carriage and a driver from the Thomas house, and conveyed to that mansion where all were cordially welcomed. Blue-coated soldiers were in evidence all about, but that was a familiar sight in that locality. Frederick Junction was a rendezvous for soldiers during the war.

The day was spent joyfully and delightfully, so much so that it required no urgent invitation to induce the visitors to remain until the next day. But who can tell what a day may bring forth?

The next day, July 5, the family were seated on the comfortable piazza enjoying the scenery and the morning freshness when up the front lawn from the Georgetown Road came a squad of Union soldiers which halted in front of those gathered there on the porch, and thereupon one of them stepped to the front and stated aloud that the three young men were under arrest. "By whose order?" was asked. "By order of General Wallace," was the reply.

Colonel Thomas seated there on the porth inquired upon what charge or ground they were arrested. The spokesman or sergeant answered and said that he could only say that he supposed General Wallace knew his own business.

The three were then marched under guard of the squad to the encampment of the 11th Maryland Regiment of one hundred day men under command of Col. William T. Landstreet, near the railroad iron bridge, a distance of half a mile or more.

Here the three were given muskets, placed in the ranks and drilled with the other men of the regiment. They were given bunks and soldiers' rations and remained at camp several days, being drilled and disciplined each day, but no uniform was given them.

On the morning of the 8th they were marched with the regiment to the west of Frederick where they were drawn up in line of battle to resist the Confederate skirmishers.

But an officer observing them in citizens' clothes

directed them to return to Frederick Junction by way of the Baltimore Pike to the stone bridge and thence down the east side to their camping ground.

The next morning, July 9, they were kept with the regiment and placed on an eminence adjacent to the railroad bridge. The firing from a Confederate battery, a mile or two to the westward, commenced and these three were kept in the ranks in the danger zone for sometime when an officer with a sympathetic nature said to them: "Young men, if you should be captured fighting in civilian clothes, you are likely to be shot. General Wallace is now at some distance and I advise you to get away from here as fast as you can."

The young men acted promptly on this suggestion, threw down their guns, and were soon on their way to the residence of Mr. James H. Gambrill, a friend and neighbor. When they arrived at the Gambrill house they found General Ricketts there seated on the east porch of the house, talking to Mr. Gambrill. After sitting there for a while on the porch with General Ricketts and Mr. Gambrill, an officer, Major Adam E. King, rode up and made a report to the general. After delivering the message and receiving instructions, the officer started away, but was brought back on a stretcher almost immediately. He had been shot and mortally wounded, as was supposed at the time, though he recovered and lived for many years after.

By this time the shells were falling fast and plowing up the earth on all sides, so the three young men and Mr. Gambrill, who was himself then a young man, upon the advice of General Ricketts, all sought shelter in the Gambrill Mill, down by the big waterwheel and remained there until the battle was over, about 5 o'clock in the afternoon.

The arrest of the young men had been brought about in this way: General Wallace, it seems, had said that it was a time when all able-bodied men should come to the defense of the flag, and mentioned these young men by name as taking no part on either side, and said that they should be made to fight. This was construed into an order and the squad, under command of a sergeant, in pursuance of that unofficial order, brought the young men away from their happy surroundings for a place and a part in the battle.

Meanwhile, what of the young ladies? They were frantic. They worried everybody with their complaints and woes. They said it was an outrage. They travelled across the fields to see Mr. and Mrs. Worthington and down the road to tell the story to Mr. and Mrs. Gambrill. Their beaux and brother had been conscripted, summarily. When the skirmishing occurred west of Frederick on the 8th, they would scream and cry. When a real battle seemed imminent on the 9th, they went to the headquarters of General Wallace to beg the release of their fiances. But he was not in. They then crossed on the dangerous iron bridge to go to the Junction, hearing that the general was there, but he got out and away without meeting them. So their efforts were in vain. But many a soldier who took part in that battle recalled for years after the vision of the two beautiful young girls who came right into camp, distresed and tearful, inquiring where they could find General Wallace. One soldier, in writing of the battle, says of this episode:

"Two extremely attractive young women are very much in evidence as they flit from place to place, obviously in deep distress over something. The last we saw of them was their rapid crossing of the railroad bridge to the westward."

It may be well to relate that both the young ladies afterwards were married to the young men to whom their word had been plighted, and no doubt the perils and dangers of that battle endeared them to each other more than ever, and doubtless, too, there was a happy reunion when the battle was over and the civilian soldiers were released from their perilous situation under the mill-wheel. After taking refuge down by the big waterwheel, the greatest danger was that someone might turn on the water and start the wheel turning. In that event all would, without doubt, have been crushed to death.

War is not a pleasant thing to have around one's home. For years after it would fret the young men to be teased about the part they took in the battle of Monocacy.

The young ladies could very well laugh about it when it was all over and everybody was safe again at home, but when the firing of cannon west of Frederick on the 8th was heard, they went into hysterics at every boom, for they knew their young men were there in danger, and on the 9th, in the morning, when the bloody struggle of that day was plainly impending, they rushed from home into the new danger zone themselves in the vain effort to obtain the young men's release.

To their dying day all of them blessed that kind-hearted Yankee officer who told the young men they might quietly leave the line of battle and seek places of safety. After concealing themselves their most fearful apprehension was that the huge overshot waterwheel might start revolving while they were taking refuge there, but during the three hours and more of their concealment, it remained motionless and they came forth, finally, unscathed.

CHAPTER XXIII.

RENEWED ALARM IN WASHINGTON

While the greater part of the Third Division of the Sixth Army Corps, under command of Gen. James B. Ricketts, reached the Monocacy in time to render material aid to General Wallace in his effort to impede the progress of General Early toward Washington, and, indeed, to bear the brunt of the battle, General Grant, in command of all the Federal armies, with headquarters at City Point, Virginia, had not, as late as July 8, awakened to the fact that a formidable force of Confederates was on Maryland soil threatening the National Capital.

On July 3 he had telegraphed General Halleck from City Point that "Early is now here." When in fact, General Early was, then at Winchester, Virginia, with the Second Army Corps of the Confederate Army, marching on Martinsburg and Harper's Ferry. General Grant had reasoned that if there was any force threatening Washington, it would only be a small force, and so on the 6th of July, only one division, the Third, was sent up the Bay to Baltimore.

As we have seen, the railroad passes the Monocacy where General Wallace had resolved to make a stand, and Ricketts' men were taken off the cars there as the trains arrived, some regiments reaching the scene as late at eight o'clock at night the day before the battle.

On July 8 at 10.30 o'clock in the evening General Halleck sent this message to General Grant:

Washington, July 8, 1864.
10.30 P. M.
Lieutenant-General Grant,
City Point, Virginia.

It is the impression that one-third of Lee's army is with Early and Breckinridge, and that Ransom has some 3,000 or 4,000 cavalry. If you intend to cut off this raid, we must have more forces here.

H. W. HALLECK,
Major-General and Chief of Staff.

This telegram finally aroused General Grant to a realization of the situation at Washington; so on the afternoon of July 9 he sent the following message to General Meade, commanding the forces besieging Petersburg.

City Point, Va.,
July 9, 1864, 6 P. M.
Major-General Meade,
Commanding, etc.

Send in balance of Sixth Corps to be forwarded to Washington. The rebels have crossed the Monocacy and Halleck gives it as his opinion that one-third of Lee's army is with them.

U. S. GRANT,
Lieutenant-General.

General Halleck himself was greatly disturbed over the situation and, as he knew that certain Union forces which had been operating in the neighborhood of New Orleans were about to arrive in Hampton Roads by transports from the Southern city, he sent the following telegram himself to the commanding officer of those troops without waiting for the order to be transmitted through General Grant, though Grant had previously been advised that they were needed in Washington and had assented to their going.

Headquarters of the Army,
Washington, D. C.,
July 9, 1864. 3 P. M.
Commanding Officer,
Fort Monroe.

Troops arriving from New Orleans will. be sent immediately forward to Washington.

H. W. HALLECK,
Major-General and Chief of Staff.

General Halleck apparently did not even take time
to find out the name of the commanding officer but sent
forward his dispatch as above addressed to the commanding officer, whoever he might be.

On the very day the battle was being fought at Monocacy, troops from Petersburg and Fortress Monroe were
being ordered to Washington, 250 miles distant. Monocacy is but 40 miles away and, but for the courageous
stand made by General Wallace, the Confederates could
easily have reached Rockville, 15 miles from Washington,
on the evening of the 9th, and have arrived at Washington
on the afternoon of the 10th. It is well to keep in mind
the narrow margin of time in order to appreciate the
effect of Wallace's resolute stand at Monocacy.

News of the defeat of Wallace's forces reached
Washington piecemeal during the afternoon of the 9th.
The President himself was greatly concerned and
awaited anxiously definite information as to just what
had happened.

During the day Mr. John W. Garrett, president of
the Baltimore and Ohio Railroad, had heard at his office
in Baltimore of the conflict going on at and near Monocacy Junction, and about four o'clock in the afternoon
he telegraphed Secretary of War Stanton that reinforcements for the Union troops engaged in the battle were

deemed of the greatest importance, and that not a moment should be lost. This dispatch was received in Washington at 4.10 P. M. on the 9th. At 5.15 the President himself sent the following dispatch to Mr. Garrett:

Washington, D. C.,
J. W. Garrett, July 9, 1864. 5.15 P. M.
Camden Station.

What have you heard about the battle of Monocacy today? We have nothing about it here except what you say.

A. LINCOLN.

Mr. Garrett replied as follows:

Camden Station, Baltimore, Md.,
July 9, 1864.
His Excellency A. Lincoln, Received 7.15 P. M.
President.

Our telegraph operator at Monrovia, which is eight miles east of Monocacy, this instant telegraphs that an aide of General Wallace has arrived there who reports that "our troops at Monocacy have given away, and that General Wallace has been badly defeated." . . .

J. W. GARRETT,
President.

AID FROM CITY POINT

By some mischance General Grant's message to General Meade to send in the remainder of the Sixth Corps was delayed. At 8 P. M. on the 9th, General Meade at Petersburg, sent the following message to General Grant at City Point:

July 9, 1864. 8 P. M.

Lieutenant-General Grant:

An accident has delayed receipt of your telegram of 6 P. M. till this moment. The Sixth Corps has been ordered and will at once proceed to City Point.

GEORGE G. MEADE,
Major-General, Commanding

Soon after the first battle of Manassas a conference
of leading military men, with the Secretary of War and
others, had been held in Washington to take into consideration the defenses of the city, and it was determined
at this conference, that Washington should be well fortified against any possible attack of the Confederates.
Brevet Maj.-Gen. J. G. Barnard was made chief engineer
and placed in charge of the defenses of Washington.
Under his supervision more than fifty forts were constructed about the city; these separate forts being connected with each other in many instances by breastworks,
with ditches and palisades and abatis in front.

It added no little to the consternation prevailing in
Washington, after the result of the battle of Monocacy
became known there, to have Major-General Barnard
write Major-General Halleck, Chief of Staff, on July 9,
a message in these words: "The militia regiments, now
garrisoning the forts, scarcely know how to load or fire
the guns."

On the 10th, about noon, General Grant telegraphed
Washington as follows:

City Point, Va.
July 10, 1864.
12.30 P. M.

Major-General Halleck,
    Chief of Staff.

Two divisions, the balance of the Sixth Corps, are
now on their way to Washington, the advance having
sailed at 10 ·A. M. The remainder are sailing as fast as
the steamers are loaded.

U. S. GRANT,
Lieutenant-General,

The following welcome telegram was also received
at Washington, from the chief-of-staff of Maj.-Gen.
Edward R. S. Canby, then commanding the 19th Corps:

Fort Monroe, Va.,
July 10, 1864.
Maj.-Gen. H. W. Halleck,   1 P. M.
Chief-of-Staff.

Steamer Crescent has just arrived with troops from New Orleans and has been ordered to Washington.

J. W. SHAFFER,
Colonel and Chief-of-Staff.

General Grant's quartermaster also telegraphed Washington concerning the movement of troops to that city, as follows:

City Point, Va.,
July 10, 1864.
10.30 A. M.
Brig.-Gen. M. C. Meigs,   Received at 4.30 P. M.
Quartermaster-General.

General Wright (commanding Sixth Corps) left at 10 A. M. His troops number 11,000. They are embarking rapidly.

RUFUS INGALLS,
Quartermaster.

All the separate forts forming together the defenses of Washington were given individual names, chiefly in honor of distinguished Union officers who had lost their lives during the war, but sometimes in honor of distinguished men in public life. The fort guarding entrance to the city by way of the Seventh Street Pike was named Fort Stevens, perhaps in honor of Thaddeus Stevens, long a leading Representative in Congress from Pennsylvania, and an out-and-out anti-secessionist.[1]

This fort was located near the northern corner of the District of Columbia, about six miles distant from the wharf at the river. West of the Seventh Street Pike, across Rock Creek, was Fort De Russey, and nearer

Tennallytown on the Georgetown Road was Fort Reno. Between these was Fort Kearney, while further to the west toward Conduit Road, were Fort Simmons, Fort Bayard, Fort Sumner, and Fort Mansfield. To the southeast of Fort Stevens were Fort Slocum, Fort Totten, Fort Lincoln, and others.

Following the battle near Frederick Junction, news reached Washington that Early was actually marching upon that city with a large force of Confederates, estimated at 20,000 or more, with cavalry, infantry and artillery.

The main road leads to Rockville and passing through Rockville, leads on directly into Washington by way of Tennallytown; while by turning to the left in Rockville, and travelling east five miles, the Seventh Street Pike is reached, which leads into the capital city by way of Sligo and Silver Springs.

All day on the 10th Early's men were traveling toward Rockville, scarcely twenty-five miles from the scene of the conflict. The day was exceedingly warm and the troops suffered from the heat, the dust and from thirst.

So when within four miles of Rockville the army was halted and there bivouacked for the night. The cavalry under McCausland went on to Rockville, his videttes being stationed on the direct road much nearer Washington. Thus rested the tired army on the night of the 10th with their great objective only fifteen or sixteen miles away by the direct route, and not more than eighteen miles by the other.

On the 10th, also, all day transports were being loaded at City Point, Virginia, 250 miles distant, with Sixth Corps veterans, and the loaded boats were steaming down the James and up the Chesapeake, headed for Washington. And at the same time other boats loaded with 19th Corps men were being forwarded from Hampton Roads to the same destination. There were 11,000 of the Sixth Corps and 6,000 or more of the 19th Corps, all travelling as fast as the transports would carry them, bound for the National Capital, to defend it with their lives against any and every assault of the enemy.

Fortunately the boats carrying these reinforcements did not have to stop to rest at night as did the weary, dusty, footsore forces of the Confederacy. All night the fires under the boilers of these transports were kept well stoked and burning under forced draft. All night propellers were revolving at unwonted speed, driving the boats carrying the needed reinforcements through the smooth waters of the Chesapeake Bay.

A Race For A Great Stake

On the early morning of the 11th the leading transport turned from the waters of the Bay into the mouth of the Potomac River, still 100 miles from the wharf at Washington.

On the same morning the Confederate Army near Rockville bestirred itself and, after a soldiers' breakfast, resumed its march toward the Capital, now near at hand. For the infantry, the route by way of the Seventh Street Pike was chosen, and under a blazing hot sun and through dense clouds of dust, they went forward. Here was a race between the two great contending forces, the stake of which was the capital of the nation, its treasure and prestige.

No wonder those in authority were anxious and alarmed.

On May 2, 1864, Col. Moses N. Wisewell had been appointed Military Governor of the District of Columbia, and every effort was made by him and by General Augur to marshal the scattered forces already in the city, and further appeals were made by the Administration to the governors of the great States of New York, Massachusetts and Pennsylvania for succor.

Gen. Montgomery C. Meigs, quartermaster-general, was requested to organize his employees and to report to Major-General McCook, near Fort Stevens with as little delay as practicable. The Veteran Reserves, under Col. Moses N. Wisewell, were also sent to the front. Men were drawn from the fortifications on the south side of the Potomac and organized for the defense of Fort Stevens. All the convalescents from the hospitals were organized and sent to the trenches. But still these were all only "miscellaneous troops," and real fighting men were needed.

Too Many Generals, Not Enough Privates

There were at the time a goodly number of officers of rank in the country and these offered their services freely, but fighting men were lacking. Among those offering their services was a new brigadier at the Fifth Avenue Hotel, New York. In reply General Halleck sent the following mirthful rejoinder:

> Washington, D. C.,
> July 11, 1864.

Brig.-Gen. J. R. West,
Fifth Avenue Hotel, New York.

We have five times as many generals here as we want,

but are greatly in need of privates. Anyone volunteering in that capacity will be thankfully received.

H. W. HALLECK,
Major-General and Chief-of-Staff.

A CONFEDERATE'S STATEMENT

Shortly after noon on the 11th the vanguard of Early's forces reached a position near enough to Fort Stevens to be deployed as skirmishers. Shells were being fired from the big guns in the forts at the advancing columns, but these went wild and high and did no damage. As General Barnard had reported, the militia regiments then garrisoning the city scarcely knew how to load or fire the guns, and the employes and Veteran Reserves were scarcely better qualified.

A Confederate veteran of Gordon's Division of Early's army, Mr. I. G. Bradwell of Georgia, but now (1932) of Brantley, Alabama, has this to say of the marksmanship of the men behind the guns within the fortifications:

"The next day, July 11, when we were several miles from the city, the enemy in the works around the town opened on us with their big guns. As these big shells passed high over our heads our boys in the ranks laughed at the marksmanhip of the "melish" behind the guns. We knew then that our enemies were a set of fellows untrained and badly frightened. When these big shells came over and exploded far in the rear, I suggested to my comrades that the enemy was shelling our wagon trains; but none of them did us or the trains any harm."

This same intelligent veteran, who was himself a witness of what occurred there that day says further on in an article in the March, 1928, *Confederate Veteran:*

"Out in front of Fort Stevens we halted and formed our line. Skirmishers were thrown out and the usual preliminaries of battle began. . . . . General Gordon ordered up a battery of Parrott field pieces, pretty good guns themselves. These brave gunners unlimbered in front of the brigade out in the open field in full view of the Yanks, about four hundred yards away, and replied, knocking up the red dirt around the muzzle of the big fellows in the fort while the enemy continued to aim at the moon and stars."

LIEUT. EDGAR S. DUDLEY' STATEMENT

In an article prepared by Edgar S. Dudley, first lieutenant, Second United States Artillery, entitled *Early's Attack* on Washington, it is said:

"During the advance of the enemy there was the greatest excitement and alarm, particularly after Wallace's defeat. The alarm in the city was intense, for it lay an easy prey to an energetic enemy. The danger of capture was great."

General Grant, in his report of July 22, 1865, says:

"The Sixth and 19th Corps reached Washington at 2 P. M. on the 11th, but Gen. Horatio G. Wright, in command of the Sixth Corps, reported 3 P. M., his troops coming up at 4 P. M. on the 11th. President Lincoln, in his anxiety, had met these troops as they landed on the wharf, his heart gladdened to see the veterans entering the city at the crucial moment[2]."

GENERAL BARNARD'S REPORT

In his report on the *Defences of Washington,* Major-General Barnard says, at page 91:

"When Early marched to Washington in 1864, the defences had been stripped of the disciplined and instructed artillery regiments (number about 18,000) which had constituted their garrison and their places supplied by newly raised 100 days regiments (Ohio National Guard) insufficient in numbers and quite uninstructed. Under such circumstances much anxiety was felt on the approach of Early's veterans, flushed with recent success, inspired by the very audacity of their enterprise and incited by the prize before the eyes. Yet inadequately manned as they were, the fortifications compelled at least a concentration and arranging of force on the part of the assailants, and thus gave time for the arrival of succor.

"One division (Ricketts') was, as we have seen, detached on the 5th of July from the lines before Petersburg and sent to Baltimore where it arrived in time to bear the brunt of the battle of Monocacy. The other two divisions did not receive their orders until the 9th and did not reach Washington till 2 P. M. on the 11th, barely in time."

Although some of the transports bearing the reinforcements arrived at the wharf in Washington between 12 and 4 o'clock in the afternoon of the 11th, it required some little time for them to disembark and march through the city several miles to the point where the enemy was and even until a late hour at night there was every indication that the enemy was preparing to attack. At 11.40 the following dispatch was sent by the assistant adjutant-general to General McCook at Fort Stevens:

> Washington, D. C.,
> July 11, 1864.
> 11.40 P. M.

Major-General McCook,
Commanding Reserve, Fort Stevens.

The chief officer of pickets says the enemy are apparently making every preparation for a grand assault, tearing down fences, bands playing, cavalry moving to our left. Cannot a part of the Sixth Corps be hurried up at once?

> C. A. RAYMOND,
> Assistant Adjutant-General.

Five minutes later the following dispatch was sent to General Wright:

July 11, 1864.
11.45 P. M.

Gen. H. C. Wright,
Commanding Sixth Corps.

General Hallack thinks your corps should all be assembled near Fort Stevens.

C. C. AUGUR,
Major-General U. S. Volunteers.

As indicative of the general alarm in the city at this time, Nicolay and Hay say in their *Abraham Lincoln, A History,* at page 169: "Captain Fox, the Assistant Secretary of the Navy, without the President's knowledge, had a vessel made ready in case of a serious disaster." The purpose of the order being to provide in advance for the speedy and safe removal of the President in case flight should become necessary. The order was given, however, without the President's knowledge. Indeed, the President displayed great courage and self-possession during the whole period of the existence of the alarm within the city.

---

[1] Since this was written it has been learned that Fort Stevens was at first known as Fort Massachusetts, and that its name was changed on April 1, 1863, to Fort Stevens, in memory of Brig.-Gen. Isaac Ingalls Stevens, who had been killed at the battle of Chantilly, Virginia, on September 1, 1862, while leading the Second Division of Reno's Corps.

[2] In his *History of the Sixth Army Corps*, George T. Stevens, surgeon of the 77th New York Volunteers (1870), says, at page 375: "At 2 o'clock we touched at the wharf at the foot of Sixth Street. President Lincoln stood on the wharf chatting familiarly with the veterans and now and then, as if in compliment to them, biting a piece of hardtack which he held in his hand."

CHAPTER XXIV.

THE ELEVENTH OF JULY. 1864

EARLY'S OWN ACCOUNT

On Sunday morning, following the day of the battle, General Early started from the battlefield with his army of invasion by the main highway, the Georgetown Road, for Washington, about forty miles distant. Besides his own infantry, cavalry, artillery and wagons, he had charge of about seven hundred Federal prisoners captured in that battle. The road leads from the Monocacy River through Urbana, Hyattstown, Clarksburg, Gaithersburg, and Rockville. The latter place is about 25 miles from the battlefield and by direct route, 15 miles from Washington. In his account of the battle, General Early says:

"The action closed about sunset. . . . All the troops and trains were crossed over the river that night, so as to be ready to resume the march on the next day. . . The march was resumed at daylight on the 10th and we had bivouaced four miles from Rockville, having marched 20 miles (or more). McCausland marched in front, driving a body of enemy cavalry before him. . . . We moved at daylight on the 11th, McCausland's Cavalry on Georgetown Pike, while infantry, preceded by Imboden's Cavalry, under Colonel Smith, turned to left at Rockville so as to reach the Seventh Street Pike which runs by Silver Springs into Washington. The previous day had been very warm and the roads were exceedingly dusty, as there had been no rain for several weeks. The heat during the night had been very oppressive and but little sleep had been obtained. This day was an exceedingly hot one and no air stirring. When marching the men were enveloped in a suffocating cloud of dust and many of them fell by the way from exhaustion. I pushed on rapidly as possible hoping to get into the fortifications around Washington before they could be manned. Smith drove a small body of cavalry before him into the works on Seventh Street Pike, dismounted his men and deployed them as skirmishers. I rode ahead of the infantry and arrived in sight of Fort Stevens on this road a short time after noon when I discovered the works were but feebly manned.

"Rodes, whose division was in front, was immediately ordered to bring it into line as rapidly as possible: throw out skirmishers and move into the works if he could. . . .

"But before Rodes' Division could be brought up we saw a cloud of dust in the rear of the works toward Washington, and soon a column of the enemy filed into them . . . . . and skirmishers were thrown out in front while an artillery fire was opened on us from a number of batteries. This defeated our hopes of getting possession of the works by surprise and it became necessary to reconnoitre. This reconnaissance consumed the balance of the day."

MAJOR-GENERAL McCOOK'S REPORT

On Monday, July 11, Maj.-Gen. A. McD. McCook was designated to command "the entire line and troops" defending the Capital on the north. In his report General McCook says:

"At 12 M. a strong line of the enemy's skirmishers came into view, advancing upon our position. The picket line at this moment was composed of 100 day men of the 150th Ohio and a portion of the 26th New York Cavalry dismounted. Being satisfied that they could not contend favorably against the enemy's line, were ordered to fall back slowly, fighting until they reached the rifle pits. Fire was then opened at proper points upon our line and the enemy was held in check until the dismounted of the Second Division of the Cavalry Corps, Army of the Potomac, 600 strong, commanded by Major George G. Briggs, Seventh Michigan Cavalry, were made ready to go out, drive the enemy back and re-establish our picket line. This was handsomely done about 1.30 P. M., the enemy's skirmishers being forced back and our line well established at 1,100 yards in front of the works. . . . Affairs remained in this condition until evening.

"About 3 P. M. Maj.-Gen. H. G. Wright, U. S. Volunteers, commanding the Sixth Army Corps, reported to me at Fort Stevens, informing me that the advance of his corps would be up in a short time. I directed him to furnish a force of 900 strong of his veteran corps for picket duty during the night, constant skirmishing being kept up between the lines until after dark on the 11th instant."

THE CLOSENESS OF THE RACE

As indicative of the closeness of the race between the Blue and Gray for possession of the great Capital of the Nation, let us take note of the relative positions of the two forces on the morning of the 11th. While Early's army was pushing forward toward its goal along the Seventh Street Pike, the first transports from City Point were plowing their way through the waters of the tortuous Potomac; as the vanguard of Early's forces reached Silver Springs, these transports were turning into the eastern branch of the river; and as Rodes' men were deploying as skirmishers, Wright's men were debarking at the wharf.

GENERAL McCOOK'S REPORT CONTINUED

"At 9 P. M. Brig.-Gen. M. C. Meigs reported at Fort Stevens with about fifteen hundred quartermaster employees, armed and equipped. They were at once ordered into position near Fort Slocum, placed on right and left in rifle pits. At 10 P. M. Colonel Price reported with about twenty-eight hundred convalescents and men from hospitals, organized into a provisional brigade composed of men from nearly every regiment in the army of the Potomac. They were ordered into position in the rear of Fort Slocum, as information received led me to believe that the enemy would demonstrate further to my right."

The report further refers to the Confederates taking possession of the Rives house, "surrounded by an orchard and large shade trees," at the right of the Silver Springs Road, and of the house of Mrs. Lay on the left of the road, and very much annoying the skirmishers during the day, the Confederate sharpshooters in these two houses killing and wounding about thirty of the Federal skirmishers.

COL. JOHN C. MARBLE'S REPORT

In his report of operations Col. John C. Marble, commanding Forts De Russey, Smead and Kearney, says, among other things:

"After establishing our skirmish line there was considerable activity along it. Noticing a considerable movement of the enemy in the vicinity of Wilson's house on the Seventh Street Road, we deemed it advisable to send in a few shells. We are assured by citizens in that direction that the enemy were surprised at the accuracy of our fire at such distance, and from information thus obtained, we are led to conclude that the accuracy and activity of our artillery and skirmish line contributed largely to deter them from making the intended assault on Monday night (the 11th)."

BRIG.-GEN. MARTIN D. HARDIN'S REPORT

In his report Brig.-Gen. Martin D. Hardin, U. S. Army, commanding a division of 22nd Army Corps in defense of Washington, says, *inter alia:*

"One company of veteran reserves, under Captain Clark, Sixth Regiment Veteran Reserve Corps, made a gallant effort to take a barn which the enemy were using to advantage against our skirmishers in front of Fort De Russey. Captain Clark was slightly wounded and many of his company were wounded. These efforts and the determined way of holding the picket line showed the enemy that he would have to make a desperate assault to carry that portion of the line, which I believe was one of the weakest points on the front. This resistance on the picket line and the advance of the Sixth Corps skirmishers, it is considered, made the enemy think we were prepared for an assault."

COL. WILLIAM H. FRY'S REPORT OF CAVALRY OPERATIONS

The aforegoing reports refer chiefly to skirmishing along the lines in front of Fort Stevens and between what is called the Seventh Street Pike or Brookeville Road and the deep ravine to the west through which flows Rock Creek. This ravine lay between Fort Stevens and Fort De Russey and hindered to a serious degree the cooperation of Confederate forces on the Seventh Street Pike with the cavalry on the Tennallytown Road. In his report General Early stated that McCausland's Cavalry proceeded from Rockville toward Washington on what was called the Georgetown or Tennallytown Road, while the infantry turned to the left at Rockville and approached Washington by way of the Seventh Street Pike, which now passes the Walter Reed Hospital, under the name of Georgia Avenue.

Against McCausland, Major William H. Fry, commanding Provisional Cavalry Regiment of 500 men, was sent out on the 10th. Major Fry passed through Rockville on the 10th at about 11 o'clock in the morning and went beyond Rockville, about three miles, where he met McCausland's Cavalry. Skirmishing commenced at once, and Major Fry fell back through Rockville toward Washington, and finally at nightfall, made a stand on a hill about one mile east of Rockville. He reports as follows:

"July 11, at daylight, I started my command in the direction of Rockville, but before reaching Old Tavern I was overtaken by Colonel Lowell, Second Massachusetts Cavalry, with two squadrons of his regiments. He immediately assumed command of the whole force, and in the vicinity of Old Tavern the enemy were again found advancing in force. We fell back, skirmishing constantly until within two miles of Tennallytown where a dismounted skirmish line was formed and held, the enemy never succeeding in driving us away."

Col. James M. Warner's Report

In his report of the operations in defense of Washington, Col. James M. Warner, command First Brigade, says, *inter alia,* concerning the opposition to McCausland on the Rockville Road:

"On the following morning, the 11th, at daybreak Colonel Lowell, Second Massachusetts Cavalry, with about three squadrons of his own regiment and one squadron of the Eighth Illinois Cavalry, relieved Major Fry's command. . . . . Skirmishing was kept up with the enemy the entire day and, although their line was visible from the Signal Station at Fort Reno, the long-range guns of the fort could not be brought to bear upon them without endangering our own men."

It will thus be seen that the skirmishing between the opposing cavalry forces was kept up during the day on the 11th. The operations consisted of contact and withdrawal, back and forth, without heavy casualties on either side. McCausland apparently being unwilling to risk his men too close to the big guns in Fort Reno and his cavalry brigade being too strong for Colonel Lowell to drive more than a short distance back.

The principal skirmishing on the 11th was in the afternoon, between the infantry at and near Fort Stevens.

General Early says that the afternoon of the 11th was taken up in reconnoitering, and evidently also in finding out by the pressure of his skirmish line the character of the resistance to be expected in case a real assault should be made.

No doubt it is true that the Confederate infantry were greatly exhausted by their marching and fighting. They had come from Lynchburg, Virginia, afoot, a distance of perhaps two hundred and forty miles; they had fought Hunter and driven him out of the Valley, they had fought Sigel at Martinsburg and Weber at Harpers Ferry, and they had fought Wallace in a real battle at Monocacy, two days previously; the weather for weeks had been exceedingly hot and dry and the roads dusty.

GENERAL EARLY'S OWN REPORT

General Early says:

"On the morning of the 11th we continued the march but the day was excessively hot even at an early hour in the morning, and the dust so dense that many of the men fell by the way and it became necessary to slacken our pace. Nevertheless, when we reached the right of the enemy's fortifications, the men were almost completely exhausted and not in a condition to make an attack. Skirmishers were thrown out and moved up to the vicinity of the fortifications."

Thus it will be seen that no vigorous assault could well have been made on the 11th. Tired, thirsty, foot-sore, dust-covered soldiers are in no condition to fight.

Soon after Early's retirement from before Washington, some newspapers stated that from Saturday, July 9, to Monday, July 11, inclusive, Washington was practically defenseless and if Early had moved promptly he could have entered the city. To that suggestion General Early replies:

"It may be true Washington was open to successful attack during those three days, but on Saturday, July 9, I was contending with Wallace at Monocacy; on Sunday I was marching as fast as the hot weather and my tired army would permit, and on Monday, the 11th, my army was too much worn out to make the attack, and besides it would have been foolhardy to rush my men against well constructed fortifications mounted with heavy artillery and every approach swept by a cross-fire from these big guns without first ascertaining somewhat of the number and character of the men behind the guns and breastworks, and in the ditches and rifle pits surrounding them."

He could observe through his field glass that the defensive works about the city were strong and scientifically constructed, but he could not ascertain at a glance what active forces were behind these forbidding and formidable looking defenses of the city. After a reconnaissance and a conference with his generals he resolved, he says, to make the assault the morning of the 12th but during the night he received information that two divisions from Grant's army had arrived in the city, and that to make an assault as he had resolved to do, would be a most hazardous undertaking and might result in the destruction of his whole force. Consequently, he reluctantly determined to retire, but to defer his retirement until the night of the 12th. He kept up active skirmishing all day on the 12th so that his purpose might not be disclosed. But for the delay at Monocacy on the

9th, Early's army could easily have reached Fort Stevens on Sunday, July 10, and allowing that afternoon for rest and reconnaissance, he could almost certainly have made a successful assault upon the works on Monday morning, July 11. On that day in the morning, not only had no reinforcements arrived from Grant's army before Petersburg, but even the employes of the Quartermaster's Department and the convalescents from the hospitals had not been organized for service. In a letter General Meigs, who organized his employees for the defense of the city says: "I marched about 5 P. M. with fifteen hundred or two thousand toward Fort Stevens." *Official Records,* Serial No. 70, page 258. So it was not until 5 P. M. that these employees are marshaled for duty, and it was as late as 9 or 10 o'clock before the whole force was in a position to defend. The crisis passed on the 11th of July for at 10 o'clock that night, C. A. Dana, Assistant Secretary of War, telegraphed General Grant at City Point:

"Five boatloads of General Wright's troops have arrived and one of the 19th Corps. General Wright and his troops have gone to Fort Stevens."

THE ITINERARY OF THE SIXTH CORPS

The critical situation at Washington on the 11th is further shown by the itinerary of the Sixth Army Corps, Maj.-Gen. H. G. Wright, U. S. Army, commanding, as published in *Official Records of the Union and Confederate Armies,* Serial No. 70, page 270, *et seq.:*

"July 10.—First and Second Divisions embarked at City Point for Washington."
"July 11.—Portion of Second Division landed and marched to Fort Stevens."

*First Brigade, Second Division, commanded by Brig.-
Gen. Frank Wheaton.*

"July 10.—At 5.30 A. M. embarked on transports
Dictator and Guide for Washington."

"July 11.—Debarked at Washington at 12 M.
marched to Fort Stevens. Arrived there at 4 P. M. At
5 P. M. Brigade marched out and relieved skirmishers
belonging to the Veteran Reserve Corps, 100 day men,
and War Department clerks, who were being driven
toward the fort. Deployed the whole brigade without
any support and drove the rebels back to a position
800 yards from the fort."

*Third Brigade, Second Division, commanded by Col.
Daniel D. Bidwell, 49th New York Infantry.*

"July 10.—Embarked for Washington at 11 A. M."

"July 11.—Disembarked at Washington and moved
to Fort Stevens."

"July 12.—Engaged the enemy at Fort Stevens."

*Third Brigade, First Division, commanded by Col.
Oliver Edwards, 37th Massachusetts Infantry.*

"July 10 and 11.—The command was shipped on
board of transports."

"July 12.—Arrived at Washington; marched through
the city and took up position at Brightwood."

*Second Division, commanded by Brig.-Gen. George
W. Getty.*

"July 10.—Embarked at 11 A. M. for Washington."

"July 11.—Disembarked at Washington and took up
position in rear of Fort Stevens; First Brigade engaged
the enemy."

"July 12.—First and Third Brigades attacked and
drove the enemy."

GENERAL WHEATON'S REPORT

From this it is most manifest that while the first
transports bearing reinforcements from City Point
arrived at the wharf in Washington on July 11, at about
12 o'clock M., the troops aboard did not reach Fort
Stevens until 4 P. M. of that day. In his report General
Wheaton says:

"Upon arrival at Washington, July 11, at 12 M.,
I was directed by General Wright to move toward the
Chain Bridge. While marching up Pennsylvania Avenue,
in compliance with the instructions of the corps commander, I was halted by Colonel Taylor, Chief-of-Staff,
Department of Washington, and informed by him that
the enemy was driving in our picket line and seriously
threatening Fort Stevens, on Seventh Street, and received
through him General Augur's instructions to march at
once in that direction instead of to Chain Bridge as at
first ordered. I turned my brigade up Eleventh Street,
and while on the march to Fort Stevens, was passed by
General Wright, Commanding the Corps, and received
verbal instructions from him to mass near Crystal Spring,
in the neighborhood of Fort Stevens, where we arrived
at 4 o'clock in the P. M. At 5 P. M. the force outside
Fort Stevens, consisting of a portion of the Veteran
Reserve Corps, War Department clerks and citizen volunteers, were driven in toward the fort by a portion of the
enemy's forces under Early. At the same time I was
ordered to move 500 men of my brigade out to recover
the line held in the afternoon. This was successfully
accomplished before 7. . . . . Skirmishing continued during the night and following day."

War Records, Serial No. 70, page 275:

The arrival of General Wheaton with his brigade of
veterans from before Petersburg practically ended the
critical situation in Washington. He drove back the Confederate skirmish line from before Fort Stevens to the
main line. Later on other regiments were sent outside
the line strengthened

"from a point opposite the center of the line between
Forts Stevens and Reno to the west, and a point opposite
Fort Slocum to the east, a distance of two miles."

During the night more transports with reinforcements from City Point arrived and were hurried forward
to the danger point so that before morning the great
fortifications defending the city were well manned and

the trenches outside were occupied by both the improvised troops from the city and by the veterans of the Sixth Corps, which was considered one of the very best fighting units in the Federal Army. The crisis had passed and Washington was saved.

CHAPTER XXV.

TUESDAY, JULY 12, 1864

About 5 o'clock P. M. the next day, the 12th, General Wheaton organized an attack on the Confederate skirmish line in front of Fort Stevens, and within range of the guns of Fort Slocum, between the Rockville or Tennallytown Road and the road to Silver Springs.

The enemy was posted in and near the Rives house on two wooded hills in front of the entrenched line of defense, the intervening space being entirely covered with scrub timber and underbrush. A spirited encounter took place here in which the Federal loss was severe. General Wheaton reporting his loss at six officers and 53 men killed and eight officers and 137 men wounded, total in killed and wounded, 204.

Col. Daniel C. Bidwell, 43rd New York Volunteers, was in command of the Third Brigade and led the attack in this encounter. This brigade bore the brunt of the fighting and lost heavily.

LINCOLN A WITNESS

President Lincoln himself witnessed this attack from Fort Stevens. The President was also a witness to the first shots exchanged between the hostile forces on the previous day.

In their *Abraham Lincoln, A History,* by John G. Nicolay and John Hay, it is stated in Volume IX, page 172:

"When Rodes' Division arrived on the afternoon of the 11th, he (Lincoln) saw the first shots exchanged in front of Fort Stevens and stood in the fort, his tall figure making him a conspicious mark, until ordered to withdraw; and on the 12th, when Bidwell's Brigade marched in perfect order out of the works to drive the enemy from the Rives house, the President again stood, apparently unconscious of danger, watching with grave and passive countenance the progress of the fight amid the whistling bullets of the sharpshooters until an officer fell mortally wounded within three feet of him, and General Wright peremptorily represented the needless risk he was running."

This engagement was also witnessed by Gen. John C. Breckinridge on the Confederate side. Prior to the war this Confederate general had been elected Vice-President on the ticket with James Buchanan in 1856, and later had been defeated as a candidate for the presidency in 1860. In 1861 he joined the Confederate Army and was made major-general. He had defeated Sigel at New Market on the 15th of May, and was with Early at Monocacy on July 9, though Gordon commanded the active division at that battle. He had marched with Early to Silver Springs on the 11th, and occupied the library in the dwelling house now owned and occupied by ex-Senator Blair Lee, as his headquarters, during the time the Confederates were threatening the Capital.

This engagement was further distinguished by being fought in full view of the National Capitol.

There was skirmishing on the 12th, also, between cavalry forces on the Rockville Road in which some infantry participated. The losses were not heavy, however. At 7.30 P. M. Surg. Robert Reyburn sent this message from Tennallytown to Surg. R. O. Abbott, U. S. Army Medical Director:

"The loss is very slight on our part of the line today. Five killed and twenty wounded."

Although Early had decided during the night of the 11th to withdraw his forces from before Washington on the following night, the state of his mind was not known to official Washington, and apprehension continued throughout the 12th. There were rumors that Longstreet's corps had left the vicinity of Petersburg and was on its way down the Valley to Washington.

The President himself telegraphed General Grant that he had heard such rumors and requested General Grant to look out for Longstreet's absence in front of him.

One officer reported that perhaps the rumor of Longstreet's approach was true and that accounted for the inactivity of the enemy on the 12th, as they were probably awaiting reinforcements.

RUMORS OF CONFEDERATE REINFORCEMENTS

Thomas A. Scott, the president of the Pennsylvania Railroad, telegraphed from Philadelphia on the 12th to Edward M. Stanton, Secretary of War, that scouts from the Valley of Virginia reported that Longstreet's corps would probably cross the Potomac at Edward's and Noland's Ferries. These ferries are not more than twenty-five or thirty miles from Washington. But all these rumors proved to be without foundation, in fact.

EARLY WITHDRAWS

After maintaining a stiff skirmish line all day on the 12th, General Early at night began to withdraw his forces from before Washington, and to retire by way of Rockville to the fords of the Potomac near Poolesville.

It appears that the Potomac was crossed principally at Edward's Ferry or ford, which is a few miles south of White's Ferry where, no doubt, a part of the retreating army also crossed, though the records are not explicit as to that.

Nelson A. Fitts, a Federal prisoner who escaped from Early's guard after crossing the Potomac, states that the crossing was at Edward's Ferry.

Col. C. R. Lowell states that the infantry crossed at "White's Ferry or Conrad's Ferry, or the ford near the mouth of the Monocacy," while C. A. Dana, Assistant Secretary of War, says:

"A signal officer at Point of Rocks says enemy crossed large wagon trains at Nolan's Ferry on the morning of the 14th, followed by the mass of their cavalry and infantry."

Another signal officer at Sugarloaf Mountain says that they crossed 400 wagons at White's Ferry, three miles below the mouth of Monocacy, while General Wright Says, "The main body of the enemy with his trains crossed at Edward's Ferry." So it seems likely that not all crossed at one place, but at several fording places. This would be the logic of the situation, for the Confederates were being pursued, and the desire was to cross over the river as speedily as possible.

A good many lives were lost and a number of men wounded on the 12th, just to maintain a stiff skirmish line in order to conceal the purpose that was in Early's mind, of retiring from before the city on the night of that day.

At 3.55 P. M. on that day the Chief-of-Staff, Major-

General Halleck, sent this message to Capt. T. S. Paddock, commanding Fort Lincoln:

"Hold your position firmly. . . . Orders have been given that every officer and man who leaves his post shall be shot." The apprehension was still great in the mind of official Washington.

On the morning of July 13th it was discovered that the great army of the Conferedates threatening Washington had gone. At 10 A. M. on that date C. A. Dana, Assistant Secretary of War, telegraphed General Grant at City Point, Virginia: "The enemy have disappeared along the entire line." McCook reported that "the rebel pickets in front of Fort Stevens were changed in the night from infantry to cavalry, and the cavalry departed just before daylight."

The Federal forces, however, were a little wary about moving out of the fortifications and the Confederates got a good start toward Rockville before the defenders ventured forth.

Consequently Early was able to cross into Virginia with his whole force and thus escape an encounter with the Army of the Potomac which pursued him with the avowed purpose of cutting off his retreat and destroying his whole army. General Wright followed across the Potomac some distance behind, but not being able to come up with him, finally returned with his forces to Washington. Indeed, some thought he did not press forward vigorously enough or as energetically as he might have done.

General Bradley T. Johnson, who had returned from Southern Maryland with his cavalry the evening of the 12th, protected Early's retreat across the river. Early retreated no further than the Valley of Virginia where he remained for weeks, sending out raiding parties into Maryland and Pennsylvania, gathering supplies for his own army and for the armies defending Petersburg, demanding $200,000 of the city of Chambersburg, which was burned when the demand was refused; fighting several battles with Federal troops, notably at Winchester, September 19, and Fishers' Hill, September 22, both of which he lost, with no decisive result until October 19 when he was disasterously defeated by Sheridan at Cedar Creek. In praise of Sheridan's part in this battle, Thomas Buchanan Read wrote his celebrated poem, entitled "Sheridan's Ride."

GENERAL GRANT HOLDS A COUNCIL OF WAR

Though not a part of the doings of the 12th of July it will perhaps be interesting to note here the council of war held in the Thomas house on Monocacy battlefield, August 5th.

As just stated, after Early recrossed the Potomac into Virginia, he retreated no further than the "Valley," where he remained, making raids into Western Maryland and into Pennsylvania and gathering supplies for his own army as well as for the army defending Petersburg. In his *Memoirs* General Grant says:

"The Shenandoah Valley was very important to the Confederates because it was the principal storehouse they now had for feeding their armies about Richmond. It was well known that they would make a desperate struggle to maintain it. It had been the source of a great deal of trouble to us heretofore to guard that outlet to the north; partly because of the incompetency of some of the commanders, but chiefly because of interference from Washington.". . . . "They were left, therefore, free to supply themselves with horses, beef cattle and such provisions as they could carry away from

"ARABY"

Western Maryland and Pennsylvania. I determined to put a stop to this."

Accordingly, General Grant left his headquarters at City Point, Virginia, and came directly to Monocacy Junction without stopping in Washington. Hunter's army had some time before returned from its long journey through the mountains of West Virginia, where it had been driven by General Early in the latter part of June, and was then encamped about the Junction, "scattered over the fields along the banks of Monocacy with many hundred cars and locomotives belonging to the Baltimore and Ohio Railroad, which he had taken the precaution to bring back and collect at that place."

GENERAL GRANT HOLDS A COUNCIL OF WAR IN THE THOMAS HOUSE

Upon General Grant's arrival he and General Hunter, together with several other major-generals, including Wright, Crook and others, assembled in an upper room in the mansion house at "Araby," over the library and held a council of war in regard to the situation in the "Valley." Scharf, in his *History of Western Maryland,* says there were eight major-generals present at that conference. But the names of all are not given. At this conference General Grant says in his *Memoirs:*

"I asked the general (General Hunter) where the enemy was. He replied that he did not know. He said that the fact was he was so embarrassed by orders from Washington, moving him first to the right and then to the left, that he had lost all trace of the enemy."

Grant had already selected General Sheridan to take charge of the forces operating in the "Valley" and at once telegraphed him to come to the Junction. Sheridan was then in Washington and came at once by special train, arriving August 6, 1864. General Grant remained over night at "Araby" and waited for General Sheridan. When he arrived the two had a conference and Sheridan was given instructions. Hunter was relieved of his command and Sheridan put in his place. It was in this upper room at the Thomas house that the strategy of the campaign against Early in the "Valley" was worked out, and it proved a success.

General Grant breakfasted with the Thomas family on the morning of August 6th. After breakfast a little incident occurred which shows how circumspect non-combatants in the border States had to be during that civil strife. One of Colonel Thomas' children was named Virginia, then about five or six years old. She was a pretty and attractive child and when the morning meal was ended the general lifted the child into his lap and said: "Well, Virginia, what are your father and mother? Are they Rebels or Yankees?"

To which the little girl replied: "Mamma, she's a Rebel, but papa, he is a Rebel when the Rebels are here and a Yankee when the Yankees are here."

Which was, indeed, the truth for while the ladies expressed themselves quite freely, the men were more circumspect.

The answer seemed to relieve a momentarily tense situation for the father was at heart rather sympathetic toward the Southern cause, and though he was careful in his acts and conversation, he feared the child might give an answer that would connect him with secession, but she sensed correctly his attitude and gave a perfectly truthful picture. It would have been embarrassing if the

child had said of the hospitable host to the distinguished
head of the Union armies that he was a Rebel.

General Grant laughed heartily at the perfectly frank
reply and the incident passed happily for all.

CHAPTER XXVI.

WALLACE'S LOST BATTLE A VICTORY FOR THE UNION CAUSE

It seems almost indisputable that had it not been for the stubborn battle fought at Monocacy on July 9, 1864, by the Union troops under Gen. Lew Wallace, whereby Early's march upon Washington was delayed fully 24 hours, Early would have captured that city on July 11th. That 24 hours gave barely time to enable the reinforcements from City Point to arrive. If Early could have reached Fort Stevens on the 10th, he would have had time to rest his men overnight and to make a vigorous assault on the city the next morning. Indeed, as the works were still but feebly manned on the 11th, he might have gone in on the 10th had he reached the city on that day. It is shown by the records that the miscellaneous troops gathered hastily together in the city for its defense were not brought even into the semblance of an organization until the afternoon of the 11th, and that they were sent the same afternoon, a heterogenous assemblage, to the fortifications and even outside, without the slightest training as a body of fighting men, to defend the city.

No wonder the skirmishers were being driven back on the afternoon of the 11th, when real fighting men from the Sixth Corps arrived just in time. Brig.-Gen. Frank Wheaton, commanding the Second Division, Sixth Corps, reported that at 5 P. M. on the 11th, his brigade "marched out and relieved the skirmishers belonging to the Veterans Reserve Corps, 100 day men and War Department clerks, who were being driven toward the fort."

General Early states that on the afternoon of the 11th, before Rodes' Division could be brought up, he saw a cloud of dust in the rear of the works and soon a column of the enemy filed into them, and skirmishers were thrown out. "This defeated our hopes of getting possession of the works by surprise."

The mere fact of these miscellaneous troops coming in when they did, and being seen by Early, caused him to hesitate until he could reconnoitre, and thereby they served a purpose, but could he at once have looked beyond the outward appearance, he would have seen that this was an improvised army and not an army of trained fighting men. He did discover this a little later the same day, but the real fighting men had then arrived.

Twenty-four hours earlier, indeed, twelve hours earlier, he could and most certainly would have gone into the city.

After the scare in Washington was over, and Early had retreated across the Potomac, it was said in some quarters that Early did not intend to capture the city, and that direful things would have happened to him had he captured it. That his whole force, in case he had gone in, would have been taken or destroyed. What would have happened had he gone in, no one can say with certainty. But if he did not intend to go in, if he could, and official Washington was convinced of that fact, why all the consternation in Washington? Why was General Grant besought to send aid quickly? Why were the governors of Northern States appealed to for troops to repel the invasion and to save the city? Why was any effort made at all, to keep Early out? Why not open the gates and let him in?

As already suggested no one can say now with confidence what would have happened if Early had actually gotten inside the breastworks with his veteran fighting force. He might have taken charge of the splendidly constructed fortifications, and with his own men, and those brought up from Point Lookout, have defied the Federal Army on the outside. The Point Lookout prisoners, as forlorn as they were in their prison camp, would have responded quickly to normal army conditions, good food, good clothes and discipline. Seventeen thousand or eighteen thousand men added to Early's experienced thousands would have made a formidable army, indeed. Well manned, the fortifications about the city were well nigh impregnable.

The audacity of attempting to take and hold the city would not have been greater than the audacity of marching more than two hundred miles from the base near Richmond; surrounded by foes on every side, threatened from every direction, without any chance of succor from any source, and menacing the seat of the National Government, in sight of the Capitol itself.

Once in possession of the fortifications and its guns, what would have become of the President and his Cabinet? What of the Treasury and its contents? What of the Navy Yard and its ships? What of the hospital stores? What would Gladstone and Louis Napoleon have done toward recognizing and aiding the Confederate States? What would have become of the morale of the Federal officials? No one can answer these questions. But it is not absurd to say, after the scare had subsided and the danger had been averted, that Early would not have gone in if he could? He could, at least have gathered the riches of the place, and the army stores collected there, burnt the shipping, captured or scattered the heads of government, and escaped. No one with reason can question but that could have been done if he had not been detained at Monocacy, and had arrived at the Capital one day earlier; and the other alternative was not impossible. Whatever may have been the language used in his communications with Early, that General Lee entertained the hope that Early might actually capture the city, is abundantly disclosed by the records.

In *Battles and Leaders of the Civil War*, Volume 4, at page 492, Early says:

"On the 9th Johnson moved north of Frederick with orders to strike (certain railroad bridges), then to move to Point Lookout for the purpose of releasing the prisoners there, if we should *succeed in getting into Washington.*"

In their *Abraham Lincoln,* Nicolay and Hay say: "The orders to Johnson form the strongest proof that Early really hoped to capture the Capital."

In his letter to President Davis of date June 26, General Lee had said: "At this time as far as I can learn, all the troops in the control of the United States are being sent to Grant, and little or *no opposition could be made by those at Washington.*" "If Early's movement could be united with the release of the prisoners at Point Lookout the advantages would be great." It was clearly in Lee's mind that the opportunity was highly favorable for the release of the 17,000 prisoners at Point Lookout and the uniting of them with the large army under Early's command already, as contemplated, in possession of the National Capital and its defenses.

Early was recognized as an officer of extraordinary vigor and promptitude, and a suggestion of that kind from Lee was sufficient to set Early to thinking seriously of what might be accomplished by a bold effort. In his official report he says:

"I determined at first to make an assault."

Further on he says: "I am sorry I did not succeed in capturing Washington, and in releasing the prisoners at Point Lookout."

In an another account he says, when his army first arrived before Washington, he immediately ordered Rodes to move into the works, if he could, upon finding the works but "feebly manned."

In an account of the operations of the cavalry brigade under his command, Gen. Bradley Johnson, after narrating the events of his raid through Maryland, July 9, 10, 11 and 12, 1864, says:

"We had failed in the *main object of the expedition, which was to relieve the prisoners at Point Lookout, convert them into a new army, capture Washington, establish communications across the Potomac by Manassas Junction with Gordonsville and Richmond,* and by making this a new base of operations, force Grant to let go his hold and come to the rescue of Pennsylvania."

By "Pennsylvania," it may be assumed he meant all the States north of the Potomac, including the District of Columbia.

The views of Col. Matthew R. McClennan have already been given. He says:

"The battle of Monocacy was one of great spirit and importance, and in my belief, saved the city of Washington from the ravages of the enemy."

In their *Abraham Lincoln, A History,* Volume 9, page 169, Nicolay and Hay have this to say of "Early's Campaign Against Washington":

"General Early left his camp near Rockville at dawn on the 11th, and pushed forward with eager hopes upon Washington. The infantry, turning to the left, advanced by the Seventh Street Road, which runs by Silver Springs into the city, with a cloud of cavalry on either flank. The day was hot and dusty, and the troops suffered greatly, but inspired by the prospect of the rich prize before them, they plodded onward with good heart and shortly after noon Early, riding a little in advance of his column, came in sight of Fort Stevens, which guarded the entrance to Washington by Seventh Street. A brief survey convinced him 'that the works were but feebly manned'; the greatest achievement of the war seemed to be within his grasp. He ordered General Rodes to 'bring his division into line as rapidly as possible, and to move into the works if he could'.

"But before the column, which was moving by flank, could be brought up, Early, who was gazing intently at the line of works in his front, saw to his infinite vexation a column of men in blue file into them on the right and left; a fringe of skirmishers was thrown out in front, and from all the batteries in range a sharp artillery fire opened. His hopes of a surprise passed away in the wreathing smoke of the National guns, and he gave orders for a close reconnaissance of the position.

"The whole of the afternoon was consumed in this work and as it proceeded, the prospect for the Confederates became every hour more discouraging." . . . . The fortifications were found to be very strong and scientifically constructed, every possible approach was raked with artillery.

"Early might well be excused for declining to rush his tired army upon those bristling works.". . . . "The newspapers had informed him of the departure of heavy reinforcements from Petersburg; and when he saw the improvised levies of General Augur filing into the works in the afternoon, he came not unnaturally to the conclusion that he had to deal with the veterans of the Army of the Potomac.

"This supposed state of affairs called for the most careful preparation and before the preparations were completed, what he imagined had become true; Wright with his two magnificent divisions had landed at the wharf, being received by President Lincoln in person, amid a tumult of joyous cheering; and the advance of the 19th Corps under W. H. Emory was also in the streets of Washington. When the rear of Early's Infantry closed up in the evening, the Capital was already safe from a *coup de main.*"

That night (the 11th) there was a conference with Early's generals. "But it was like parting with soul and body for Early to give up his hope of seizing Washington, and he broke up the conference, saying he would assault the works at daybreak the next morning, unless it should previously be shown to be impracticable."

"During the night he received false information that the two corps from the Army of the Potomac had arrived. He therefore delayed his attack until he could make one final reconnaissance; he rode to the front and found the parapets lined with troops. With the dome of the Capitol in his sight, gilded by the rays of the rising sun, he gave up all hope of capturing Washington."

Nicolay and Hay describe the information concerning the two corps of the Army of the Potomac arriving, as *"false information."* As a matter of fact, it was not false. It was not accurate in the sense of *two full corps* arriving, but it was true as to some regiments from two corps, the Sixth and the Nineteenth, arriving. At 10 o'clock on the night of the 11th C. A. Dana, Assistant Secretary of War, telegraphed General Grant that five boat loads of General Wright's troops had arrived, and one of the Nineteenth Corps.

On the 13th he telegraphed that 4,360 men of the

Nineteenth Corps had arrived which, together with those of the Sixth Corps already up under General Wright, made a total of about fifteen thousand men. He stated that General Emory of the Nineteenth Corps reported that the remainder of two divisions of that corps was close at hand. As the boats carried from twelve hundred to fifteen hundred men or possibly more, a large reinforcement had arrived by 10 o'clock on Monday night, and boats were arriving every little while with more men of the Sixth and Nineteenth Corps. In substance, Early's information was true.

In his report Early himself says of the conference with his generals:

"After interchanging views with them, I determined to make an assault on the enemy's work at daylight the next morning. But during the night a dispatch was received from General Bradley T. Johnson from near Baltimore that two corps had arrived from General Grant's army and that his whole army was probably in motion. As soon as it was daylight, I rode to the front and found the parapet lined with troops. I had therefore to give up all hope of capturing Washington."

In his book entitled *The Ninth New York Heavy Artilley,* Alfred Seelye Roe, says at page 134:

"The truth of the whole matter was that Washington was badly scared, and with justice; only the timely arrival of the First and Second Divisions of the Sixth Corps saved the city from pillage and conflagration, and it was our heading off Early at Monocacy that permitted such result. Early himself in 1888 told the writer that the sight of the Greek cross on the works north of Washington was what induced him to retreat."

The Greek cross was the emblem of the Sixth Corps; the Third Division of which fought Early at Monocacy, and the First and Second Divisions of which arrived at Washington barely in time to save the city.

Gen. Lew Wallace felt very strongly that his stand at Monocacy was the crucial act in the defense of the city. He says: "Orders have been given to collect the bodies of our dead in one burial ground on the battle-field, suitable for a monument, upon which I propose to write:

"THESE MEN DIED TO SAVE THE NATIONAL CAPITAL
AND THEY DID SAVE IT."

In his *Memoirs* General Grant has this to say of the battle:

"If Early had been but one day earlier he might have entered the Capital before the arrival of the reinforcements I had sent. Whether the delay caused by the battle amounted to a day or not, General Wallace contributed on this occasion, by the defeat of the troops under him, a greater benefit to the cause than often falls to the lot of a commander of an equal force to render by means of a victory." (Grant's *Memoirs*, vol. 2, p. 305.)

Few men were in a position to judge accurately the possibilities of Early's invasion of Maryland and attack upon the Capital better than Lucius E. Chittenden, Register of the Treasury, under Mr. Lincoln at the time of the invasion. In an interesting volume, entitled *Recollections of President Lincoln and His Administration*, published by Harper in 1901, Mr. Chittenden devotes two chapters to this invasion and together with his own experiences as an official of the Treasury, he gives his conclusions after a comparison of the evidence from different sources as to what would have happened had not General Early been detained at Monocacy for 24 hours or more.

He says, page 408: "I went into the treasury. I found General Spinner, the treasurer, Mr. Tuttle, the cashier, and three or four of his principal clerks engaged in filling mail sacks with Treasury notes and other securities; all working with great earnestness and expedition. General Spinner said: "I have a small steamer ready,—no matter where. We will carry nothing but money or securities if we decide to move.". . . . "Within two hours my family and some friends were speeding northward at 40 miles an hour."

Speaking of the coming of the First and Second Divisions of the Sixth Army Corps, Mr. Chittenden says: "They had just returned into a fort which they had previously garrisoned for a year and knew the range of every tree and object."

Then after reviewing the evidence, he says: "It must, therefore, be accepted as a fact of history that the capture of Washington and the release of the prisoners at Point Lookout were the objectives of Early's campaign."

"Had he made the attack on the morning of the 11th, he would have found the city in the condition supposed by General Lee when the campaign was projected. The Confederate Army would have met with no resistance except from raw and undisciplined forces which in the opinion of General Grant, and it was supposed of General Lee, also, would have been altogether inadequate to its defense. Its capture and possession for a day would have been disastrous to the Union. Early would have seized the money in the Treasury, the archives of the departments, the immense supplies of clothing, arms and ammunition in store, he would have compelled General Grant to raise the siege of Richmond; he would have destroyed uncounted millions in value of property, and he would have had the same opportunity of retreat of which he availed himself the next day.

"But with his veterans behind the defenses he would

have had no occasion to retreat. The released prisoners at Point Lookout in two days would have added 20,000 to the strength of his army. The Confederates of Maryland would have swarmed to his assistance and he could certainly have held the Capital long enough to give Great Britain the excuse she so much desired to recognize the Confederacy and break the blockade. After the danger had passed, when its magnitude became apparent, there was but one opinion among the friends of the Union. It was that we had escaped a loss of prestige and of property, compared with which previous disasters would have been trifling and probably a blow fatally destructive to the Union cause. And then there is another record which will be held in honor so long as and wherever courage is held to be a virtue among men. It is the page which is filled with the story of Monocacy where the streams ran blood, inexperienced men fought like veterans and veterans like the legionnaires of Caesar. When the children of the Republic are asked what was it that brought Early's campaign to naught and saved the Capital, let them be taught to answer: 'General Wallace and his command at the battle of Monocacy and the arrival of the Sixth Corps within the defences of the Capital.'

In an earlier part of his consideration of the circumstances and evidence concerning the battle, Mr. Chittenden says: "If that (battle) fought at Monocacy did delay General Early so as to save the Capital from assault and probable capture, it was one of the decisive battles of the world, and with the events that immediately followed, deserves a much more complete account than it has hitherto received."

As Mr. Chittenden appears to have written his views of the battle a number of years after the war, when he had had time to consider all the evidence and to weigh it, and besides as he had intimate personal knowledge of many of the events about which he writes, his views are worthy of no light consideration. As his conviction was that the battle fought at Monocacy on July 9, 1864, did save the National Capital from capture, and did therefore contribute immeasurably to the preservation of the Union, it was, in the opinion of a capable, well informed and unprejudiced critic, "One of the decisive battle of the world," and as such it is assuredly entitled to an important place in the history of our country.

The measure of praise that Mr. Chittenden bestows upon the forces of General Wallace at Monocacy need not be minimized so far as the great majority of Nationals engaged there are concerned. They fought courageously and stood their ground nobly until ordered to retreat.

And no less a measure of praise is due the men in gray who contended there on that bloody field with the forces of General Wallace. They showed their courage in the sharp fighting at the Jug Bridge, at the fords above the railroad, at the wooden bridge near Frederick Junction and in the conflicts between McCausland's dismounted cavalry and the skirmish line of General Ricketts, but the brunt of the battle was when Gen. John B. Gordon with his depleted ranks of one division only of foot-sore, travel-worn veterans, went against the fresh Third Division, Sixth Army Corps, under Gen. James B. Ricketts, posted behind the fences and in the fields of the Thomas farm, and after a bloody encounter in which the Confederate losses were much greater than the Federal, dislodged and drove it.

In his *Reminiscences* General Gordon says of this battle:

"The Union lines stood firmly in this second position, bravely defending the railroad and the highway to Washington. Between the two hostile lines there was a narrow ravine down which ran a small stream of limpid water. In this ravine the fighting was desperate and at close quarters. To and fro the battle swayed across this little stream, the dead and wounded on both sides mingling their blood in its waters; and when the struggle was ended a crimsoned current ran toward the river. Nearly half of my men and large numbers of Federals fell there."

If there be honor and glory in killing and being killed in battle, then there is honor and glory for the soldiers who wore the gray no less than for the soldiers who wore the blue at Monocacy.

CONFEDERATE MONUMENT

CHAPTER XXVII.

MONUMENTS

Several monuments have been erected on the battlefield by the States whose troops fought there on July 9. Pennsylvania has a monument to the regiments of volunteers from that State, set up in the middle of an half acre of land which the State bought. It is a fine, durable monument in granite, located near the ground where the regiment was posted just before and during the battle.

Vermont also has a monument at the intersection of the Baker Valley Road with the Georgetown Road, dedicated to the Tenth Vermont Volunteers who were posted nearby during the engagement.

New Jersey also has erected a monument in honor of her brave soldiery who fought so well at Monocacy; the 14th New Jersey Regiment. All these troops were of the Sixth Corps, Third or Ricketts' Division.

THE CONFEDERATE MONUMENT

The Daughters of the Confederacy have also set up a stone marker or boulder on the west side of the Monocacy, along the highway to Washington, about a mile northwest of the bridge over the river. It is known that Ramseur's Division went that way when attacking the Federal force defending the bridges. A battery of Confederate artillery was operated from a wood that stood then on the west side of the turnpike, near where this boulder now stands.

Another battery was on the east side of the turnpike, not far from the Frederick branch of the railroad. It was between this Confederate boulder and Frederick Junction that Ramseur's men contended with the Federal skirmishers under Capt. George E. Davis, occupying the triangle already referred to.

The boulder was dedicated just fifty years after the battle. The inscription on the bronze tablet affixed to the front is as follows:

THIS BOULDER OVERLOOKS
THE MONOCACY BATTLEFIELD
AND IS ERECTED IN MEMORY OF
THE SOUTHERN SOLDIERS WHO
FELL THERE IN BATTLE FOUGHT ON
JULY 9, 1864,
WHICH RESULTED IN A CONFEDERATE
VICTORY.
ERECTED JULY 9, 1914,
BY THE FITZHUGH LEE CHAPTER,
UNITED DAUGHTERS OF THE CONFEDERACY,
FREDERICK, MARYLAND.

THE NEW JERSEY MONUMENT.

The first of the several monuments to be erected on the battlefield was that of the 14th New Jersey Regiment. It was unveiled on July 11, 1907. The State of New Jersey was represented by Rev. W. W. Case of Trenton. The services were largely attended. One hundred and eighty survivors of the regiment and their friends arrived by special train the night before. Prayer was offered by Rev. John Handley of Vineland, New Jersey, and a history of the regiment was given by Major John C. Patterson, of Monmouth, New Jersey. There was music by the Braddock Band and the memorial was unveiled by Miss Alice Patterson and Miss Nettie Foster.

Major Patterson presented the monument to the State of New Jersey, and it was accepted on behalf of the State by Rev. Dr. Case. Henry C. La Rowe of Brooklyn, New York, accepted for the Reunion Association. Reverend Handley and Judge William H. Vredenburgh, of Freehold, New Jersey, also delivered addresses, and an ode prepared for the occasion was read by E. D. Smith, of Elizabeth, New Jersey, and a poem by E. L. Cowart, Jr., son of Quartermaster E. L. Cowart of Elizabeth. The monument stands west of the Monocacy and southwest of the highway bridge over the railroad-cut on the Georgetown Road. It is of granite, about twenty-four feet high, surmounted by the energetic figure of an infantryman cut from granite, displaying much life and action.

On the front of the monument is carved the Greek cross, and there are two handsome, artistic bronze tablets affixed to the front containing inscriptions. Major E. Y. Goldsborough, who served on the staff of Gen. E. B. Tyler during the battle, and who was a resident of Frederick, had charge of the arrangements, and the occasion was in every respect a great success.

The inscriptions on the bronze tablets are as follows—upper tablet:

"Erected by the State of New Jersey to commemorate the heroic services of the 14th Regiment New Jersey Volunteer Infantry, 1st Brigade, 3rd Division, 6th Army Corps, Army of the Potomac, at the battle of Monocacy, Md., July 9th, 1864." . . . .

"The 14th Regiment New Jersey Volunteers was organized on the Monmouth Battleground and mustered into the United States Service near Freehold, New Jersey, August 26, 1862, and mustered out on June 18, 1865, near Washington, D. C.,

Lower tablet:

"The United States Forces commanded by General Lew Wallace on this battlefield, so stubbornly opposed the Confederate troops under General Jubal A. Early, as to assure the safety of the National Capital."

"Commission to erect the monument—Major John C. Patterson, president; Adjt. William H. Foster, secretary; Corp. R. A. Clark, treasurer; Capt. Jarvis Mauser, Serg. John Grover."

ADDRESS OF MAJOR PATTERSON

In his address, Major John C. Patterson, the chairman of the Monument Commission, said in part:

"On this ground we became part of the little army of Gen. Lew Wallace, 5,400 strong with one battery, (Alexander's) of six guns and two or three odd pieces besides. . . .

"Our orders were to stop the advance of Gen. Early and his picked body of men, commanded by such able officers as Breckinridge, Rodes, Ramseur, Wharton, Evans, Rosser, Johnson and Gordon.

"We were greatly outnumbered, yet we took our position against an army known to be eighteen or twenty-five thousand strong, with 40 pieces of artillery. Weak in numbers, we were reinforced with the thought that the hour for the destruction of the National Capital was at hand. Here, on these fields in the face of such great odds, the brave men of General Wallace's army fought with a courage and resistance scarcely paralleled in the annals of war. From eight o'clock in the morning with the thermometer in the nineties we fought there until five o'clock in the afternoon of that hot July day.

"At that hour General Wallace ordered us to withdraw from the field, but before we went we had accomplished the purpose for which the brave men from Ohio, Pennsylvania, Maryland, Vermont, New York and New Jersey had been sacrificed. We had delayed General Early in his march on Washington one day. How much that one day allowed to be done, history will tell you.

"It allowed the First and Second Divisions of our own corps to hasten from City Point on the James River and reach Washington, where, encouraged by the immortal Lincoln in person, they marched through the city and to Fort Stevens, where they deployed in line of battle just as Early was preparing to attack."

"We had by this delay given time to man the works protecting Washington with tried veterans of the Army of the Potomac, thereby saving our Nation's Capital.

"The 14th New Jersey went into this battle with about two hundred and fifty-six rifles, one lieutenant-colonel, one adjutant, eight captains, and I think five lieutenants. The next morning was a sad roll call for the 14th New Jersey. Only 92 answered to their names. We had lost one lieutenant-colonel wounded, one adjutant wounded, three captains killed or mortally wounded, one lieutenant killed and I think two lieutenants wounded.

"You will learn from this that out of 15 officers engaged, we lost four killed and eight wounded. We lost our color-sergeant killed, and out of seven men of the color guard, two were killed and three wounded. Besides this a large number of the rank were killed, wounded and captured. With all this loss, we fought until ordered out."

REVEREND DOCTOR CASE'S REMARKS

In accepting the monument on behalf of the Governor of New Jersey, Reverend Doctor Case said:

"There can be no doubt but that the battle fought here on July 9, 1864, was one of the most important battles of the Civil War. Washington at that time had a very small available force for its defense. Most of the troops from the entrenchments surrounding the city had been sent to reinforce General Grant, who was pressing the siege of Richmond and Petersburg by slow but sure processes.

"At Point Lookout below the city of Washington on the Maryland side was a camp of 20,000 prisoners. It was Early's purpose to release them. . . . His army was not the proud army that swept through the beautiful valleys of Maryland to the Monocacy, but shattered and broken with a loss of over twelve hundred, he was delayed for more than twenty-four hours, so that when he reached the outworks of Washington, he found that this twenty-fours hours had allowed the First and Second Divisions of the old Sixth Corps to reach the entrenchments, where, under Gen. Horatio G. Wright, they were ready for battle. After a feeble attack, easily repulsed, Early hastened to put the Potomac between him and the Union forces."

Comrade La Rowe Speaks

Dr. Case then presented the monument to the Reunion Association of the 14th New Jersey Volunteers, and in accepting it on behalf of the Association, Comrade Henry C. La Rowe, of Brooklyn, N. Y., said:

"This is, indeed, a memorable day in our lives, the counterpart of which we are not likely ever to see again, but with all our pride and rejoicing comes a feeling of sorrow and sadness. We almost hear a 'voice that is still,' we almost 'feel a touch of a vanished hand'— a voice we heard and a hand we clasped, for the last time 43 years ago today. Memory recalls forms and faces that we shall not see again until we 'pass over the river and rest with them under the shade of the trees.'

"But after all, comrades, don't you think it paid to stay here? . . . What if men were maimed for life! What matters it if we did redden the sheaves of grain with our blood! Who regrets it now, in view of the tremendous, undreamed of beneficent results which followed the mighty struggles of the Civil War."

"May this monument be an inspiration to future generations."

NEW JERSEY MONUMENT

The above is a reproduction of the picture of the monument
erected by the State of New Jersey to the Fourteenth New Jersey
Regiment of Volunteers. It was unveiled July 11, 1907, and is
located on a plot of ground on the west side of the Washington
Highway from Frederick, adjacent to the main line tracks of the
B. & O. R. R. southwest of the over-pass bridge, and about 200
yards northwest of the wooden bridge over the Monocacy. It is
also about 350 yards west of the station at Frederick Junction.
One of Best's barns in the background.

THE PENNSYLVANIA MONUMENT

The monument to the Pennsylvania regiments was the second to be unveiled on the battlefield. It was erected by the State of Pennsylvania at a cost of $8,000 (estimated) and unveiled on November 24, 1908.

A large number of the survivors of the regiments were present at the unveiling exercises and many townspeople also. Lieutenant-Governor Murphy was present, accompanied by the staff of Governor Stuart.

The exercises were opened with an invocation by Rev. Dr. Osborne Ingle of All Saints Episcopal Church of Frederick.

Mayor George Edward Smith of Frederick made an address of welcome, and Capt. William H. Lanius, chairman of the Monument Commission, presented the monument to the State of Pennsylvania.

Lieutenant-Governor Murphy accepted the monument on behalf of the State, and the oration of the day was delivered by Capt. Robert T. Cornwell of West Chester, Pennsylvania; after which Major E. Y. Goldsborough of Frederick made appropriate remarks.[1]

DESCRIPTION OF THE PENNSYLVANIA MONUMENT

The monument is of blue westerly Rhode Island Granite, a shaft 35 feet high standing on a base ten feet square. Surmounting the base is a polished die with four Doric columns at the corners. On the die is a cylindrical shaft with a carved cap, bearing on its top a polished ball of westerly granite, three feet six inches in diameter. On its front is cut the Greek cross which was the emblem of the Sixth Army Corps. The inscriptions are on the four sides of the die upon which rests the cylindrical shaft. On the face of the 12-ton base has been cut the coat-of-arms of Pennsylvania.

On the front of the monument, which faces the old Georgetown Road, is cut on the granite the following inscription:

"ERECTED BY THE COMMONWEALTH OF
PENNSYLVANIA, IN COMMEMORATION
OF THE BRAVERY, SACRIFICES AND
PATRIOTISM OF THE 67TH, 87TH
AND 138TH REGIMENTS THAT
FOUGHT ON THIS BATTLEFIELD
JULY 9TH, 1864."

"COMMISSIONERS
"WILLIAM H. LANIUS, CAPTAIN, CO. I, 87TH
ROBERT T. CORNWELL, CAPTAIN, CO. I, 67TH
WILLIAM V. COPPLEBERGER, PRIVATE, CO. A, 138TH"

On the base in front is a bronze plate bearing the inscription:

"VIRTUE, LIBERTY AND INDEPENDENCE."

The motto of Pennsylvania.

INSCRIPTIONS

On the north face of the die is the following inscription:

"138TH PA. VOL.
138TH REG. PA. VOL. INF.
2ND BRIGADE, 3RD DIVISION, 6TH CORPS
ORGANIZED AT HARRISBURG, PA., AUG. 26, 1862
MUSTERED OUT JUNE 28, 1865
NEAR WASHINGTON, D. C."

On the east face is the following:

"67TH PA. VOL.

67TH REG. PA. VOL. INF.

2ND BRIGADE, 3RD DIVISION, 6TH CORPS

ARMY OF THE POTOMAC

ORGANIZED AT PHILADELPHIA IN THE

SUMMER AND FALL OF 1861

MUSTERED OUT JULY 14, 1865"

On the south face is this inscription:

"87TH PA. VOL.

87TH REG. PA. VOL. INF.

1ST BRIGADE, 3RD DIVISION, 6TH CORPS

ORGANIZED AT YORK, PA.

SEPTEMBER 14, 1861

MUSTERED OUT JUNE 29, 1865"

The monument is surrounded by a fence made of granite posts and two rails of galvanized iron piping. Granite posts, weighing a ton each, mark the four corners of the plot of ground, about a half an acre, which was purchased as a site for the monument. A fine view of Frederick Valley is to be had from this plot of ground.

Owing to a change of location of the Georgetown Road, this handsome monument is seldom seen by the traveler along the highway, and a tall hedge fence obscures it from view even to those who pass by on the old road.

THE VERMONT MONUMENT

The third monument to be erected on the battlefield by a northern State is the Vermont monument which was unveiled in 1915.

It stands at the intersection of the Baker Valley Road with the Georgetown Road, and occupies a triangular piece of land right in the corner of the Thomas farm, now owned by Messrs. John H. and William G. Baker.

The plot purchased as a site for the monument is marked by three granite posts, one at each corner of the triangle.

The monument itself is a solid granite monolith, rectangular in shape, about four feet wide, two and one-half feet thick, and six feet high, standing on a granite base, with a sub-base about six feet long and four feet wide. The height of the whole is about eight feet.

On the front is a bronze tablet in the shape of a Greek cross set into the granite upon which is inscribed in bronze letters the following:

"THIS MONUMENT WAS ERECTED BY THE STATE OF VERMONT TO DESIGNATE THE POSITION OF THE TENTH VERMONT INFANTRY DURING THE BATTLE FOUGHT HERE ON THE NINTH OF JULY, 1864, TO SAVE WASHINGTON,"AND WE SAVED IT."

"SEVEN COMPANIES OCCUPIED THE WASHINGTON PIKE WHILE THREE COMPANIES OCCUPIED THE BUCKEYSTOWN ROAD OPPOSITE THE THOMAS HOUSE."

The Vermont Monument stands at the intersection of the old Georgetown Road and the Baker's Valley or Buckeystown Road. It is erected on a triangular plot of ground marked by three granite posts. It was erected in 1915, and upon the bronze tablet let into the face of the monument is this inscription: "This monument was erected by the State of Vermont to designate the position of the Tenth Vermont Infantry during the battle fought here on the 9th of July, 1864, to save Washington, 'and we saved it,' Seven companies occupied the Washington Pike while three companies occupied Buckeystown (Baker's Valley) Road opposite the Thomas house."

The base of the monument stands a little higher than the public road, on a slight embankment and is reached from the road by three granite steps. While not as large or imposing as the other monuments, it is a handsome memorial to the brave Vermonters who stood so valiantly against the invading hosts of Early on that bloody field.

[1] For an account of the dedicatory ceremonies at the unveiling of the Pennsylvania monument see post, page 241.

INTER-CHAPTER

COL. JUDSON SPOFFORD'S REMINISCENCES AND VIEWS

Among the Union veterans of the War Between the States, still surviving, is Col Judson Spofford, now of Boise, Idaho. He took part in the battle of Monocacy as a "high private in the front rank of Company 'K,' Tenth Regiment Vermont Infantry Volunteers," and was one of the seventy-five picked men sent with others to the north side of Monocacy at Frederick Junction to hold back the Confederate division of Gen. Stephen D. Ramseur, who was trying to capture the wooden bridge over the Monocacy on the highway to Washington, during the battle of July 9, 1864. After the war Colonel Spofford removed from Vermont to Idaho and has been engaged in the insurance business in Boise City for a number of years. He is past department commander Grand Army of the Republic of Idaho. A few years ago Colonel Spofford visited Frederick and manifested great interest in the project of creating a national park on the Monocacy battlefield. He is a veteran of a number of battles during the war, including Gettysburg, Wilderness, Spottsylvania Court House, North Anna, Cold Harbour and others; and was several times wounded. He is tall, erect and still active notwithstanding his wounds and four score and more years, and is besides a man of intelligence. Although familiar with the big battles of the war he declares that

Monocacy was the most important of them all because that battle decided something whereas the other battles, including Gettysburg, decided nothing. This he declares to be the case more than sixty years after the last of those many sanguinary struggles which took place during that four years of mortal strife, and more than sixty years after the "muffled drums have beat their last tattoo." As his views coincide entirely with the general tenor and purport of this book, I am inserting a synopsis of what he has written on the subject in the form of an Inter-Chapter. It will be found interesting reading.

I have also inserted excerpts from a York newspaper containing an account of the unveiling of the Pennsylvania Monument on the battlefield, and other data.

MONOCACY, THE DECISIVE BATTLE OF THE CIVIL WAR

By Col. Judson Spofford, Boise City, Idaho.

I am aware that in the caption of this story I make a broad assertion, one with which all readers will not readily coincide. It is not my plan or desire to change current history; but rather to add a new chapter to that which others have written. I am going to tell you a story, a historical story if you please, from my personal viewpoint, from the viewpoint of a soldier who fought in the ranks during this great battle. If, after reading this and weighing the testimony I offer in its support, you are convinced that Monocacy was a great battle, and that it, and the men who fought it, have not been accorded their rightful place in history, then the object of the story will have been accomplished.

As a high private in the front rank of Company "K," Tenth Regiment Vermont Infantry Volunteers, I served throughout the battle of Monocacy, as I had served through many a one preceding it. I was one of the seventy-five picked from my regiment under the command of Lieut. George E. Davis, and, in the early morning sent across the old wooden bridge, to the north side of the river, where we were instructed to hold the bridge and the turnpike crossing it and the railroad bridge, at all hazards. The turnpike was the only direct road leading to Washington, the Capital of the Nation and it was the one thing which the Rebel army were fighting to possess. I was in an advantageous position, where I had a full view of the two contending armies, and of General Wallace's headquarters throughout the battle.

As far as I know or have been able to find out, I am the only survivor of that band of Green Mountain boys who fought on the north side of the river. I mention these little personalities, not to boast of my service, but to show that I was an actual, active participant in the battle, and that I am better qualified to tell about it than one who was not there but miles away and personally knew nothing about it.

SYNOPSIS OF THE BATTLE

July 7, 1864.—Gen. Jubal A. Early with 30,000[1] Confederate veteran soldiers, picked men from Lee's army, were at Frederick, Maryland, only 40 miles north of Washington, the capital of the nation. General Grant having taken all available troops with him to the Army of the Potomac, Washington was in a defenseless condition, it was threatened, and liable to be captured and destroyed by the approaching Rebel army.

Gen. Lew Wallace, with a small force of One Hundred Days Men, with his headquarters at Baltimore, was the only opposing Union force between Washington and the Rebel army of 30,000 marching on the nation's capital.

General Wallace, seeing the danger, determined to oppose and delay Early's march on Washington as long as possible, so as to give General Grant time to get troops from the Army of the Potomac to Washington, before the Rebel army reached there.

General Halleck, Chief of Staff in Washington, ignores General Wallace, gives him no information of the conditions, no details of the impending dangers, no orders and no encouragement that reinforcements will be sent to him.

General Grant has information from Halleck that a small enemy force is raiding in Maryland and Pennsylvania. Grant sends the Third Division of the Sixth Corps by transports to Baltimore.

General Halleck orders General Ricketts, commanding that Third Division, to take his force to Harpers Ferry, and report to the officer in command there.

The general in command of Harpers Ferry at that time was Gen. Jubal A. Early of the Confederate Army.

To obey the order of General Halleck, to take his division to Harpers Ferry, General Ricketts would have to take his command through General Wallace's department, right past General Wallace, who was then fighting with the advance of Early's army at Frederick.

General Wallace stopped Ricketts' Division of veterans at Monocacy Junction. Ricketts at first was peeved at this interference with his orders. Wallace explained matters to Ricketts, who at once grasped the situation and not being anxious to report to General Early, put himself and his division at General Wallace's disposal and asked for orders.

July 8.—General Wallace, after fighting Early's advance all day at Frederick, during the night moved his force to Monocacy Junction, formed his line on the Monocacy River in such a way as to command the turnpike leading to Washington over the wooden bridge, the Baltimore and Ohio Railroad leading to Harpers Ferry, and the pike leading to Baltimore, over the stone bridge. He placed the 3,350 veterans of Ricketts' command to guard the pike leading to Washington. A squadron of the Eighth Illinois Cavalry, 250, he placed at the ford some distance below the wooden bridge. His 2,500 raw and undiciplined men were placed at the stone bridge on the Baltimore Pike, and Alexander's battery of 6-inch guns he divided between Ricketts and Tyler. Seventy-five men had been picked from the Tenth Vermont, and early in the morning sent across the old wooden bridge to the north side of the river with instructions to hold the turnpike leading to Washington at all hazards. Thus he had a force of 6,100 men, nearly one-half of them raw and undisciplined, to meet and contend with Early's army of 30,000 veterans, picked from Lee's army for this particular job to capture Washington.

HALLECK AND WALLACE AT ODDS

General Halleck was of the Regular Army. General Wallace had volunteered as a private at the outbreak of the war. Owing to his quick grasp of military affairs and his undaunted skill and bravery, he had received rapid promotion and in the early part of 1862 had been promoted to a major-general, same rank as General Halleck, though General Halleck ranked him because of length of a service of almost a lifetime. General Halleck seemed to have had an idea that a volunteer should not be allowed to obtain rank above a corporal. General Halleck displayed the same disposition toward Grant that he had toward Wallace, until President Lincoln took the bit in his teeth and promoted Grant to a position where he outranked, not only outranked, but commanded Halleck. Then Halleck poured out his wrath in double portions on General Wallace.

July 9.—By daylight General Wallace had formed his little army in position for the coming fray. He was ready to fight, and he did fight one of the noted battles of the world. At 7 o'clock the skirmish line of the Tenth Vermonters were engaged in a rather spasmodic fire with the overwhelming numbers of their opponents.

The Thomas Mansion—The Three Young Men

Colonel Thomas, owner of the Thomas mansion, a retired merchant from Baltimore, had an unmarried daughter, and she had a young lady friend, a Miss Tyler, visiting her from one of the "border State" cities. The Thomas mansion, a fine old Southern home, was located in a picturesque locality and "green-walled by the hills of Maryland."

Colonel Thomas had purchased this palatial home and moved from Baltimore to avoid *war* and all its terrible consequences and, as he thought, to be far removed from the strife and ravages of the conflict which he felt sure would rage about Baltimore. But his mansion now became the centerpiece of a great conflict and his productive fields were transformed into the bloody battle-field of Monocacy where Union men fought like demons for the preservation of their National Capital and Rebels fought like maniacs for its destruction. Colonel Thomas, also, had a son in Baltimore who, about this time had come out to the old home and brought with him two young gentlemen friends, Anderson and Gatchel, ostensibly to spend the Fourth of July but really to visit the young ladies: Anderson to see Miss Thomas and Gatchel to visit Miss Tyler.

Brig.-Gen. Erastus B. Tyler, who was in command at this point until General Wallace came down from Frederick, saw these young men and suspected them of lingering there with the intention of joining the Rebel army. He arrested them, put them in United States uniforms, armed them with Springfield rifles and told them to "Fight for Uncle Sam." The young grief-stricken ladies were employing every device known to true lovers for the deliverance of the young men from their impending dangers. From my position I saw the young ladies, after the skirmishing preliminaries of the battle had commenced, hastening across what soon became a bloody battlefield, past the Union lines to General Wallace's headquarters, pleading for the release of the three young men, but the absorbing difficulties of that critical hour made it too late for him to act and the two weeping, heart-broken girls returned to the Thomas mansion and with the rest of the family took refuge in the cellar during the day. All day long the battle surged above and all around them, and the yards and fields were strewn with the dead and wounded from the contending armies.

WALLACE HAD LOST—BUT WON

Late in the afternoon General Wallace had won that for which he was fighting, TIME. He had gained time for General Grant to get troops to Washington before the Rebel army could reach there. He withdrew what was left of his little army and the battle was closed.

All day the battle raged with unabated fury. Charge after charge upon the Third Division was made by the picked veterans of General Lee's army, every time with increased numbers and more determination to break through the Union lines and get possession of the Washington Pike, but all to no purpose.

Of the Third Division veterans there was but a single line, and in places it was stretched until it seemed that it would break of its own tension. It had not support, not a man in reserve.

In Wallace's little army there were three general officers, Generals Wallace, Ricketts and Tyler.

The first charge, made by McCausland on Ricketts' left flank, was made with a single line of battle and handsomely repulsed by the veterans of the Third Division. Each succeeding charge throughout the day was increased by the addition of another line until at 4.30 o'clock in the afternoon the enemy charged with four solid lines of battle. When the first line reached the Third Division they were handsomely repulsed and with heavy losses sent staggering back into the three supporting lines. This created a momentary panic and taking advantage of it, General Wallace ordered General Ricketts to get his men off the field in the best and quickest way possible. Ricketts withdrew his men taking a circuitous route to avoid the raking fire from the infantry and an enfilading fire from the forty pieces of artillery, and they finally reached the Baltimore Pike east of the stone bridge.

The Vermonters' skirmish line were still fighting on the

north side of Monocacy. All day they had been an army unto
themselves. Isolated from all other Union troops and opposed
by several times their numbers and often called upon to surrender, they still maintained their position. Earlier in the day
the old wooden bridge had been burned. This left the little band
of Green Mountain boys cut off from all other Union forces with
no way of exit except by the ties and stringers on the railroad
bridge and that 40 feet in the air.

Lieutenant Davis, our commander, ordered us to "get over"
the best we could. He selected a read guard to hold back the
pursuing foe and some of us succeeded in getting over, some were
shot and fell through the ties into the raging river 40 feet below,
others were wounded and taken off to Libby Prison, while a few
joined the regiment on the Baltimore Pike, leaving more than
a third of their number on the battlefield. From that point
General Wallace with his command fell back toward Baltimore
and soon bivouacked for the night.

WALLACE RELIEVED AND REINSTATED

In the dead of night while General Wallace was sharing a
blanket with General Ricketts and trying to get a little sleep,
the first he had had for three consecutive days and nights, he
was routed out of his blanket by a dispatch bearer from General
Halleck's office who delivered an order to General Wallace telling
him that he was removed and General Ord would succeed him
in command.

Thus was one of the greatest and one of the most successful generals removed from his high sphere of usefulness to the
Government by a man who, from some cause or another, had got
into a position which he was nowise qualified to fill, and which
he, with no apparent qualifications, continued to hold. When
the rank injustice of Wallace's removal became known to General
Grant and President Lincoln, General Ord was transferred to
another command and General Wallace was restored to his rightful position in spite of Halleck's persistent opposition.

Here there is to me a mystery. Why was Halleck not
removed?

General Wallace had proven himself to the satisfaction of
President Lincoln and General Grant to be a military genius,
quick to perceive the dispostion, plans and intentions of his
adversary, and with a masterful knowledge of the best and most
proficient way to handle men. It was through his masterful

efficiency in all these matters that he early gained the confidence of General Grant, and a little later the full confidence of President Lincoln. At the close of the war he was called by the Government to fill high positions in State and in diplomatic affairs of the nation.

MY REASONS FOR CLAIMING THAT MONOCACY WAS THE MOST IMPORTANT AND REAL DECISIVE BATTLE OF THE CIVIL WAR

In July, 1864, Washington, the Capital of the Nation, was in a defenseless condition. At that time a Confederate Army of 30,000 veterans selected from Lee's army for the sole purpose of capturing Washington was within 35 miles of that city. Only two days easy marching, or one day and a night forced march. With the exception of Gen. Lew Wallace with a little force of about 6,100, about one-half of whom were raw and undisciplined troops, there was no protecting force between the Rebel army and the city of Washington.

General Wallace, who was under the ban of General Halleck, decided to delay the Rebel army as long as possible. In other words he decided to fight. Not with the idea of beating the Rebel army, but for *time*. To delay the onrushing enemy long enough to give General Grant *time* to get troops from the Army of the Potomac to the defense of Washington before the Confederate Army would get there. By maneuvering and fighting he held them all day of the 7th and 8th at Frederick. The Tenth Vermont joined General Wallace the morning of the 8th. During the night of the 8th he withdrew his force from Frederick and took a position on the Monocacy River, guarding the two turnpike roads leading, one to Washington, the other to Baltimore. Here on the 9th of July, 1864, he fought one of the most determined and sanguinary battles of the war. The enemy did most of its fighting to get possession of the Washington Pike and the wooden bridge. General Wallace's force at this point consisted of 3,350 men of Gen. James B. Ricketts' Third Division of the Sixth Army Corps. The one-hundred-days men were posted at the stone bridge on the Baltimore Pike to protect Ricketts' veterans from being flanked.

All the time General Wallace had been counting off the time, first by half a day, then by hours, then by quarter hours, and then by minutes. *Time* was the main thing he was fighting for. TIME was the essence of all considerations.

About 4.30 P. M. General Wallace decided that he had won

that for which he was fighting. He had won *time*. TIME, which in effect had saved Washington and given him the *victory*. He knew the old Third Division had given General Early's army such a severe drubbing that it could not move until the next day, and that he had given Gneral Grant *time* to get troops to Washington before the Confederate Army could get there. *Washington was saved.*

General Wallace ordered Ricketts to withdraw his division from the field which he did in good order, although under a terrific fire from infantry and an enfilading fire from the 40 guns of King's artillery. He had left 1,600 of his men on the field. A terrible cost. But it had saved the Capital of the Nation and saved the Union from dissolution.

General Wallace had gained just what he fought for, and instead of being defeated, as is generally stated in encyclopedias and most histories, he fought the greatest and fiercest, the decisive battle of that war. No other battle of the Civil War or of the world accomplished as much or was so far-reaching in its consequences for the destinies of this Republic and for the welfare of the world.

If General Wallace had not taken the desperate chances he did and fought that sanguinary battle "of forlorn hope," as General Grant termed it, General Early would have captured Washington, the Capital, in spite of anything that could have been. Then the Capital of the United States of America would have been in the possession of the Confederate States of America.

Early then would have released the 20,000 Rebel prisoners at Point Lookout.

Then he would have had an army of 50,000 veteran Rebel troops in the Union Capital.

Early would have looted the Treasury and destroyed the public buildings.

General Grant would have been compelled to raise the seige of Richmond and Petersburg.

France and England, having the excuse they had been so long and so impatiently waiting for, would have acknowledged the independence of the Confederate States of America.

The United States of America would have been split in two. The only real republic in the world would have been severed and utterly destroyed.

PENNSYLVANIA MONUMENT

This shaft was erected by the State of Pennsylvania and was unveiled
November 24, 1908. It is a tribute to the valor of the Eighty-seventh
and One Hundred and Thirty-eighth Pennsylvania regiments, and to
the other Pennsylvania Federals who participated in the battle. It is
located on a plot of ground along the old Washington Road, nearly
opposite the intersection of the Baker's Valley or Buckeystown Road.

DEDICATION OF THE PENNSYLVANIA MONUMENT[2]

At the dedication of the Pennsylvania monument on the battlefield on November 24, 1908, Capt. William H. Lanius, of York, presided, there being 250 survivors of the 67th, 87th and 138 Regiments of Pennsylvania Volunteers present, and in all about five hundred persons on and about the broad platform erected for the dedicatory exercises. Rev. Osborne Ingle of the Episcopal Church in Frederick offered the opening prayer. After which Mayor George Edward Smith of Frederick sang the "Star-Spangled Banner," the veterans joining in the chorus.

Captain Lanius then made a brief address, as follows:

"Comrades, Ladies and Gentlemen—We are here today to dedicate a monument to the memory of the Pennsylvania soldiers who took part in a battle, prolonged and stubborn, with far-reaching results generally accredited in history as having resulted in saving Washington from falling into the possession of the Confederates under Gen. Jubal Early.

"Because of the larger operations of armies under Grant and Lee, before Petersburg at the time, this battle never reached the prominence necessary to fill the public eye and stamp its importance upon the history of the day, but passed as only one of the many skirmishes constantly reported. Fighting against odds finally of five to one in a single line of battle with the knowledge that no reinforcements were available, this fight took on somewhat the form of a forlorn hope, and is so described by General Grant in a communication to General Wallace.

"General Grant, in his *Personal Memoirs*, makes this interesting reference to Monocacy: 'The force under General Wallace was small in numbers to move against Early. The situation in Washington was precarious. He, Wallace, moved with commendable promptitude, and met the enemy at Monocacy. He could hardly have expected to gain a victory, but hoped to cripple and delay the enemy until Washington could be put in a state of preparation to meet Early. With Ricketts' Division at Monocacy on time Wallace succeeded in stopping Early for the day on which the battle took place.

" 'The next morning Early started on his march to the Capital of the Nation, arriving before it on the 11th. Learning of the gravity of the situation I had ordered Meade to send the other two divisions of the Sixth Corps to Washington for the relief of the city. The latter reached there the very day that

Early arrived before it. The 19th Corps, under General Emory, arrived in Washington from Fortress Monroe about the same time.

" 'Early made his reconnaissance with a view of attacking the city on the 12th, but the next morning he found our intrenchments fully manned. He commenced to retreat, with the Sixth Corps following. There is no telling how much this result was contributed to by General Lew Wallace's leading at Monocacy what might well have been considered almost a forlorn hope. If Early had been but one day sooner, he might have entered the Capital before the arrival of the forces I had sent there.

" 'Whether the delay caused by the battle amounted to a day or not, General Wallace contributed on this occasion a greater benefit to the cause than often falls to the lot of a commander of an equal force to render by means of a victory[2].'

"It now becomes my pleasure to turn this monument over to the Governor of the Commonwealth of Pennsylvania."

In response to the address of Captain Lanius, Lieutenant-Governor Murphy then spoke, first expressing the regret of Governor Stuart at being unable to attend in person. The Lieutenant-Governor is a polished orator and his praise of the veterans who had participated in the struggle which the occasion commemorated drew prolonged cheers. So did his mention of the names of General Lew Wallace and General Ricketts.

Captain Lanius read a letter of regret from Brig.-Gen. Adam E. King, of Baltimore, who had been a member of Ricketts' staff. Ill health made it impossible for him to attend.

Captain T. Cornwell, an aide on the staff of General Ricketts, whose home is at Chester, was next called. He delivered the oration of the day, pointing here and there over the field as he drew word pictures of the battle.

Major E. Y. Goldsborough, of Frederick, a past commander of the Grand Army of the Republic, followed. At the conclusion of the exercises the band, which had been playing patriotic selections during the afternoon, sounded taps. The exercises had occupied about two hours, beginning shortly before 12 o'clock and concluding a little before 2 P. M.

If Washington Had Fallen

As has already been stated in the aforegoing pages, a most competent judge of the significance of the sanguinary conflict at the Monocacy was Lucius E. Chittenden, Register of the United States Treasury under President Lincoln, who has written a chapter in his book, hereinbefore referred to on the subject of this battle. There are two editions of the book, one dated in 1890 and the other in 1901 (as I recall now) many years after the war. Mr. Chittenden seems to have read widely on the subject and discusses the different versions of the battle pro and con at length. Besides he was in Washington at the time of the battle and knew conditions existing there at the time. As a witness to events transpiring in Washington during the exciting times of Early's invasion and attack upon Washington, and as an extensive and intelligent reader of reports and accounts of the invasion, Mr. Chittenden's views and conclusions concerning the battle are entitled to weight and consideration.

A summary of his conclusions will be found at the close of this chapter, expressed in a few words.

Entirely aside from the possibility of English or French intervention the fall of the National Capital would have been a serious set back to the Union cause. What would have happened thereafter no one can with confidence say. But whether given over to pillage and burning or stripped of its treasure and supplies, or strongly held with the reinforcements from Point Lookout, certainly the President and his Cabinet and the officials of Government would have been captured unless they saved themselves by ignominious flight. The consequences of its capture could hardly be considered as little less than disastrous to the Union cause. Already,

after the appalling Federal losses at Cold Harbor the
Peace Party at the North was clamoring for a peace on
what terms could be obtained, and this party, too, was
growing stronger and the Government itself was beginning to be influenced by the cry of "Stop this slaughter."
Had Washington fallen the demands for peace might have
prevailed. Who knows?

The battle that saved the National Capital from
capture and mayhap saved the Union itself, was fought
at Monocacy by the courageous stand of Gen. Lew Wallace
at that river in the effort to impede the daring and alarming progress of Gen. Jubal A. Early in his march upon
the Federal city.

In this view the Legislature of Maryland at its
January session in 1931 passed the following Joint Resolution and Memorial:

SENATE JOINT RESOLUTION No. 10

WHEREAS, the sanguinary battle fought at Monocacy on
July 9, 1864, between the Federal forces under Gen. Lew Wallace
and the Confederate forces under Gen. Jubal A. Early, caused a
delay of at least twenty-four hours in Early's march upon Washington, and thereby enabled General Grant to send several divisions of seasoned Federal veterans to the defense of the city
just in time to man the fortifications, then poorly and inadequately manned, before the arrival of the Confederate hosts bent
upon the capture of the city, and

WHEREAS, this delay of twenty-four hours, caused by the
battle fought at Monocacy to impede the progress of the invading
army toward the National Capital, saved the Capital from capture and all the direful consequences thereof, and has for that
reason been denominated "one of the decisive battles of the
world," and

WHEREAS, the valor displayed by the officers and men on both
sides in that important conflict, reflects honor and glory upon
the citizen soldier of America, both North and South, and

WHEREAS, the battlefield is located on the National Highway
from Washington to the West, over which many thousands of
American citizens travel to and fro every year, and moreover,
is a picturesque spot with the winding Monocacy flowing through
and adding to its beauty; therefore be it

Resolved by the General Assembly of Maryland, That the
Congress of the United States be and it is hereby memoralized

and earnestly requested to create on the Monocacy battlefield a National Military Park to commemorate the battle fought there on July 9, 1864, by which the Federal Capital was saved and possibly the Union itself; such park would, if established, become a resting place and shrine where thousands of travelers and tourists could rest and renew their patriotism by a contemplation of "the lofty deeds which there have been wrought; of the great hearts which spent themselves there.

The denomination of the battle of Monocacy as "one of the decisive battles of the world" is taken from a book by Lucius E. Chittenden, Register of the United States Treasury, under President Lincoln. In concluding his summary of the battle Mr. Chittenden says: "When the children of the Republic are asked what it was that brought Early's campaign to naught and saved the Capital, let them be taught to answer: "General Wallace and his command at the battle of Monocacy, and the arrival of the Sixth Corps within the defenses of the Capital'."

[1]The records do not bear out Colonel Spofford's statement that there were 30,000 men in Early's army of invasion, but it is printed as he wrote it.

[2]This account of the dedicatory services at the unveiling of the Pennsylvania monument are largely excerpts from a York, Pa., newspaper of date November 25, 1908.

CHAPTER XXVIII.

A FEDERAL PRISONER'S NARRATIVE

Among the prisoners taken at Monocacy by the Confederates was Alfred Seelye Roe of the Ninth New York Heavy Artillery.

He writes an interesting account of his experiences as a prisoner, from which the following excerpts are taken:

"Captured in battle on Saturday, the ninth day of July, 1864, at Monocacy, or Frederick Junction, Maryland, the sun was well up his eastern way when we, under Confederate guard and guidance, turned our backs on the burning stubble of the battlefield, dotted here and there with the naked bodies of our comrades slain, and took a road of which we knew only that it led southward. I have since learned that it was called the Georgetown Pike. It was crooked and dusty; but not so much so as those we had found in Virginia. . . .

"The ascent from the valley is gradual and as we wend our way we repeatedly turn to look at the scene that is to be indelibly painted on memory's canvas. The river; the railroad with its iron bridge; the turnpike bridge, now smoking in ruins; the big stone mill, near whose base I heard the last order, 'Elevate your pieces, men,' Colonel Thomas's house, around which the tide of battle had surged the day before, and lastly, the wheatfield, whence on that ninth day of July, we had seen two harvests gathered; the one in the early morn of wheat, the staff of life, and the other at eve of men, and the reaper thereof was death. Every feature of this scene prints itself on our memories, till finally the friendly hill shuts off the view and we can now give ourselves entirely to our immedate surroundings. . . .

"Marching in any way under a July sun in the Southern States is not particularly pleasant. . . . . It soon became obvious, however, that we had more friends among the people whom we met than our guards had. It was a very common thing to find tubs of water newly drawn placed by the roadside to satisfy the tormenting thirst engendered by the excessive heat. . . . .

"There were between six hundred and seven hundred of us, many from the Third Division of the Sixth Corps, and others from the one hundred days men whom Ohio sent into the fray. It was their first and only experience, and many of them were in for longer stays in Rebel prisons than their whole term of enlistment called for. . . . . Our first halt was at a pleasant little village called Urbana, where a kind citizen, perhaps Columbus Windsor by name, of strong Union sympathies, sets out several barrels of sweet crackers for our comfort and bids us help ourselves. Many intervening years have not wholly effaced the regret that was mine over my inability to get what I deemed my share of those toothsome morsels, nor my admiration for the man who thus remembered those in bonds as bound with him. . . . . We had gone only about four miles from our starting place, and the time must have been near noon, but the command, "Forward," to a soldier, bond or free, is seldom more welcome than the parental summons to arise in the morning is to the farmer's sleepy and tired boy. The country through which we were marching seemed a veritable paradise. . . . .

"Our forward movement is unfraught with special interest until we pass through the hamlet of Clarksburg. Near the outskirts of the village an aged man is sitting at an open window, the house being very near the street. An elderly lady, apparently his wife, is leaning past him with hands extended upon the window sill. So dust-begrimed are we that I do not wonder at her long mistaking us for a part of the Rebel throng which all day had been passing her door. Suddenly light dawns upon her, and raising her hands with an astonished tone, she exclaims: 'Why, they are our men!' At once I eagerly

ask, 'Who are our men?' 'Why, Union men, of course.'
Utterly heedless of the laws supposed to govern prisoners,
we forgot our situation and cheered. But the nearest
guard, not liking such demonstrations thrust his bayonet
through the window and thus drove from sight the good
old dame who seemed to us for the nonce another Barbara
Fritchie. . . . .

"Our first camp was south of Clarksburg, and as
our haversacks, filled on the field of Monocacy, were yet
distended, there was nothing unusual in our preparation
of coffee and consumption of hardtack, nor in the refreshing sleep that soon fell upon us.

"All the way down our guards had jokingly told us
of the gay time expected by them on their entering Washington, remarks that we took more in the spirit of banter
than otherwise, hardly thinking it possible that Early
would have the temerity to beard the lion in his den.
When, however, on the next day, Monday the 11th, we
turned to the left on passing through Rockville, we knew
that at least a feint was to be made. This was a little
before noon, about the time the Confederates reached
the head of Seventh Street, and found that the delay at
Monocacy had been fatal to success here, for old soldiers
from the Sixth Corps had reached the Capital in time to
save it. . . . .

"Between Rockville and Washington we were drawn
up in line and thoroughly searched. . . . . It was here,
thus drawn up, that I first saw ex-Vice-President Breckinridge. I remember him as one of the finest looking men
I ever saw. His face was so classically cut, and his eye
so piercing at any distance, that now with an interval
of nearly twenty-four years, I can see him as he sat on
his horse and directed his men.

"In addition to seeing General Early often, we saw
Gordon, Rodes and McCausland, who were the most
conspicious leaders in this expedition. . . . .

"The day itself was one of the hottest of a very hot
summer, and many, both Federal and Confederate, were
overcome by the heat. While travelling this road southeast from Rockville, we saw mortar shells sent up from
the defenses, and the curves described by them were most
beautiful. Exploding high in the air at times, they gave

a superb display of pyrotechnics, though I must confess that our admiration was somewhat tempered with apprehension lest 'some droppings might fall on us.' To be killed or wounded was not longed for at any time, but certainly we didn't fancy blows from the hands of our friends.

"The afternoon was half spent when we filed to our left into an apple orchard and were ordered to camp. We had passed Silver Springs, the home of Montgomery Blair, and from the nearness of the firing I concluded that we were pretty close to the head of Seventh Street. I recall very vividly that several times during that afternoon, the early evening and the day following, shells from our own batteries went shrieking through the tops of the trees under which we were lying. It required, however, no great acumen to understand that the Confederates were not finding matters to their satisfaction. The noise of the encounter on the 12th was great, and the Rebel yell, varied with Union shouts, seemed as vivid as ever. Our Confederate foes must have thought the Sixth Corps well nigh ubiquitous, for they had left behind them the blue cross at Monocacy, and here they were confronted by the same emblem, though the color was white. The red was there, too, ready for the fight, if necessary. Little did we think then that President Lincoln was himself witnessing the discomfiture of the enemy and the victory of our friends and comrades. . . . .

"The night of the 12th had shut down upon us and was well advanced when we were ordered out, and this time our faces were set away from the Capital. By the light of Montgomery Blair's burning mansion, we marched away for the Confederacy. We then said that the house was destroyed in retaliation for the destruction of Governor Letcher's home in Lexington, burned by Hunter; but General Early has since disclaimed any complicity in the matter. . . . . He had not, from the moment of finding Sixth Army Corps men there, entertained the possibility of getting into Washington. Opposed as we were to the cause of the Rebellion, yet I think we can afford a little praise for this affair, though an unrelenting foe, in his leading his men by forced marches over many hundreds of miles, through a not over friendly country, in some cases, down to the very Capital of the Nation. Nothing but final success was wanting to make him the Alaric of the Century."

"The morning light was breaking when on the 13th we passed, for the second time, through Rockville. It may have been five o'clock, for I know the citizens were beginning to make their appearance, and one good old lady quite touched my heart when, through her glasses, she beamed kindly on me and in the sweetest of voices said, 'Good morning.' How those two trite commonplace words, so often misapplied, lightened the burdens of that long, toilsome day! It was a good morning to me only in the thought that I had seen one kind, sympathetic woman who, as she spoke to me, may have been thinking of a boy of her own, possibly at that moment in distress somewhere in this troubled land. All through the hours of that weary day, at high noon and at sultry eve, still rang in my ears those pleasant tones, so that even when our march was prolonged all through the night, it was still to me, 'Good morning'."

. . . "During the 13th we found our guards not quite so disposed to discuss the capture of Washington as they had been on Sunday and Monday. In fact, they were exceedingly waspish, and on very slight provocation shouted, 'Dry up, Yank!'

". . . Passing through Poolesville, in the gray of dawn, we came to White's Ford on the Potomac, only a short distance above the scene of the terrible disaster of Ball's Bluff. The river here is wide and shallow, affording an easy passage so far as the depth of water is concerned. But appearances are often deceptive, for the bottom of the stream is exceedingly slippery. I profited by the misfortunes of those in front of me. Many, trusting to themselves alone, would undertake the passage, but slipping upon a smooth stone covered with weeds, down would go their heads and up would turn their heels, thus giving the soldiers involuntary baptisms. Seeing many instances of this, I joined arms with a like-minded friend and thus bracing each other we made the transit, dry as to the upper portion of our bodies. This was on the morn of the 14th, and soon after we went into bivouac at a point called Big Spring, so named from the immense pool of water, the first of the large number of ever-flowing springs that we were to encounter on our march. It was nicely walled about and large enough for a hundred cattle to drink from it at the same time. Here we rested, and for the first time, essayed to cook our own food, as our escort had been obliged to do all along. When I contrast the living facilities of the Union and Confederate armies, I am amazed that the latter held out as long as they did. The Northern soldier, when he went into camp, tired from his day's march, made his coffee, ate his hard-tack, perhaps gave it a little relish from the piece of salt pork that he had in his haversack, and in twenty minutes was getting welcome rest from 'tired nature's sweet restorer."

"But not so with his Southern foe. When bivouac came he had no coffee to boil, unless there had recently been a flag of truce, and there was no bread, hard or soft, for him. In the wagons were numerous long-handled, three-legged skillets, having heavy iron tops. These must be obtained, and the flour dealt out to the men had to be cooked, each mess by itself. As there were not dishes enough for all to cook at once, some had to wait their turn. In fact I learned that during a halt someone was cooking constantly. As they did not carry yeast nor anything like it, and as they had but little salt, it must be seen that their bread would not have offended the most advanced hydropath, nor have troubled a Jew, even during the 'Feast of the Passover.' Our Monocacy rations had given out and we were supplied with raw flour, the result, I suppose, of some part of the Maryland foray. Bread-making, thus, was a new experience to us, and we didn't like it. As for myself I must state that I gave up the skillet entirely, and mixing the flour with as little water as possible, adding what salt I could spare, I strung the dough out something like maccaroni, and having wound this around a stick proceeded to warm it through, rather a hot task on a July day. I may say that I seldom burned my food thus. I couldn't wait long enough. In summing up the advantages held by our side, let us not forget to lay great stress on the superiority of our commissariat, and among the items there found put among the very first, coffee, an article more worthy the praises of Burns than the barleycorn that he has immortalized.

In A Confederate Prison

" 'When I was in prison!' How many people I have seen shrink away from me on my uttering this expression; but the appendix 'Rebel prison' invariably draws from them the words, 'What! were you in a Rebel prison? In what prison, and how long? How did they use you?'

"From intense aversion, the expression has changed to one of the utmost interest, and there are indications of awakening sympathy when I reply, 'Yes, in Danville, Virginia. Between seven and eight months, and as well as they could; but their best was bad enough.' The men, captured at Monocacy, Maryland, by foot and rail, have finally reached the most considerable place in Southern Virginia, and on the morn of July 29, 1864, the heavy prison door opens and shuts upon our party. I have always rated the total number entering the building at about six hundred. Of these prisoners, 106 were members of my regiment. . . . .

"Just 27 out of our 106 succumbed to prison hardships, and in dying found their release. . . . . It is a very moderate estimate to claim that fully one-half our number fell victims in less than a year to the results of our imprisonment. Then, too, any prisoner who had passed beyond the period of boyhood never fully recovered from his months of hunger, cold and anxiety. When, at the end of the following April, I rejoined my regiment and a comrade undertook to tell me how much I escaped through my capture, I quite silenced him by asking if any company had lost more than half its men during my absence; if the Valley campaign, hard though it was, had resulted in the death of one-quarter of the members of the regiment. . . . .

"As to our location, we were in a brick building, erected some years before for tobacco manufacturing purposes, but which had been pressed into the service of the Confederate government for prison use; and I have since been informed by the owner he never got a red cent for it. In the list of prison houses in Danville, it is No. 1. Just back of us, on the bank of a mill race, is the cookhouse, where Yankee workmen mix up and bake strange combinations, called corn bread. My mother still preserves some of this bread as a Rebellion relic after more than a quarter of a century. I think it is as good now as it ever was. . . . .

"It does not take us a great while to recover from the fatigue incident to our long journey. Then begins a protracted hunger, to last until we see our own lines again. During the months of August and September we are given corn bread and occasionally a soup made of refuse bits of bacon, sometimes of fresh meat—including lights or lungs. The bacon is rancid, and the vegetables in it are not very inviting, consisting of stray cabbage leaves and a leguminous article known to us as 'cowpea.' The well-worn statement that every pea has a worm in it had no exception here. In fact we thought it had a double verification, but poor as this soup was there came a time when we would have joyously hailed its advent. The bread, mentioned before, was composed of corn and cob ground together, and was baked in large tins—the whole upper surface being marked off into rectangles, so that when carried to the floor for distribution, by a knife in the hands of the designated party, it is cut into parallelopipeds of about two-thirds the size of an ordinary brick. To each man one of these is given and on it he may sustain nature till the next morning. If he tries to save any of it for a meal, later in the day, unless he puts it in his pocket, the chances are that it will be stolen, so really the safest plan for him is to eat it an once and then solace himself on recollection and expectation till the next meal. . . . .

"The day is very hot and clothing is voted a nuisance. Item after item is cast aside till nothing is retained save what decency requires and decency, it will be remembered, is a relative term. . . . .

"Ah! what have we here! A party of men are hilarious about something. In the centre of the group are four men playing poker. They have the only pack of cards in the prison. Soiled hands have used them till they are in truth of mother earth, and from the usual rectangular form they have been worn to a uniform oval. The pack belongs to boys on the lower floor, and these men are using them through having given to the possessors some part of their rations of bread. Every looker-on is getting enjoyment from the game, watching most intently its progress. It is safe to say that the jackpot is not very full. . . . .

"Sometimes on the still air are borne sounds that leave a fadeless impression. From the first floor came, once, strains of harmony so sweet that I thought myself in heaven and that angel voices were making true the fancies of my childhood. Only the wounded men, sweet singers they were, beguiling the long tedium of night with song, and it was that delightful ditty, 'Kitty Wells,' that for the first time in my life fell on my ears. For several days delirium had possessed the brain of a young boy from Ohio who was just beneath us. During the day the hum of conversation drowned his voice; but when sleep had pressed down nearly all the eyelids, then it was that his plaintive tones came to us, and how he pleaded for mother! Ineffectual tears filled our eyes at the sound of his cries; but with him we wandered amid the scenes of his earlier years, and we saw that mother leading him by the hand, and we saw her bidding her darling 'Goodbye' as he became a soldier, and we reflected how little that Ohio mother knew of the sufferings of her dying boy. His spirit, ere long, forsook the frail tenement and was at rest. . . . .

"December 20th, in spite of a drizzling rain, I remained in the yard till I was quite wet. This was at nightfall. By 8 o'clock I was down with an attack of diphtheria. All through the night I had great difficulty in breathing. The next day I grew worse, but there was nothing to be done for me. The 22nd, in the morning with several others, I was trundled off to the hospital in a condition which, I have always thought, arising at home, would have finished me. There was no rehabilitating sympathy around me, and I had no relish for a grave in Virginia, sacred though its soil be. I was in no condition to appreciate the view of the streets, though I remember passing No. 6, and we are finally landed at the hospital. Here I am assigned to a cot and the German steward proudly refers to me as the first case of diphtheria, and so far as I know I am the only case during our imprisonment. In a few days my disease yields to lunar caustic and flax-seed poultices, and I then have a chance to look about me. The doctor makes his rounds and asks me, 'Well, how are ye comin' today?' He is a kind man and I respect him. Dr. Dame, the Episcopal rector, New Hampshire born, and a second cousin of

Caleb Cushing, calls almost daily on us, and on his asking me what he can do for me, I suggest a book. The next coming brings 'Paradise Lost'—there being a degree of fitness in his selection that I don't believe occurred to him. In December last (1888, the 24th) I called on the aged clergyman and said to him, grasping his hand, 'You don't know me; but I was sick and in prison and ye visited me.' With what cordiality came the response, 'Is that so? I am glad to see you. Come, let us sit and talk.' For nearly an hour we discourse of these remote times, and he tells me that wherever it was possible he sent a letter to the friends of the dead prisoners. Whatever of improvement there was in our treatment above that given to men further South, I think was largely owing to him. To my mind, he filled, in the broadest sense, the definition of the Christian. Though Northern born, his early going to the South, his education at Hampden-Sidney, his marriage and long residence in Virginia, all combined to make his prejudices in favor of secession; but he was more than a Rebel or Federal, he was a Christian man. Going into one of the prisons one Sunday to preach he found a second cousin, by the name of Cushing, from the old Bay State, and he led the singing. So thoroughly did the war mix up families. His talks to the men were always most respectfully received, and when in the following April, the Sixth Corps entered Danville, no one received more considerate attention than the Reverend George W. Dame.

"As I convalesced I explored. I found that our hospital was built for Confederate occupancy; but necessity had filled it with Yankees. So far as I could observe, we received as good as our captors had to give. A good lady living near, whose name I have never learned, daily sent to us some sort of delicacy, and that was honestly given to us. The two Confederate officers who were about our ward held converse as to the approaching Christmas, and great expectations were had over a visit to the home of one of them. The principal present to be taken was a pair of shoes made by one of our men to be given to a sister. The poverty of the country was apparent in the most commonplace conversation. On their return from their festival they dilated on the pleasure afforded by that one pair of Yankee-made shoes. The next May I met one of these lieutenants at Boston Station, on the Richmond and Danville Railroad, the same being near his home, and I recall his wonder at my rehearsal of his pre and post Christmas talks. . . . .

"Once, at least, a seeming corpse was carried out before it was really thus, and revived by the clear air, Jimmy O——ds arose and, naked, marched into the ward proclaiming himself 'not dead by a d——d sight.' Weeks afterward I saw Jimmy peacefully smoking his dudeen in Annapolis."

* * * * *

Another prisoner writes in a somewhat lighter vein. He says:

"When captured I had $1.40 in my pocket. They told me to hand over the dollar and to keep the 40 cents as I would need it before I got back, which I found was gospel truth. That Rebel was honest, anyway. . . . . Our dinner the first day was one loaf of bread cut into four pieces for four men. I can say that none of us had to let out our trouser straps.

"We marched 30 miles the first day and were pretty well tired out by night when they issued to each of us one pint of flour. This we mixed with water and slapped on a flat stone, which we propped up opposite the fire and baked it. This tasted good to us but I fear it would not have passed muster at the Waldorf-Astoria. Armstrong said he could not eat his without butter, but we told him his complexion would be better if he abstained from butter. Finally he concluded that we were right and let it go at that.

"A lieutenant came along and asked how we were making out. We told him we were perfectly delighted with the menu. He said, 'I am glad you have nothing to complain of. . . . .

"The next day we had no breakfast though our appetites were in fine shape. At noon we had a bountiful feast. They cut a loaf in two for two men. It tasted good while it lasted but the time seemed so short. . . . .

"That afternoon Ghormley said he was going to make

a break into the bushes and get away. He jumped off his mule and had not gone more than ten feet when a guard spied him and fired six shots into the bushes. Ghormley came back in a hurry. He told the guard that he only wanted to get a few blackberries."

CHAPTER XXIX.

COMPOSITION OF THE FEDERAL AND
CONFEDERATE FORCES AT
MONOCACY

EIGHTH ARMY CORPS (FEDERAL)
MAJ.-GEN. LEW WALLACE, COMMANDING

Brig.-Gen. Erastus B. Tyler
Commanding First Separate Brigade.

First Regiment, Maryland-Potomac Home Brigade. Five
companies. Capt. Charles J. Brown, commanding.

Third Regiment, Maryland-Potomac Home Brigade.
Colonel Charles Gilpin, commanding.

Eleventh Maryland. Col. William Landstreet, commanding.

One Hundred Forty-fourth Ohio, three companies; One
Hundred Forty-ninth Ohio, seven companies.
Col. Allison L. Brown, Commanding

Baltimore Battery, Capt. Frederic W. Alexander. Six
pieces, three-inch rifles.

One howitzer at the railroad bridge in charge of Capt.
William H. Wiegel.

SIX ARMY CORPS (FEDERAL) (THIRD DIVISION)
BRIG.-GEN. JAMES B. RICKETTS, COMMANDING

First Brigade
Col. William S. Truex

Fourteenth New Jersey—Lieut.-Col. Caldwell K. Hall.
One Hundred Sixth New York—Capt. Edward M. Paine.
One Hundred Fifty-first New York—Col. Wm. Emerson.
Eighty-seventh Penna.—Lieut.-Col. James H. Stahle.
Tenth Vermont—Col. William W. Henry.

Second Brigade
Col. Matthew R. McClennan

Ninth New York Heavy Artillery — Col. William H. Seward, Jr.
One Hundred Tenth Ohio—Lieut.-Col. Otho H. Binkley.
One Hundred Twenty-second Ohio (detachment)—Lieut. Charles J. Gibson.
One Hundred Twenty-sixth Ohio—Lieut.-Col. Aaron W. Ebright.
One Hundred Thirty-eighth Penna.—Major Lewis A. May.

Cavalry
Lieut.-Col. David R. Clendenin

Eighth Illinois—Lieutenant-Colonel Clendenin.
One Hundred Fifty-ninth Ohio (detachment of mounted infantry)—Capt. Edward H. Lieb and Capt. Henry S. Allen.
Detachment of mixed cavalry—Major Charles A. Wells.
Loudoun (Va.) Rangers.

The Federal forces belonging to the Eighth Corps consisted of about two thousand five hundred men.

The Third Division of the Sixth Corps, under command of Gen. James B. Ricketts, consisted of about five thousand men, but the 67th Pennsylvania, part of the 122nd Ohio and the Sixth Maryland did not arrive at the battlefield. These were detained at Monrovia on the Baltimore and Ohio Railroad, about eight miles away, by some misunderstanding, mistake or delay.

Col. John F. Staunton seems to have commanded the 67th Pennsylvania.

Of those actually participating of the Sixth Corps, the First Brigade, commanded by Col. W. S. Truex, consisted of 1,750 men, and the Second Brigade, under command of Col. Matthew R. McClennan, of 1,600 men, or a total of 3,350 actually present and taking part. These figures are taken from General Wallace's official report as printed in *War Records,* Serial No. 70, at pages 195 and 196.

There was also the Eighth Illinois Cavalry, 230 men; a detachment of the 159th Ohio Mounted Infantry; a detachment of mixed cavalry under Major Charles A. Wells, and the Loudoun Rangers. Just how many cavalry in all is not recorded.

CONFEDERATE FORCES ENGAGED IN THE BATTLE
OF MONOCACY

In *Battles and Leaders of the Civil War,* Vol. 4, at page 492, General Early has set forth the numbers of the regiments and the names of the States to which they belonged, comprising the brigades and divisions of the Second Confederate Army Corps with which he invaded Maryland and threatened Washington City. But this recital when compared with other sources of information appears to be inaccurate and incomplete. While in the main, perhaps correct, yet there are omissions and inaccuracies if the reports of other military officers are to be considered. Taking all the information obtainable together the composition of the Confederate forces seems to have been as follows:

SECOND ARMY CORPS, C. S. A.
LIEUT.-GEN. JUBAL A. EARLY, COMMANDING

(Note: While General Early was in command of the corps, he appears to have assigned to General John C. Breckinridge the command of two divisions, to-wit: (1) That commanded by Gen. John B. Gordon, and (2) That commanded by Gen. John Echols. The first mentioned consisted by Evans', York's, and Terry's brigades, and the second of Wharton's, Smith's and Patton's brigades. General Breckinridge was thus a corps commander but subordinate to General Early.)

GORDON'S DIVISION—*Three Brigades*
Commanded by Maj.-Gen. John B. Gordon.

Evans' Brigade
Commanded by Brig.-Gen. Clement A. Evans.

13th Ga., Colonel Baker; 26th Ga., Col. E. N. Atkinson; 38th Ga. ———; 60th Ga., ———; 61st Ga., Col. J. H. Lamar; 12th Ga. Battalion, Major Harvey; 31st Ga., Col. J. H. Lowe. Six regiments and one battalion.

York's Brigade
Commanded by Brig.-Gen. Zebulon York.

(Note: This brigade consisted of the remnants of Hays' and Stafford's brigades which had been almost wiped out by previous fighting.)

Hays' Command

5th, 6th, 7th, 8th and 9th Louisiana. Five fragmentary regiments.

Stafford's Command

1st, 2nd, 10th and 14th Louisiana. Four fragments of regiments.

Terry's Brigade
Comanded by Brig.-Gen. William T. Terry.

2nd, 4th, 5th, 27th and 33rd Virginia. (Remnants of the old Stonewall Brigade, commanded by Col. J. H. S. Funk.) 21st, 25th, 42nd, 44th, 48th, 50th Virginia. (Remnants of J. M. Jones' Brigade, commanded by Col. R. H. Dungan). 10th, 23rd, 37th Virginia. (Remnants of Stuart's former command, and being the remains of the 14th Regiment of Edward Johnson, most of which was captured by the enemy May 12, 1864.) Lieut.-Col. S. H. Saunders, commanding. In all fourteen fragmentary regiments.

ECHOLS' DIVISION
Commanded by Brig.-Gen. John Echols.

Wharton's Brigade
Commanded by Brig.-Gen. John A. Wharton.

45th, 51st and 30th Virginia. The latter a mere battalion. (Two regiments, one battalion).

Smith's Brigade
Commanded by Brig.-Gen. Thomas Smith.

36th and 60th Virginia. (Two regiments.)

Patton's Brigade
Commanded by Brigadier-General Patton.

The composition of Patton's Brigade at the time of the battle could not be ascertained.

(George E. Pond, associate editor of the *Army and Navy Journal,* in his volume, entitled, "The Shenandoah Valley in 1864," says: "The division described as Echols' was Breckinridge's old command temporarily given to Elzey at Lynchburg, and afterwards at Staunton, temporarily transferred to Vaughan; but Echols received it in Maryland." Further on he says, "Breckinridge was assigned to something like a corps command having under him two divisions, Gordon's and Echols'. While the other infantry divisions and the cavalry reported directly to Early.")

(In his *Autobiographical Sketch,* Early says, in speaking of the battle fought at Monocacy, "Echols was ordered up but was not needed." This evidently refers to the sending for reinforcements by General Gordon as mentioned in his report of the battle.)

RODES' DIVISION

Maj.-Gen. Robert E. Rodes, Commanding.

Grimes' Brigade

32nd, 43rd, 45th, 53rd North Carolina and 2nd North Carolina Battalion. Four regiments and one battalion.

Cook's Brigade

4th, 12th, 21th and 44th Georgia. Remnants of four regiments.

Cox's Brigade

1st, 2nd, 3rd, 4th, 14th and 30th North Carolina. Six regiments.

Battle's Brigade
3rd, 5th, 6th, 12th and 61st Alabama. Five regiments.

Ramseur's Division
Maj.-Gen. S. D. Ramseur, Commanding.

Lilly's Brigade
13th, 31st, 49th, 52nd and 58th Virginia.   Five regiments.

Johnson's Brigade
5th, 12th, 20th and 23rd North Carolina.   Four regiments.

Lewis' Brigade
6th, 21st and 54th North Carolina, 1st North Carolina Battalion.   Four broken regiments and one battalion.

Cavalry
Maj.-Gen. Robert Ransom, Commanding.

Gen. John McCausland's Regiment.
Gen. John D. Imboden's Regiment.
Gen. W. L. Jackson's Regiment.
Col. Bradley T. Johnson's Regiment.

Johnson was sent before the battle of Monocacy to cut the Northern Central and Pennsylvania railroads.

Imboden had been sent to cut the B. & O. Railroad and destroy it above Martinsburg.

The only Confederate cavalry participating in the battle at Monocacy was the command of Gen. John McCausland.

Artillery.
Lieut.-Col. Lloyd King, Commanding.

Composed of Nelson's, Braxton's and McLaughlin's Batteries, also Massie's, Jackson's, Carpenter's and Kirkpatrick's.

In his official report to General Lee, of the battle of Monocacy, General Early says:

"My infantry force did not exceed ten thousand, as Breckinridge's infantry (normally much larger) really did not exceed two thousand five hundred muskets."

There has been considerable criticism of this part of Early's report; the opinion being expressed by many officials in the Union army, that Early's force at Monocacy was much larger than he reported it to be.

Even after Early had retired from before Washington, it was reported by observers that he had with him from twenty thousand to thirty thousand men, besides cavalry and artillery.

On July 13th, Major-General Halleck, Chief-of-Staff, telegraphed to General Grant at City Point, Virginia, that "From the most reliable estimates we can get of the enemy's forces, it numbers from 23,000 to 25,000, exclusive of cavalry."

In their *Abraham Lincoln, A History,* Nicolay and Hay have this to say, page 170:

"Early might well be excused for declining to rush his tired army upon the bristling works; he had less than twenty thousand men—he says 'about eight thousand muskets,' but he always looked at his own force through the wrong end of his fieldglass."

This *Life of Lincoln* was prepared about 1884 or 1885, more than twenty years after the war, and yet it was claimed that Early had a force of something less than twenty thousand men, and the claim of only eight thousand muskets was ridiculed.

Just how many men constituted his whole army is not satisfactorily established. George E. Pond, in the volume prepared by him, called *The Shenandoah Valley in 1864,*" has tables purporting to show the strength of Early's army on August 20, 1864, then operating in the Valley. The table showing the number fit for duty is quite different from the one showing actual numbers on the roster. An estimate of fifteen thousand would perhaps cover all, but satisfactory data is not available to show numbers with accuracy.

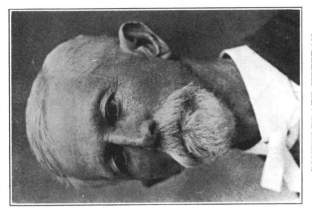

UNION VETERAN

"Colonel" Judson Spofford, Company K, 10th Vermont Volunteers, who took part in the Battle of Monocacy, July 9, 1864. He was one of the picked men sent to defend the bridges on the west side of the Monocacy under Lieut. George E. Davis of the same regiment.

CONFEDERATE VETERAN

"Major", I. G. Bradwell, Company I, 31st Georgia Regiment, Gordon's Division, Old Stonewall Corps, Army of Northern Virginia, who took part in the Battle of Monocacy, July 9, 1864, and who claims to have fired the last shot at the retreating foe.

Two known survivors (1932) of that great struggle of July 9, 1864.

CHAPTER XXX.

CONCLUSION

With the result of the four years of Civil War, or "War between the States," everybody is familiar. The South having submitted the question of the right to secede, to the arbitrament of arms and the question having been decided against it, had no alternative but to yield obedience to that decision and to the supremacy of the Union. Their theory had been that as the thirteen original States were sovereign and independent before the ratification of the Constitution to which they adhered, and as these States had voluntarily entered the compact, and as other States had since, upon their own application, been admitted on an equality with the original thirteen, each having voluntarily entered the compact, each had the right to voluntarily withdraw.

"South Carolina, who led in this fateful business, adjourned her legislature and called a constitutional convention together: a body like that which had declared her assent to the Constitution of 1788. By formal ordinance of that convention, the ordinance of the convention of 1788 was repealed, and the connection of the State with the union was authoritatively severed. That was her act of 'secession' taken in the highest sovereign fashion known to her law and tradition." Wilson's *History of the American People,* Vol IV, page 271.

The other States followed her example.

The Northern States, represented by the Government at Washington, said this thing could not be done. That

once having given assent to the Constitution and having
become an integral part of the National Union, no State
so entering in could voluntarily withdraw or secede.

This was the issue submitted to the decision of the
tribunal of war and it was decided against the right to
secede. No matter how sovereign and independent the
States may have been before entry into the Union, once
in, there can be no withdrawal, but nevertheless each
State shall enjoy an independent sovereignty in the
Union. Thus it has been said that the United States of
America is "an indissoluble Union of indestructible
States."

But for four years, while the issues were being
argued on the battlefields, a most terrible, destructive,
and desolating war raged between brothers and former
friends.

In his *History of the American People,* Vol. IV, at
page 265, Woodrow Wilson says:

"It had cost the country more than seven hundred
men for every day of all four long years of campaign and
battle: four hundred killed or mortally wounded on the
field, the rest died of disease, exposure, accident, or the
slow pains of imprisonment.

"The Federal Government had spent $3,400,000,000
upon the war, nearly $2,500,000 for every day it had
lasted: and less than $800,000,000 had come into its
coffers from taxes. 'More than $2,600,000,000 had been
added to the public debt.'

"The Confederacy had piled up a debt, upon its part,
of nearly $1,400,000,000 and had spent besides, no man
can say how much; for the scant yield of the taxes had
been supplemented by direct requisitions on the farmers
for the food supplies of the armies; States had undertaken so far as they could, to support their own volunteers in the field; private purses had been opened to pay
for the equipment of sons and brothers sent to the front—
every public and every private source had been drained."

He further states that:

"In all 1,700,000 men out of a military population of 4,600,000 in the Northern States had been enlisted for service in the field. Of these, 360,00 lost their lives; 110,000 by actual casualties of the field.

"But the sacrifices of the South had been greater yet—immeasurably greater. . . . . Nine men out of every ten of fighting age had gone from countrysides and towns to the field, reckoning only those who enlisted for at least three of the four years of the struggle. Before the war ended, mere half-grown boys and men grown old were included in the muster.

"The total military population of the South was but 1,605,000. Of these, 900,000 she drew into her armies for at least three years of service.

"The lives of close up to 300,000 she gave as her sacrifice of blood—more than one-fourth of all fit for the field. Of these, 94,000 lost their lives in actual battle."

The result of the war was to make us a great nation. It is our proud boast that the United States is the greatest power on the face of the earth today, and that we are citizens of the Great Republic.

When the nations of Europe were struggling with each other in 1914-1918; when France was bled white and England was fighting with her back to the wall, America came to the rescue just in the nick of time and saved the day for the independence of the nations and the freedom of the seas. Proudly, we assert that there is no intention or dispostion to use our power for conquest but only for the maintenance of peace at home and of peaceful relations abroad.

In his *Memoirs*, General Grant says that after the surrender of Lee at Appomattox, he went to the house of Mr. McLean:

"Here the officers of both armies came in great numbers and seemed to enjoy meeting as much as though they had been friends for a long time while fighting battles under the same flag."

Grant showed great magnamity at the surrender. The most honorable terms were granted. Both men and officers were to be released on parole. They were to keep their horses, "because they would need them for the spring plowing and farm work."

Some advised Lee to scatter his men and gather them again from time to time for guerrilla warfare. He spurned the suggestion. He said, "For us, as a Christian people, there is but one course to pursue. We must accept the situation; these men must go home and plant a crop; and we must proceed to build up our country on a new basis." The whole country is proud to proclaim these two men as great Americans, and both entitled to the place they have in the Hall of Fame.

Then there are Wallace and Early, both distinguished American soldiers. Wallace gained more fame with the pen than with the sword, but he achieved the purpose for which he fought at Monocacy, for was he not FIGHTING FOR TIME?

Early was both blamed and praised for his part in the war. After the struggle ended, Northern newspapers criticised him for not going into Washington when he was so near. He was also criticised by some Southern writers. He wrote *A Memoir of the Last Year of the War*, and also a biography to justify his course.

What was said by Gen. Bradley T. Johnson in his report does justice to his commander. In speaking of the object of the expedition under Early for the release of the prisoners at Point Lookout and the capture of Washington, General Johnson says:

"I have always considered the movement one, the audacity of which was its safety, and that no higher military skill was displayed on either side than that shown by General Early in this daring attempt to surprise the Capital of his enemy with so small a force."

Gen. John B. Gordon and Gen. James B. Ricketts were both able commanding officers. The former, after the war, served his native State in the United States Senate, and General Ricketts was breveted major-general for meritorous services through the war, and was retired in 1867 because of wounds received in battle.

Most of these brave men who fought so gallantly for one side or the other during that four years struggle are dead, but let us hope that they are now fraternizing on that farther shore, and that they look down together upon our re-united country to revere and bless it.

The battle of Monocacy was not one of the major battles of the war. So far as numbers engaged are concerned, it was a minor affair, but considered from the viewpoint of results, not one of the big battles surpassed it in importance. The loss of a nation's capital and seat of government to the enemy can never be lightly regarded.

When Richmond fell, the collapse of the Confederacy was not long delayed.

The affair of the Trent, when an American man-of-war seized the English vessel on the high seas and took therefrom Mason and Slidell, the Confederate Commissioners to England and France, had roused great indignation in England as it was a gross breach of international law. England made instant protest, accompanied by preparations for war, and the act was disavowed by the United States Government, but England's

wrath was not fully appeased; and moreover her statesmen looked with disfavor upon the blockading of the
Southern ports, for from the Southern ports she obtained
much of the raw cotton for her busy looms.

There was also a distinctly hostile feeling between
the United States and France, under Napoleon III, because the latter had established a throne in Mexico for
the Archduke Maximilian, and had maintained it by
force of arms, in spite of the well known Monroe Doctrine.

The relations between the United States and these
European powers were greatly strained throughout the
four years of the American conflict, at times, apparently,
almost to the breaking point.

What effect the possession of Washington by the
forces of the Confederacy, the seizure of the treasury, and
the flight of the officials of the Government and of the
officers in charge of headquarters of the army and of the
Navy of the United States, would have had on these un-
friendly powers no one can say.

The affairs of mankind and of governments are so
complex that it is difficult to surmise what would have
taken place, if something else had happened, but surely
it cannot be gainsaid that the saving of the National
Capital from capture by the Confederate forces under
Early was a great victory for the Union cause; and un-
questionably the battle that saved the Capital from capture was fought at Monocacy.

Is it possible for anyone now to say with absolute
certainty that the result of the war would not have been
different if Washington had been taken by Early? The
Nation's Capital in the hands of the enemy, the President and heads of Government in flight; many persons
already discouraged by the long drawn out conflict and

the already appalling loss of life and treasure; England and France both seeking an opportunity to recognize the Southern Confederacy. Might it not have happened that had Washington fallen into the hands of Early, the result of the war would have been a divided instead of a reunited country?

In his *Memories of My Youth,* Mr. George Haven Putnam, himself a veteran of the Civil War and a student of history, says:

"The later history has shown that, in co-operation with John Delane, Lord Palmerston was in correspondence with Louis Napoleon for an early intervention on the part of Great Britain and France, an intervention that would, of course, have brought about the destruction of the Republic.

"They had convinced themselves that the breaking up of the Republic would be on the whole an advantage to the interests of Great Britain."

In another place he says:

"He (Early) could fairly have expected to have captured the President, while he certainly would have secured the money supplies of the Treasury and could probably have destroyed munitions of all kinds in the armories and army warehouses. At this time Louis Napoleon was still pressing upon England the policy of recognizing the establishment of the Southern Confederacy. The news that, more than three years after the beginning of the war, a Confederate force had been able to penetrate into the lines of the National Capital would certainly have been used as a text or argument for the contention that the Confederacy was fairly established and that success for the North was impossible."

In another part of this interesting volume Mr. Putnam says:

"The more influential members of her Majesty's Government, Lord Palmerston, Lord Russell, and Mr.

Gladstone were entirely unsympathetic with the cause of the North. They had convinced themselves that the task of what they called reconquering the South, and thus of maintaining the existence of the Western Republic, was a hopeless one."

In view of this attitude of both England and France it is not going beyond the bounds of reasonable conjecture to say that had Early gotten into Washington the probable event would have been a divided country? With all the vast expenditure of money, the loss of property, the unspeakable death list, the sorrows of the maimed and permanently disabled, having been endured and suffered in vain! We cannot answer the question, with assurance, one way or the other. But we know that at the time Washington was great and justly alarmed, for the danger was real and the peril imminent. The capture of the city was most happily averted. The battle for delay fought at Monocacy saved Washington. Was it not, therefore, in its immediate consequences more important than any other single battle of the great Civil War?

In Benedict's *Vermont in the Civil War,* the author says:

"The battle of Monocacy was overshadowed by other less important events attending Early's raid against Washington; and so made less stir at the time and occupies much less space in history than it deserves. It was a stout and most creditable fight: and though a defeat in name and fact, it accomplished as much as many a victory, for it delayed Early's march upon Washington two days."

The delay was in fact but one day, unless we count the skirmishing west of Frederick on the 7th and 8th of July as causing another day's delay; but whether two days or one, that was sufficient to prevent the disastrous consequences of the fall of the Capital City into the hands of the Confederacy.

The purpose of Gen. Lew Wallace as expressed in his report of the battle, that he had given orders "to collect the bodies of our dead in one burial ground on the battlefield, suitable for a monument, upon which I propose to write: "These men died to save the National Capital, and they did save it"; cannot now be literally carried into effect.

But something perhaps more appropriate still may be done. Would it not create a patriotic shrine to appropriately mark the battlefield, lay out drives and walks and erect a monument there bearing this or some similar inscription:

"HERE WAS FOUGHT ON JULY 9, 1864, THE BATTLE OF MONOCACY, BETWEEN UNION FORCES UNDER THE COMMAND OF MAJ.-GEN. LEW WALLACE AND CONFEDERATE FORCES UNDER THE COMMAND OF LIEUT.-GEN. JUBAL A. EARLY, WHICH RESULTED IN A PRESENT VICTORY FOR THE CONFEDERATES, BUT WHICH DELAYED GENERAL EARLY'S MARCH UPON WASHINGTON LONG ENOUGH TO ENABLE GENERAL GRANT TO SEND, BY TRANSPORTS FROM THE SIEGE OF PETERSBURG, TO THE FEEBLY-MANNED FORTIFICATIONS AROUND WASHINGTON, VETERAN FEDERAL TROOPS WHICH ARRIVED ON JULY 11, JUST IN TIME TO SUCCESSFULLY DEFEND THE CITY AND TO FORESTALL A PREMEDITATED ASSAULT, THEN IMPENDING, BY THE ARMY OF INVASION, UNDER GENERAL EARLY, AND THUS TO SAVE THE NATIONAL CAPITAL, WITH ITS PUBLIC BUILDINGS, TREASURE AND MILITARY STORES FROM FALLING, THE PRESIDENT AND HEADS OF DEPARTMENTS FROM FLIGHT OR CAPTURE, AND TO PREVENT OTHER DISASTROUS CONSEQUENCES TO THE UNION CAUSE. THIS MONUMENT IS ERECTED TO

SIGNALIZE THE IMPORTANCE OF THE BATTLE AND TO DO
HONOR TO THE VALOR OF THE AMERICAN SOLDIERS ON BOTH
SIDES WHO HERE BRAVELY FOUGHT FOR THE CAUSE THEY
WERE READY TO LAY DOWN THEIR LIFE TO UPHOLD. HONOR
THE BRAVE."

"HENCEFORTH:

"LET OUR OBJECT BE OUR COUNTRY, OUR WHOLE COUNTRY
AND NOTHING BUT OUR COUNTRY: AND BY THE BLESSING OF
GOD MAY THAT COUNTRY ITSELF CONTINUE A VAST AND
SPLENDID MONUMENT, NOT OF OPPRESSION AND TERROR, BUT
OF LIBERTY, OF PEACE, AND OF FRATERNITY, UPON WHICH
THE WORLD MAY GAZE WITH ADMIRATION FOREVER."

On another face of the monument could be placed
the words of Lincoln and of Lee, as follows:

"THAT THIS NATION, UNDER GOD, SHALL HAVE A NEW
BIRTH OF FREEDOM; AND THAT GOVERNMENT OF THE PEOPLE,
BY THE PEOPLE, FOR THE PEOPLE, SHALL NOT PERISH FROM
THE EARTH." (Lincoln's Gettysburg address.)

"I BELIEVE IT TO BE THE DUTY OF EVERYONE TO UNITE
IN THE RESTORATION OF THE COUNTRY AND THE RE-ESTAB-
LISHMENT OF PEACE AND HARMONY." (R. E. Lee, letter to
Capt. Josiah Tatnall.)

To such a shrine patriotic Americans would come,
from the North, from the South, from the East and from
the West, and there on the ground where brave men,
North and South, fought and fell, rekindle the flame of
patriotic devotion to flag and country; renew their
allegiance to the Constitution and the Union, and each
and all feel the thrill of one who with exalted pride
exclaims:*"Thank God, I—I too—am an American."*

APPENDIX

MONUMENT TO THE PRISONERS OF WAR WHO DIED AT POINT LOOKOUT

The mortality among prisoners of war whether confined in Northern or Southern prisons, was high. Sanitary precautions and measures were then not nearly so well understood as at the present day, consequently death from camp fevers, typhoid, dysentery and kindred diseases, claimed its daily and weekly toll. In this respect Camp Lookout was no exception. The total deaths in the camp from about August 6, 1863, when the place was first used as a prison camp, until the last of the prisoners were released in the spring of 1865, is officially reported to have been 3,430. Originally the remains of these dead were buried near the camp in two separate cemeteries, each grave being marked with a wooden headboard on which was inscribed the name, rank and command of the deceased whose remains were there interred. The ground where these interments were made, was, however, low and swampy, and wholly unsuited as a burial place for the dead. Moreover in a few years these original cemeteries became overgrown with grass, weeds and briers. In 1870 the attention of the legislature of Maryland was called to the conditions existing at these burial places, and by Chapter 85 of the Acts of Assembly of that year an appropriation was made for the removal of the remains of all these prisoners who lay buried there to some more suitable location and their reinterment in that place. Accordingly a plot of ground of about one acre was obtained one mile inland, the remains were disinterred and removed to the new location.

Unfortunately, some time previously, a fire had run over the ground occupied by the graves, which destroyed not only the undergrowth but also the headboards, thus rendering it impossible to identify the remains buried in any grave. Consequently all the remains were gathered together and buried in one large mound or grave and a small white marble monument was erected to mark the place. This monument was surrounded by a neat iron fence and a substantial wooden fence was built around the whole plot of about one acre. By act of 1874 the Legislature of Maryland made a further appropriation for the purpose of improving and ornamenting this place of sepulture. After the lapse of several years, however, the new burial ground seems to have again become neglected and overgrown with bushes.

On March 9, 1906, a bill, introduced in the Senate of the United States by Senator Joseph B. Foraker, of Ohio, providing for the locating and appropriate marking of the individual graves of all Confederate prisoners of war who had died in Northern prisons, having passed the two House of Congress, was approved by the President. By this act of Congress a sum of money was appropriated, and under it a Commissioner was appointed to carry the law into effect. In accordance with its provisions the graves of many deceased Confederate prisoners of war were marked with neat white marble headstones bearing appropriate inscriptions. The act also provided for the perpetual upkeep of all these cemeteries. (See 34 Stat. L. 56; 35 Stat. L. 56; 36 Stat. L. 875-1453.) Because of the neglected condition of the State Cemetery at Point Lookout, request was made of the Commissioner appointed under the Foraker Act to care for that place of sepulture as was being done in other places. The Commissioner for the United States at the time was ex-Senator James H. Berry, of Arkansas, who undertook to comply with Maryland's request. To that end the Legislature of Maryland by Act of 1910, Chapter 543, ceded the acre of ground where the remains of the prisoners were then buried, to the United States Government. It developed, however, that the State had never obtained title to the property, and consequently conveyance of the same was made to the United States by James Hall and wife, in whom the title was found to vest.

The Act of Congress provided for the separate marking of the individual graves. As the remains of the dead in this burial ground were all buried in one mound, the only method that could be pursued in the marking of this large grave of unidentified dead, was by a central structure, and as the small monument erected by the State was not adapted to the style of marking approved by the War Department, it was replaced by a tall monument made of granite blocks, with twelve bronze tablets on and around the base on which are inscribed the names and commands of the one unknown and the 3,383 known Confederate dead. Besides these there were 44 or 46 civilian prisoners of war who died in this prison camp and whose remains are buried in this large mound. This monument is about 85 feet high and can be seen from afar. A bronze tablet showing the purpose of the monument and that it was erected by the United States, is also attached to it, at the height of about twenty feet

from the ground. The wooden fence enclosing the acre
has been replaced by a wrought iron fence and double
gate entrance. The ground has also been graded and
drained and sown in grass. The small marble monument
erected by the State of Maryland was removed and re-
erected on the site of the cemeteries where the remains
had originally been interred, being enclosed by the small
iron fence which had surrounded it where it was first
erected. The register for the cemetery shows 3,429 known
and one unknown dead, as follows: Soldiers, 3,385;
Unknown, 1; Citizens, 44. Total, 3,430. The expenditures
by the United States Government in connection with the
work, amount to $22,111.06. (See *Report of the Com-
missioner for Marking Confederate Graves.*" Final
report December 6, 1912, p. 28. 62nd Congress, 3rd
Session.) The new cemetery is still fairly well kept and
cared for, and within the enclosure standing by the tall
monument and noting the many names engraved on the
bronze plates, one senses an aspect of war not often
considered. Here lies in a promiscuous heap the remains
of the more than 3,300 young men who died, not in battle
or from wounds, but from sickness and suffering, on
prison cots, lonely and forlorn, far from home and
loved ones. Many a mother's son here lingered in pain
and anguish of mind, longing hopelessly for a mother's
love and tender care, until, after many tedious hours and
days of suffering, the pulses ceased to beat, the raging
fever departed and the aching brow became cold and
clammy in death. The slow turning wheels of weary
life at last stood still and thus the sufferer found relief
from all his woes. No wonder statesmen everywhere are
seeking to outlaw the horrid monster—WAR.

GEN. BRADLEY T. JOHNSON'S ACCOUNT OF HIS DESIGNS
AND PLANS TO CAPTURE POINT LOOKOUT.

In a narrative of the Maryland Campaign of 1864, Gen. Bradley T. Johnson, in command of a cavalry regiment, gives the following account of his raid in the direction of Point Lookout with the purpose in view of capturing the place and liberating the Confederate prisoners confined there, he says:

"It was now the morning of Tuesday, the 12th. I was due that night at Point Lookout, the extreme southeast point of Maryland, in St. Mary's County. It was physically impossible for men to make the ride in the time designated. I determined, however, to come as near it as possible. I sent an officer with a detachment to ride at speed through the country, impressing fresh horses all the way, and inform the people along the route that I was coming. They were unanimously my friends, and I requested them to have their horses on the roadside so I could exchange my broken-down animals for their fresh ones, and thus borrow them for the occasion. During the preceding day I had been taking horses by flankers on each side of my column and kept a supply of fresh ones at the rear of each regiment. As soon as a man's horse broke down he fell out of the ranks, walked until the rear of his regiment came up, got a fresh horse, left his old one and resumed his place. By this means I was enabled to march at a trot which with a cavalry column is impossible for any length of time without breaking down horses, and broken-down horses speedily break down men. With fresh horses, however, I hoped to make a rapid march and get to Point Lookout early on the morning of the 13th. After returning from the pursuit of Wilson's Cavalry, I turned the head of the column towards Upper Marlboro and had proceeded only a short time when I was overtaken by a courier from General Early. He brought me orders to report at once to headquarters at Silver Springs, on the Seventh Street Road. I moved down the Washington Road to the

Agricultural College and thence along the line of the Federal pickets, marching all night, occasionally driving in a picket and expecting at any moment to be fired upon from the works, within range of which I was moving. I reported to General Early after midnight and found the whole army in retreat."

This report furnishes irrefragable proof of Early's purpose to capture Washington if possible.

HISTORIC FREDERICK

The battle of Monocacy was fought quite near Frederick City. The preliminary skirmishes on the 7th and 8th of July took place just west of the city and the real tug of war occurred on the 9th three miles south. Both Federal and Confederate wounded were brought to the city for nursing and treatment after the battle. Many private homes took in wounded men and cared for them. Hotels and churches were used as hospitals. There were probably as many as eight hundred cared for in homes and in these improvised hospitals. Not a few died of their wounds, and of these, as well as of the dead from the battlefield, many were brought to Mt. Olivet Cemetery and buried there. The greater number of these being Confederate dead, the Federals being transferred to the National Cemetery at Antietam or forwarded to their former homes for interment. The Confederate dead buried in Mt. Olivet number perhaps six hundred or more, some being from the battlefield of South Mountain ten miles west. The city is identified with the war and especially with the battle of Monocacy in an intimate way.

BRADDOCK'S VISIT

Frederick is an interesting historic city. Here came Gen. Edward Braddock on his ill-starred campaign against Fort duQuesne in 1755 when Frederick was only a small town of a few hundred inhabitants. Meeting here for consultation and conference Benjamin Franklin, George Washington and Governor Sharpe of Maryland, on April 22, 1755. A large quantity of army stores and supplies were collected here. From Frederick the British army moved over the mountains toward Fort duQuesne, well supplied with horses and wagons and other necessaries for carrying on the war. As is well known Braddock was disastrously defeated at Fort duQuesne on July 9, 1755, he himself being mortally wounded. A fine spring of water on the mountain side five miles west of Frederick where Braddock's army encamped is still known as Braddock Spring and the beautiful resort on the mountain top as Braddock Heights.

STAMP ACT REPUDIATED

It was the Levy Court at Frederick that first officially repudiated the odious Stamp Act. The Act had been denounced in many places and by many men, but on November 23, 1765, the Levy Court of Frederick County ordered its clerk to issue a writ without the use of the stamped paper. John Darnall, the clerk, fearing the consequences of a non-observance of the law refused and was, by order of the court, committed to the custody of the sheriff of the county. Darnall afterwards submitted and expressed his willingness to comply with the court's order; whereupon he was released and the writ issued. Frederick then held a funeral in which the Stamp Act was the corpse. A fine tablet bearing the names of the twelve immortal judges who passed the order of repudiation was erected in the court room with elaborate ceremonies at the unveiling on November 23, 1904.

Thomas Johnson

One of the most distinguished citizens of Frederick was Thomas Johnson, revolutionary patriot and hero, the nominator of George Washington for Commander-in-Chief of the Continental Army, friend of that great man, first Governor of Maryland and indefatigable worker for the cause of independence. His remains lie buried in beautiful Mt. Olivet. Mr. Johnson was a member of the Continental Congress that adopted the Declaration of Independence, and the reason he was not one of the signers was because he was in Maryland at the time of the signing, working for the cause amongst the people of his native State. He might have gained greater and wider fame had he signed his name to that Declaration, but he was doing more practical things and much less agreeable by coming to Maryland, his native State, and using his untiring energies and efforts to raise troops for the field, to gather together supplies to clothe and feed the army, and to provide arms, powder and ball for the war that he knew was impending. So devoted were he and Washington to each other that when they met they embraced each other warmly. Washington afterwards proffered Johnson the position of Secretary of State, later appointed him a judge of the Supreme Court, and later made him chairman of a commission to lay out the District of Columbia and to locate the public buildings therein. It was this commission of which he was chairman that located the Capitol at Washington. His memory has been neglected and his great services have been overlooked, but recently there has been erected in court square in the city of Frederick a monument to his memory. His former residence on the outskirts of the city, known as "Rose Hill Manor," is pointed out with pride to the stranger within or near its gates.

OLD STONE BARRACKS

In the grounds of the State Institute for the Deaf and Dumb at Frederick are located the old stone barracks erected during the Revolution in pursuance of an Act of Assembly of 1777, it being Chapter X of that year. The purpose of the barracks originally was "to remove as far as possible the necessity of quartering troops in private houses." Though used at first as a place for housing American soldiers of the Revolution, they were later used as a military prison and in them were quartered prisoners of war taken at Saratoga, at Trenton and at Yorktown. Many Hessian soldiers captured at Yorktown were liberated from this prison at the close of the War for Independence and became in large part good American citizens, their descendants being still respected residents of Frederick County.

CHIEF JUSTICE TANEY

Here also in 1801 came Roger Brooke Taney, a young attorney, to practice law, and here he remained until 1820. In 1806 he married Miss Anne Phebe Charlton Key, a sister of Francis Scott Key. In 1811 he defended Gen. James Wilkinson at Frederick before a court martial assembled in that city to try General Wilkinson on several charges brought against him, including some entanglement with Aaron Burr's alleged treason. Wilkinson was acquitted. Mr. Taney afterwards became Attorney-General of the United States and later Chief Justice of the Supreme Court where he served for 28 years. Next to Marshall he is regarded as the greatest of the chief justices of that court. Judge Taney lies buried in the Catholic graveyard in Frederick by the side of his mother, Monica Taney. On September 26, 1931, a memorial in his honor was dedicated in court house square in Frederick; Chief Justice Charles Evans Hughes being the principal speaker.

Francis Scott Key

Frederick County is also the birth place of Francis Scott Key and his remains lie buried in Mt. Olivet Cemetery. A handsome monument to his memory was erected over his remains in 1898, the orator of the occasion being Hon. Henry Watterson of Kentucky. Mr. Key's fame rests chiefly upon his authorship of the "Star-Spangled Banner," but he was also a prominent attorney-at-law. He and Chief Justice Taney were brothers-in-law and close and intimate friends for many years. Mr. Key died in 1843 and Mr. Taney in 1864. Frederick City reveres their memory. Peace to their ashes.

Barbara Fritchie

Frederick was the centre of many military operations during the Civil War. On September 6, 1862, General Lee's army reached Frederick on its way to South Mountain and Antietam. In marching through the city the soldiers passed the home of Barbara Fritchie, located on West Patrick Street near Carroll Creek which flows southeastwardly through the town. Mr. Jacob Englebrecht who was a respected citizen of the town, being at one time mayor of the city, and who kept a diary right regularly for many years, has this to say concerning the coming of the Confederates:

"September 6, 1862.

"This morning the Rebels took possession of our good city of Frederick without opposition."

"September 11, 1862.

"The passing of the Rebel army continued all day yesterday until night and this morning, three hours more. In passing through town it took them about seventeen hours, altogether. We estimate their numbers at about seventy thousand. They were generally young and hardy men and had been in the service so long that they were much fagged out. Many were barefooted and some had one shoe on and one bare foot. They really looked ragged and tough—but I must say the Rebels behaved themselves well."

It was during this invasion of the city that the incidents are alleged to have happened that gave rise to the celebrated poem by Whittier, entitled: "Barbara Fritchie." As a matter of fact Jackson himself did not pass the Fritchie home, but the poem has made the town famous and Dame Barbara a heroine. A beautiful monument has been erected to her memory over her remains in Mt. Olivet. A replica of her house has been erected near the site of the old one, which is visited yearly by thousands.

MEADE SUCCEEDS HOOKER

It was near Frederick City that Gen. Joseph Hooker was superseded in command of the Federal Army just before Gettysburg by Gen. George Gordon Meade. This occurred June 28, 1863, in a field on the George W. Smith farm about one mile west of the city. General Hooker had been thwarted in some of his plans by Maj.-Gen. Henry W. Halleck, Chief-of-Staff at Washington, whereupon he immediately relinquished his command of the Army of the Potomac and the same was transferred to General Meade. The battle of Gettysburg followed a few days later, July 1, 2 and 3, and resulted in a victory for General Meade. On June 28, 1930, a large boulder taken from near Devil's Den on the battlefield of Gettysburg, to which was affixed a bronze tablet suitably inscribed, was unveiled on the highway near where the transfer occurred. Governor Fisher of Pennsylvania and other prominent men attended the unveiling. Hon. Isaac R. Pennypacker of Ardmore, Pa., delivered the address.

ADMIRAL SCHLEY

Frederick also claims with pride as one of her sons, Winfield Scott Schley, the hero of Santiago Bay. In the war with Spain for the independence of Cuba, the Spanish fleet was sunk by the American fleet under Admiral Schley off the south coast of that island. Admiral Schley was born near Frederick and after that victory the admiral was invited to the city where he was given a great ovation. Bells rang, whistles blew and the people of the city acclaimed him with one accord the hero of the naval battle of Santiago Bay. For this victory he was presented with a gold sword by the people of Pennsylvania; a silver sword by the Royal Arcanum, a gold and jeweled medal, and a silver service by the Legislature of Maryland.

JOHN GREENLEAF WHITTIER'S POEM

Perhaps nothing was ever done or written that added to the fame of historic Frederick as did the poem by John Greenleaf Whittier, entitled: "Barbara Fritchie," which purports to describe a scene occurring before the home of Dame Barbara in Frederick City on September 11, 1862, during the march of the Confederate hosts through the city on their way to the battle-

fields of South Mountain and Antietam. The first mentioned of these battles took place about twelve miles west
of Frederick on the 14th day of September, and the
second or Antietam battle about twenty miles west on
the 16th and 17th days of the same month.

Whittier puts Stonewall Jackson at the head of the
column of marchers that passed Dame Barbara's house
on West Patrick Street, close to the bridge over Carroll
Creek, and makes him give the order to his men to fire
on the Union flag that she is stated to have waved from
her upper window in the face of the marching Confederate hosts. As a matter of fact Jackson did not pass
the Barbara Fritchie home but entered West Patrick
Street, a short distance west of the Fritchie home, from
a side street known as Bentz Street.

Besides this fact it is stated in the diary of Mr. Jacob
Englebright, a Unionist, that he sat at his window in a
house opposite the Fritchie home all day of the 11th
and watched the passing Confederate Army and no such
incident as that related by Whittier occurred.

Nevertheless, though there be more poetry than history in the poem, it has brought great fame to Frederick
and many tourists come to visit the house recently built
on or near the site of the Fritchie home in replica thereof.

A fine concrete bridge over Carroll Creek on Bentz
Street is named the "Stonewall Jackson Bridge" because
by that way came Jackson to the main highway over
which the Confederate hosts were marching that day.

However, there is a well-established tradition that
the old lady had not infrequent clashes with rebel
soldiers at the doorstep of her humble home. It is also
shown that she owned and treasured a Union flag, and
waved it. In truth the name and fame of Barbara

Fritchie are interwoven with the folds of the flag and the replica of her dwelling place is a veritable patriotic shrine.

A handsome monument to Barbara Fritchie stands in Mt. Olivet Cemetery at Frederick erected by her admirers after her fame was spread afar by this beautiful poem:

The Ballad

Up from the meadows rich with corn,
Clear in the cool September morn,

The clustered Spires of Frederick stand,
Green-walled by the hills of Maryland.

Round about them orchards sweep,
Apple and peach tree rooted deep.

Fair as a garden of the Lord
To the eyes of the famished Rebel horde.

On that pleasant morn of early fall,
When Lee marched over the mountain wall,—

Over the mountains winding down,
Horse and foot into Fredericktown.

Forty flags with their silver stars,
Forty flags with their crimson bars.

Up rose old Barbara Fritchie then,
Bowed with her four score years and ten.

Bravest of all in Fredericktown,
She took up the flag the men hauled down.

In her attic window the staff she set
To show that one heart was loyal yet.

Up the street came the rebel tread,
Stonewall Jackson riding ahead.

Under his slouched hat left and right
He glanced, the old flag met his sight.

"Halt!" the dust-brown ranks stood fast.
"Fire!" Out blazed the rifle blast.

It shivered the window pane and sash.
It rent the banner with seam and gash.

Quick as it fell from the broken staff
Dame Barbara snatched the silked scarf.

She leaned far out on the window sill
And shook it forth with a royal will.

"Shoot if you must, this old gray head,
"But spare your country's flag," she said.

A shade of sadness, a blush of shame,
Over the face of the leader came.

The nobler nature within him stirred
To life at that woman's deed and word.

"Who touches a hair of yon gray head,
Dies like a dog, March on," he said.

All day long through Frederick street,
Sounded the tread of marching feet.

All day long that free flag tost
Over the heads of the Rebel host.

Ever its torn folds rose and fell
On the loyal winds that loved it well.

And through the hill gaps sunset light
Shone over it with a warm good night.

Barbara Fritchie's work is o'er
And the Rebel rides on his raids no more.

Honor to her! and let a tear
Fall for her sake on Stonewall's bier.

Over Barbara Fritchie's grave
Flag of freedom and Union wave.

Peace and order and beauty draw
Round thy symbol of light and law.

And ever the stars above look down
On thy stars below in Frederick town.

The End.

Read, Thomas Buchanan,
Wrote "Sheridan's Ride," 204.
Richmond, Confederate Capital, 11.
"On to Richmond," 10.
Ricketts, Gen. James B., 74.
Sketch of, 78.
Commands Third Division, 75.
Arrives morning of 9th, 87.
Conversation between Wallace
and Ricketts, 87.
His veterans to defend wooden
bridge, 88.
Liaison with Tyler, 88.
Meets a fusillade, 109.
Brigades waiting, 122.
Confers with Wallace, 149.
At the Gambrill home, 171.
Able officer, 271.
Rives House,
Near Fort Stevens, 190.
Rockville, Maryland,
Road to, 180.
To Seventh Street Pike, 180.
McCausland's videttes at, 180.
Confederate Army bestirred it-
self, 181.
Road to Washington, from Fred-
erick over wooden bridge, 89.
Roe, Alfred Seeley,
His book, 19.
Describes march in and voyage
on the water, 76.
Account of the battle, 111.
Burning of the bridge, 111-112.
His account of the battle, 150-151.
Washington badly scared, 215.
Account of capture and march to
Washington, 246.
Prison life at Danville, 252.
Ill, 254.
Rodes, Gen. Robert E.,
To demonstrate against Jug
Bridge, 94.
Skirmishing at, 107-122.
Romance, a, 162.
A half romance, 163.
Ross, Col. James R.,
To flag trains, 79.
Directs Ricketts where to post his
forces, 90.
Rides through the bridge to warn
defenders on the other side, 112.

S

Sandy Hook,
Location, 42, 66.
Message from, 65.
Scharf, J. Thomas,
History of Western Maryland 205.
Account of conference, 205.
Schley, Admiral, hero of Santiago
Bay, 288.
Welcomed to Frederick, 288.
Scott, Thomas A.,
Hears Longstreet is coming, 201.
Scott, Winfield,
Lieutenant-General, 10.
Seconds,
A question of, 155.
Senate,
Modified House bill to mark Mon-
ocacy battlefield, 30.
Seventh Street Pike,
Early's route by, 181.
Seward, Col. William H.,
Commands 9th New York Heavy
Artillery, 89.
Arrives, 89.
Son of Lincoln's Secretary of
State, 156.
Gets away on a mule, 156.
Shenandoah Valley,
Crows flying in, 11.
Sheridan, Gen. Philip,
Appointed to command in the
Valley, 205-206.
"Sheridan's Ride," 204.
Shiloh, 9.
Shrine, patriotic, 275-276.
Sigel, Gen. Franz,
Sent to Valley of Virginia, 11.
Defeated at New Market, 12.
Retreats, 38.
Joins Weber on Maryland
Heights, 39.
Held by small force, 39.
Reports enemy at Winchester, 50.
At Sandy Hook, 65.
Message to Wallace, "Strong force
of enemy, 66.
Isolated on Maryland Heights, 93.
Succeeded by Gen. Albion Howe,
93.

Additional Photos and Material compiled and edited by Brian C. Pohanka.

The following four accounts from Federal enlisted men who served in the Battle of Monocacy first appeared in the *National Tribune*, weekly journal of the Grand Army of the Republic. The *National Tribune* is one of the great untapped sources of personal anecdotal material relating to the American Civil War.

Monocacy, and the Gallant Stand of
the 106th New York Against Early
by Peter Robertson, 106th N.Y.V.I.
National Tribune, January 24, 1884

"On the morning of July 6th, the 3rd Division marched from the left of the line in front of Petersburg to City Point, where the 106th embarked for Baltimore. Arriving on the evening of the 7th, we went by cars to Frederick, reaching there on the forenoon of the 8th. Here General Ricketts reported his division to General Wallace, commanding the department. After maneuvering about Frederick until sundown, we marched to Monocacy Junction, and went into camp about 2 o'clock on the morning of the 9th on the south side of the railroad, near the old stone mill. At early daylight the enemy opened from one of their batteries and landed a few shells in our camp. We moved to the left and deployed in line of battle, our left resting on the Frederick and Washington Turnpike. We remained in this position until about 10 a.m., when we were ordered to the left on the double-quick, and took position on the west side of a wheatfield, where the turnpike turns at a right angle south. The 1st Brigade was formed on the left of the 2nd Brigade, from right to left as follows: 151st and 106th New York, 14th New Jersey, 10th Vermont, and 87th Pennsylvania. Off to the right of our line, toward the Monocacy River, was a cornfield, on the edge of which the enemy had a skirmish-line which partially enfiladed our line. The 151st and 106th New York, and the 14th New Jersey, made a charge, on a right-wheel, and captured nearly all of this skirmish-line. My regiment captured one lieutenant-colonel, one captain, two lieutenants, and twenty privates. If I remember rightly they belonged to the 17th Virginia Mounted Infantry. On questioning the Rebel Colonel he informed me that General Early's entire force of about 20,000 infantry, besides cavalry and artillery, was in our front. This was rather blue news, as General Wallace's entire force was less than 6,000, including hundred-days men, and we were very deficient in artillery. From the position we now occupied we could plainly see the movements of the enemy, as the country toward Frederick was open and level.

About 2 p.m. the enemy commenced to move a heavy column of infantry to our left and into a piece of woods. They soon advanced a heavy skirmish line, closely followed by two lines of battle, which, making a left-wheel, threatened our left flank. Their skirmishers commenced enfilading our line, and change of front of our three regiments became necessary. The command, 'Rise up, about-face, left-wheel, double-quick, march!' was given, and this movement brought us into the same position we occupied before making the charge above referred to, with the 87th Pennsylvania and 10th Vermont on our left, near the Thomas house. In our front was an open, level field about 400 yards across. At the further side of this field the enemy's skirmish line halted, and their lines of battle closed up to the fence, with the evident intention of charging our line. The order had been passed to our boys not to fire until the command was given. On came the Rebels in two lines of battle, their field officers in front of their lines.

The command 'fire!' rang out along our line; then 'load and fire at will', and such a fire was kept up that no mortal power could face and cross that field. At one time I counted five riderless horses running back and forth in front of the Rebel lines. Twice did the Rebel officers reform their lines and advance to face that banquet of death, and as often were they repulsed. About this time (4 p.m.), it seems orders had been given for the troops to fall back toward the Baltimore Pike, but no such orders were received by any of the regiments of the 1st Brigade, as far as I could learn.

As the line on our right had been withdrawn, the enemy moved a force on our right and rear, and, with the force in our front, made it rather hot for us. With a prospective view of Libby and Andersonville looming up, we concluded to try what virtue there was in legs to place ourselves between Early and Baltimore. In doing so we had to run the gauntlet in crossing the wheatfield to the old mill, and thence across the railroad track, up the mountain side to the Baltimore Pike, where we took up the line of march for Ellicott's Mills. We reached that place on Sunday evening, the 10th, footsore and weary. The loss of my regiment in this battle was 81 killed and wounded and 64 missing out of 320 that went into the fight. The loss of the other regiments of the 1st Brigade must have been as great.''

PETER ROBERTSON
106th N.Y.V.I.
Ogdensburg, N.Y.

Account of Monocacy by W. T. McDougle
Co. K, 126th Ohio Volunteer Infantry
National Tribune, February 21, 1884

"On the evening before the Battle of Monocacy we landed at the junction and camped nearby. I was on the detail for picket, and was placed in
charge of the post on the Frederick City and Georgetown Turnpike. During
the night nothing occurred to disturb our peace. The morning dawned with
a halo of sunshine and beauty. The birds (which we had been so unaccustom-
ed to hear during our late journey from the Rapidan to Petersburg) never appeared to be so joyful. The large farmhouse on the hill to our left seemed
almost a paradise, with its surroundings of horses, hogs, cattle, fowls, etc.
I remember the gathering of the wheat from the field. These things, in the
absence of our accustomed routine for the past two months, were to me most
impressive. We could scarcely believe it possible that before the setting of the
sun this beautiful place would be the scene of such deadly strife.

At length the clouds began to gather. The refugees were coming in in
great numbers — men, women and children, old and young, black and white,
appearing to be moving with them all their household effects. Firing was heard
in the direction of Harpers Ferry and, we were told by the refugees that the
Rebs were coming in great numbers. Nearer and nearer came the sound of
the distant guns, till, at length, we heard the shrieks of the shells as they pierc-
ed the air. The enemy had now passed in our front, and were preparing for
a charge. Their batteries having opened, we were greeted with a volley. A cannon ball struck the tree by which we were posted; another dropped a few feet
to our rear and went bounding across the valley like a schoolboy's rubber ball;
another struck and buried itself in the earth a few feet to our front. All was
now commotion. The orderlies were galloping from place to place, the officers hurrying hither and thither with their commands. The pickets were
ordered in. I found my regiment down on the right, near the river bridge. The
regiment was immediately ordered to the left of the 1st Brigade, and near the
picket post we had just vacated.

An incident occurred on our way which I think will bear a passing
notice. The enemy, perceiving our move, brought their batteries to bear upon
us. A high board fence was to be crossed. As I took hold of the top board
I was crowded back by a more anxious comrade. As he swung himself over
the fence his knapsack was riddled with a grapeshot. Again I made the attempt with the same success. But this time my predecessor, as he swung himself
over the fence, was struck in the left arm above the elbow by a grapeshot,
his arm falling by his side. I again made the attempt and cleared the fence,

barely escaping a large cannon ball that struck the board from which I had just alighted.

We found the enemy bearing down hard on the left of the 1st Brigade. They halted on a hill in our front. A large washout, with a stiff growth of weeds on its banks, extended up the hill. I was among the nine who crawled up in this to surprise the Rebs, two of our number receiving severe wounds. Judge of our surprise when, in a short time, it was discovered that the Rebs had flanked us on the right and gobbled up the most of our regiment and held undisputed control of the field. I crawled on the bank but could see no chance of escape. I had my gun loaded, but in the excitement it occurred to me that I could not surrender with a loaded gun. A Rebel flag, surrounded by some fifteen or twenty of its followers, was on a knoll nearby. The Confederates did not appear to notice me as I raised my gun and sent my best wishes into their midst. I then threw down my gun and sat down — a prisoner! It was the most horrid thought that had ever entered my mind. Never before had I fully realized the blessings of liberty, and now I had a fair prospect of being sent to Andersonville, Libby, or some other prison. I could not stand it and springing to my feet and seizing my gun, I started for the North. They ordered me to halt, but without effect, and then sent shot after shot after me, till the air appeared alive with their gentle missiles, but still without effect. One of them then undertook to run me down; but, after throwing away my knapsack, in which were two knapsacks, viz. my diary and the picture of 'the girl I left behind me', I managed to make good my escape."

A Day's Skirmish
by Daniel B. Freeman, Co. G, 10th Vermont
in the *National Tribune*, March 18, 1897

"On the morning of July 9, 1864, when a part of the Third Division, Sixth Corps, stood in front of Gen. Jubal Early's much superior force in numbers on the battlefield of Monocacy, Md., the writer, with upwards of 75 others, was detailed early in the morning for the skirmish-line, under command of Capt. George E. Davis, of my regiment — the 10th Vt.

We went across the river, and deployed in circular form, extending from the Washington Pike Bridge along the pike around towards the river some distance above the railroad bridge.

I was posted on the Pike Bridge over the railroad with George Douse in the ditch at my left, only a few feet away.

I lay alongside and behind one of the stringers, top of the plank — which was a large square stick of timber — firing over it, then lying low to reload, until after awhile the heat became so intensely hot I moved into the ditch with Douse, and we dug a pit, throwing the dirt in front of us with our plates, against some rails that crossed the end of it, and soon had a hole in the sand so we could sit and partly stand, and at the same time be protected from bullets.

About 8 o'clock a dash was made by the enemy under cover of artillery fire, to drive us from our position, hoping to gain the pike, and proceed on their way to Washington. This, at the time, was miserably defended. Early hoped by a forced march to capture it before reinforcements could be thrown in to protect it.

Here we saw a ruse of the enemy — their skirmishers, dressed in our uniform, driving before them some pickets of 100-days men, who went to our rear; but we could not long be deceived by their dress. We opened fire, and made them seek hiding places for protection, but they did not withdraw entirely.

Towards 11 o'clock another effort was made to dislodge us, and Gen. Lew Wallace, in command, ordered the Pike Bridge, over the river, burned, which left the skirmishers under Capt. Davis cut off from the rest of our troops, with no way of retreat except to swim the river or cross the railroad bridge, 40 feet in the air, stepping from tie to tie.

The enemy shortly moved a large part off by the Buckeystown Road, a mile east of us, to a ford below, crossed, formed line of battle and charged our men on the other side of the river.

Again and again, with two and three lines of battle did they charge, to be each time hurled back defeated.

Now the skirmishers were busy, for they were being pressed by the enemy's sharpshooters, firing from concealment in trees and grainfields, where we could not locate them.

I was now left alone, my comrade having been carried off wounded, and every time I raised my head above a certain rail, a bullet would hit the rail, embankment of dirt, or go whistling past.

I was called to the reserve, and Corporal Wright sent to post me as a vidette outpost, and relieve the comrade on duty there, some 200 yards to our left, in the cornfield.

As we came to this comrade, Wright stretched up to take observations, and was shot through the head. We carried him back to the reserve, and I returned to the outpost alone, just in time to see in the distance across the river, the enemy on their fourth charge, with as many lines of battle.

On and on I saw them come, and our troops were being withdrawn. I heard Lieut. Wilkie calling to me to come in quickly. As I crossed the pike I saw our reserve on the railroad bridge, and a little in the rear was Lieut. Wilkie urging me on.

As I neared the depot and looked back along the railroad I saw one of my comrades under the Pike Bridge fighting a dozen Johnnies charging down the railroad toward him. He was riddled with lead.

I sped on, paying no heed to the orders to halt. I reached the bridge, and, stepping from tie to tie, crossed over in safety under a crossfire from others of the enemy at the bend in the river a few rods below.

Capt. Davis ordered us to fall in behind the railroad after getting across, and I fired one or two shots more, and heard the order, 'Every man for himself!'. I arrived at the Relay House the next evening.

As I look back to that day I can but think my escape a miracle; and of the heroic comrade covering my retreat, who, riddled with lead, sacrificed his life there under the Pike Bridge that I and others might be spared.

The veterans of the Third Division, Sixth Corps believed then — and they believe it today — that Washington was saved from capture by the heroic struggle and defeat at Monocacy; for, let it be remembered, Early's entire army was arrested, bruised, and detained for 36 hours, at an awful sacrifice of life to both sides, allowing barely time for the First and Second Divisions of our Sixth Corps to be thrown into Washington from in front of Petersburg in the nick of time.

Who can say what the damage to the Union cause might not have been, had the Battle of Monocacy not been fought?"

DANIEL R. FREEMAN
Co. G, 10th Vt.
Chicago, Illinois

Corporal Roderick A. Clark,
Co. F, 14th New Jersey
National Tribune, April 15, 1886

"July 9, 1864, is a day that will long be remembered by the surviving members of the 14th N.J., and particularly so by your humble correspondent. It was on that day that the Third Division, Sixth Corps, under Gen. Lew Wallace, was attacked by the Rebels under Gen. Early at Monocacy, Md.

About 12 o'clock the Rebel pickets drove in our cavalry outposts on our left, and took a position with a strong skirmish-line on a high ridge west of Mr. Thomas's house, and south of the Washington Pike. Our regiment was placed in position in Mr. Thomas's lawn, north of the house, behind a large hawthorne hedge, from which position we charged the Rebel line and drove them toward the river, killing and capturing many of them, among the latter a Colonel badly wounded in the groin. We remained quietly in this position till about 3 o'clock, when we discovered the enemy advancing on us, in two lines of battle, mostly on our left flank, at least a half a mile away, without a tree or obstruction of any kind to hide them. It was certainly a grand sight as they advanced, in good order, with their numerous battle flags waving in the breeze. We began firing at once, but it made no difference. On they came with quick step until they got within 300 yards of us. Then our regiment and the 87th Pa. was moved by the left flank and changed front to prevent them from flanking us.

At the beginning of this movement I was hit in the left ankle by a minie-ball, completely crushing the joint. I started to retreat, but found I could not walk; so I stood there until two of my comrades placed me on their gun, and, with my arms around their necks, started to the rear with me. But ere they got 20 steps I was struck with another minie-ball under the shoulder-blade just to the right of the back-bone, penetrating the right lung, stopping just under the skin in my breast. It felt about the size of a cannon-ball. I don't know how long I lay unconscious, but when I came to the Rebels were all around me. Our men had retreated to the Washington Pike, and were making it hot for me as well as the Rebels. Although very weak I managed to crawl about 20 feet to the fence.

The Rebels were now very demoralized, and were skulking behind everything that afforded shelter. Their officers were compelling them to get up and move forward, and they used their swords freely. I heard several of the men say they had no ammunition, and with horrid oaths they were ordered to 'take that dead Yank's', meaning me. I never heard minies fly so fast or sound so spiteful as they did there, cutting the weeds and throwing the dirt all over me. Behind the rail fence were a good many Rebels firing at our men.

Two of them were right behind me, and as they fired the muzzles of their guns were within a few inches of me, and, to prevent burning my face, I put my hat over my eyes. I had just taken my hand away when a ball from our men struck the hat and came so close that it burned my forehead, passed on, and killed a Rebel stone dead. I thought at the time that the ball had struck the rail, but after the fighting was over I saw that it had hit one of the Rebs just over the eye.

Now my worst troubles began. I was dying with thirst, and, to make matters still worse, a big Rebel came along and pulled off my shoes; the pain caused was almost unbearable. When he discovered the bullet-hole through the one, he threw it down in disgust, and said it was a d--n shame to spoil so good a shoe.

The next one that came along took my watch, telling me that I wouldn't be able to see what time it was very long; also my pocketbook, empty though, knife and picture album; but when I beseechingly held out my hand and asked for the latter, he threw it back with an oath. (I have the album and contents yet.) My next visitor was a mere boy, whom I asked for a drink of water. He placed his hand on his bayonet and said, 'I would rather give you this.' But he gave me neither, but passed on about 10 steps, turned, and walked briskly toward me with his hand still on his bayonet. I thought then my time had come, but I did not care much, for I thought it was impossible for me to live long anyway; but, instead of hurting me, he handed me his canteen, saying, 'Drink, I will let you see that we are not as bad as you think us.' But he took good care to give me a severe lecture for coming down there to fight 'We uns'.

During the engagement the Rebels put a battery in position close to where I lay, so that I could hear every command given the gunners. This battery stayed there all night, and to one of the gunners I owe that comfort I got that night, but that was not much. This man found me when he was returning from the river with water for his horse, propped me up on knapsacks and blankets, and left his bucket, half full of water, so I could reach it with my hand. He also sat and talked with me a long time. When I told him what regiment I belonged to, he looked over toward our old campground of 1862 about a half mile away, and said, 'That was the regiment that guarded about 900 of us to Fort Delaware after the battle of Antietam. You used us well, and I will do the same for you.' He came to me several times through the night and changed my position. At sunset he came and got his bucket and bade me goodby.

I lay on the field until 10 o'clock July 10. All through the night the doctors of both sides and their assistants called on me frequently. The Rebel doctor gave me a drink of liquor, but the Union doctor had only a little for his own regiment. This same Rebel doctor, with two stretcher bearers, came after me, and carried me down to the big buttonwood tree and put me in the ambulance with two wounded Rebels and started us for Frederick City, where we arrived about 11 o'clock, 17 hours after I was wounded.

At the beginning of the engagement our pioneers burned the bridge, which made it necessary for the ambulance to ford the river. As the front wheels ascended the steep bank I was nearly thrown out in the water; both legs went in up to my knees. I only saved myself by grabbing the hoops at the side of the ambulance. On the hill where the block house stood the Rebs had two guns firing at the railroad bridge to destroy it. They burned all the depot buildings, water tanks, etc. On our way to Frederick we passed a vast number of cavalry, each man with three or four stolen horses loaded with plunder.

When we reached the hospital we found that all the nurses had been sent away to prevent their capture, but the citizens of Frederick came nobly to our assistance — especially the ladies. One young lady, Miss Lizzie Ott, was the first to come to my assistance with a basin of water and soap. After 30 minutes hard scrubbing I began to look like a white man and feel very much better. For 12 long weeks Miss Ott was untiring in her efforts, bringing me every delicacy that could be thought of, and sitting by me hour after hour, fanning me and speaking words of cheer. And, comrades, do you blame me for falling in love with her and marrying her? I think I hear you say 'You did just right!' My good old mother was also with me for four weeks, and nursed me as only a mother can.''

RODERICK A. CLARK
Co. F, 14th N.J.
Commander, Post 87, G.A.R.
Department of New Jersey,
Point Pleasant, Ocean County, N.J.

Confederate Accounts

The diary of Captain Robert E. Park, of the 12th Alabama, originally appeared in the *Southern Historical Society Papers,* Volume I. I. G. Bradwell's article appeared in *The Confederate Veteran* of January 1928.

This rare photograph of Confederate troops on their march through Frederick dates either from September 1862, during the Antietam Campaign, or July 1864, during Early's occupation of the town.

Courtesy, Mrs. Benjamin Rosenstock

Diary of Robert E. Park,
late Capt. Twelfth Alabama Reg't.
Southern Historical Society Papers, Volume I

July 1*st*, 1864—Marched twenty-two miles to-day—from Newmarket
to two miles beyond Woodstock, where we remained for the night. This is
the anniversary of the first day's battle at Gettysburg, Pennsylvania; and one
year ago, late in the afternoon, just before my brigade entered the city, I was
wounded. I well remember the severe wound in the head received that day
by Lieutenant Wright near my side, and his earnest appeal to me to tell him
candidly the nature of this terrible wound. And I shall never forget the generous
forgetfulness of self, and warm friendship for myself, shown by Captain John
J. Nicholson, of Company "I", when the command was temporarily forced
back by overwhelming numbers. I had been wounded; and fearing that I would
be captured, hobbled off after my regiment, as it fell back under a very close
and galling fire from the rapidly advancing Yankees. Nicholson, noticing my
feeble and painful efforts to escape, suddenly stopped, ran to me, and catching my arm, offered to aid me; but, appreciating his well meant kindness, I
declined his proffered assistance, and begged him to hurry on, telling him,
to induce him to leave me, and save himself, that I would stop unless he went
on. Captain N. was once a teacher in Mobile, associated with Major W. T.
Walthall, is a native of Annapolis, Maryland, and graduate of Saint Johns
College. While on furlough, and recovering from a wound, received at Seven
Pines, he married an elegant lady in Amelia county, Virginia. After Captain
N. left me, the enemy fell back again, and I was carried to our brigade hospital,
near Gettysburg, and soon joined by Captains A. E. Hewlett and P. D. Ross,
and Lieutenants Wright and Fletcher, all wounded officers of my regiment.
The last mentioned, a brave young soldier, bled internally, and died during
the night.

July 2*d*—We passed through Middletown and camped at Newtown.

July 3*d*—Marched through the historic old town of Winchester, and
encamped at Smithfield. The Good people of W. received us very kindly and
enthusiastically.

July 4*th*—Declaration of Independence Day, but as we had other
business before us, we did not celebrate the day in the old time style. We marched through Halltown and Charlestown, near the old field where that fanatical
murderer and abolitionist, John Brown, was hung, and halted under a heavy
cannonading at Bolivar Heights, near Harper's Ferry. This place on the
Baltimore and Ohio railroad, and on the Potomac river, surrounded by lofty
mountains, was once a United States Arsenal and Government foundry. The

Yankee camps had been hastily forsaken, and our men quickly took possession of them and their contents. After dark General Rhodes took his old Alabama brigade (now Battle's) into the town, where a universal pillaging of United States Government property, especially commissary stores, was carried on all night. The town was pretty thoroughly relieved of its stores, and the 4th of July was passed very pleasantly. Corporal A. F. Henderson, while in a cherry tree gathering fruit, was wounded by a minie ball or piece of shell, and carried to a hospital in the afternoon. Fuller Henderson is a son of Rev. S. Henderson, D. D., a distinguished Baptist minister of Alabama, and is a true and unflinching soldier.

July 5th—In company with Captain J. P. Smith, A. I. G., Captain R. M. Greene, of Sixth Alabama, and Sergeant A. P. Reid, I returned to town again in the morning, and procured some envelopes, writing-paper, and preserved fruits, etc. The enemy's sharpshooters from Maryland Heights fired pretty close to us repeatedly, and bullets fell so rapidly it was dangerous to walk over the town. But as we were on a frolic, resolved to see everything, we heeded the danger very little. We returned to camp, near Halltown. I was sick and restless during the night.

July 6th—As I was weak from my sickness of the past night, I rode in an ambulance all day. Rhodes' and Ramseur's divisions crossed the Potomac at Shepherdstown, and marched through the famous town of Sharpsburg. Signs of the bloody battle fought there in September, 1862, between Generals Lee and McClellan were everywhere visible. Great holes, made by cannon-balls and shells, were to be seen in the houses and chimneys, and trees, fences and houses showed countless marks made by innumerable minie-balls. I took a very refreshing bath in Antietam creek, upon whose banks we bivouacked. Memories of scores of army comrades and childhood's friends, slain on the banks of this stream, came before my mind, and kept away sleep for a long while. The preservation of such an undesirable union of States is not worth the life of a single Southerner lost on that memorable battle-field. Lieutenant John Fletcher, of my company, and Captain Tucker, commanding Twelfth Alabama, were killed at Sharpsburg.

July 7th—Left the Antietam and marched through a mountainous country towards Harper's Ferry, where constant cannonading could be heard. Our brigade halted near Rohrersville, three miles from Crampton's Gap, and the Third, Fifth, Sixth, Twelfth and Sixty-first Alabama regiments, of which the brigade was composed, were sent in different directions to guard roads. The Twelfth Alabama remained on picket all night, leaving outpost for the brigade at three o'clock P.M.

July 8th—Rhodes' division was taken within a short distance of the Ferry, halted for an hour or two, and then marched across the mountain at Crampton's Gap, where General Howell Cobb's brigade of Georgians fought in 1862, and where Lieutenant-Colonel Jeff. Lamar, of Tom Cobb's Legion, was killed. Here Tom Irvine, of Oxford, Georgia, one of my earliest schoolfellows, and a very intelligent and promising youth, was also slain. We passed through Burkettsville and stopped near Jefferson. The sun was very hot indeed to-day, and marching very uncomfortable. The mountain scenery in this section is very beautiful.

July 9th—Marched through and beyond Frederick City, but neither saw nor heard anything of the mythical "Barbara Freitchie," concerning whom the abolition poet, Whittier, wrote in such an untruthful and silly strain. We found the enemy, under General Lew. Wallace, posted on the heights near Monocacy river. Our sharpshooters engaged them, and Private Smith, of Company "D", was killed. General Gordon attacked the enemy with his division and routed them completely, killing a large number. Colonel John Hill Lamar, of Sixtieth Georgia, who had but six months before married the charming Mrs. C————, of Orange county, Virginia, was killed. There is a report that General Early levied a contribution on Frederick City, calling for $50,000 in money, 4,500 suits of clothes, 4,000 pairs of shoes, and a quantity of bacon and flour. Battle's brigade was in line of battle all the evening, and marched from point to point, but was not actively engaged. Two divisions of the Sixth Army Corps and some "hundred days men" opposed our advance. The latter were very easily demoralized, and ran away.

July 10th—Marched nearly twenty-five miles to-day on the main road to Washington city, passing through Urbana, Hyatstown and other small places. It was a severe march. We camped near Rockville. My negro cook, Charles, left me; I sent him off to cook a chicken and some biscuits, and he failed to put in an appearance any more. My opinion is that he was enticed away or forcibly detained by some negro worshipper, as he had always been prompt and faithful, and seemed much attached to me.

July 11th—Passed through the neat village of Rockville, and marched under a very hot sun towards Washington city. Halted about two miles from the inner fortifications, where we were exposed to a close and rapid shelling nearly all the afternoon. The men are full of surmises as to our next course of action, and all are eager to enter the city. We can plainly see the dome of the Capitol and other prominent buildings, Arlington Heights (General Lee's old home), and four lofty redoubts, well manned with huge, frowning cannons. Several 100-pound shells burst over us, but only one or two men in the entire division were hurt. All the houses in our vicinity were vacated by their inmates on our approach, and the skirmishers in front were soon in them. Many articles of male and female attire were strewn over the ground. This conduct was against orders, but a few men, led by an Italian, familiarly known as "Tony", who was once an organ-grinder in Mobile and now belonging to the "Guarde La Fayette," Company "A", of my regiment, exerted themselves to imitate the vandalism of Hunter and Milroy and their thieving followers while they occupied the fair Valley of Virginia. Private property ought to be—and is, generally—respected by Confederate soldiers, and any other course is ungentlemanly and unsoldierly. Yankee soldiers are not expected to appreciate such gentility and self-respect. United States Postmaster-General Montgomery Blair's house and farm, called "Silver Spring," were less than a hundred yards from my regiment. General Breckinridge is an old acquaintance of General Blair, and had placed a guard around it, and forbade any one to enter the house or at all disturb the premises. This course was in great contrast to that pursued by General Hunter when he caused the destruction of the residence of his cousin, Hon. Andrew Hunter, in Virginia. Breckinridge is the very soul of honor, as are all our leading generals. The meanest private in our army would not sanction the conduct of Milroy and Hunter.

July 12*th*—Some heavy skirmishing occurred to-day, and one of my regiment was wounded. The sharpshooters, and Fifth Alabama, which supported them, were hotly engaged; some of the enemy, seen behind their breastworks, were dressed in citizens' clothes, and a few had on linen coats. I suppose these were "Home Guards," composed of Treasury, Postoffice and other Department clerks.

I went to Roche's and other houses near the picket line, and was shown some very disreputable letters, received and written by young ladies, which had been found in the houses, and which showed how utterly demoralized the people of the North had become. It was a day of conjecture and considerable excitement, in momentary expectation of being ordered "forward." But we were disappointed in our expectations and wishes, and late at night we evacuated our position, and left Washington and its frightened inhabitants. The object of the daring expedition was no doubt accomplished, and Grant was forced to send large reinforcements to the threatened and demoralized Capital from his own army, and thus largely diminish his own force and lessen his ability to act upon the offensive. I believe we could have taken the city when we first reached it, but the delay brought heavy battalions from Grant— ten times our small number—who could have readily forced us to abandon it. About twelve o'clock at night we commenced falling back towards Rockville, and I regret to say, our march was brilliantly illuminated by the burning of the magnificent Blair mansion. The destruction of the house was much deplored by our general officers and the more thoughtful subordinates, as it had been our policy not to interfere with private property. It was set on fire either by some thoughtless and reckless sharpshooter in the rear guard, or by some careless soldier stationed about the house.

July 13*th*—Marched on our retreat the remainder of the night, passed through the very friendly Southern town of Rockville, and halted near Darnestown. I slept all the afternoon, not having enjoyed any rest the previous night. At dusk we commenced marching, *via* Poolsville, to White's Ferry on the Potomac river. Did not march over five miles the entire night, though kept awake, and moving short distances at intervals of a few minutes.

July 14*th*—Recrossed the Potomac, wading it, and halted near the delightful little town of Leesburg. We have secured, it is said, over 3,000 horses and more than 2,500 head of beef cattle by this expedition, and this gain will greatly help the Confederate Government.

July 15*th*—Rested quietly "under the shade of the trees."

In The Battle of Monocacy, MD.
by I. G. Bradwell, Brantley, Ala.
Confederate Veteran, January, 1928

The article by Judge Worthington in the January *VETERAN* is a vivid reminder to me of the engagement at Monocacy, Md., in which so many of my comrades lost their lives and in which I came so near to being killed myself — a very important event in the history of our country which caused a delay of one day that saved Washington, D. C., and perhaps Lincoln from falling into the hands of the Confederates under Early. On the Worthington plantation and those adjoining, the battle took place. Although this battle was fought nearly sixty-four years ago, and the great battles I had just passed through were on a much greater scale than this one, it still clings to my memory.

In writing of this, I must go back to the beginning and mention other things leading up to this battle, otherwise the reader might not understand much that he ought to know at this time when facts have been so distorted and misrepresented as to make them appear as present-day historians would have them understood by a new generation.

The Confederate forces engaged in this campaign under General Early having just passed through the battles of the Wilderness, Spotsylvania, Cold Harbor, etc., were fearfully decimated. Brigades were only regiments, divisions were brigades in numerical strength, but all were veterans of much experience in battle. His numbers have been greatly overestimated, even by his friends.

I cannot say whether General Lee had in mind a demonstration against Washington at the time he detached General Early and his command to meet Hunter at Lynchburg, but something had to be done to stop his triumphal march. Accordingly, to our surprise, we were ordered out of the works at Cold Harbor, where we were facing Grant's army, and went into camps in the rear, where we rested two days of precious time. Long before day we set out for Lynchburg on a forced march to meet that Falstaff and his army before he could enter that city.

Early's force consisted of Gordon's division, about twenty-seven hundred strong, in advance, followed by General Rodes and the artillery. We pushed on over the railroad track, now utterly torn up by Sheridan's Cavalry, until we were met by trains of old ramshackle cars sent to meet us. On these we climbed and were carried to our destination, where we arrived just as the sun was sinking in the west. We detrained immediately and marched through the town. Hunter had already arrived there and had thrown up a long line of earthworks, on which he had mounted cannon to protect himself from a few old men, citizens of the place, and twelve- and fourteen-year old boys, who had taken up arms to defend their homes. These were throwing up breastworks on the edge of the town as we passed out.

Finding the enemy so numerous and strongly posted, General Gordon decided to await the arrival of General Rodes and the artillery before making an attack. These came up during the night and took position on our right at daybreak, skirmishers were thrown out to see what the enemy could do, and all that day a lively exchange of compliments passed between the opposite forces, while the artillery on each side assisted in the exercises of the day.

In the meantime, General Early was perfecting his plans to assault the enemy at daybreak the next morning, but when we approached the works not a gun was fired, and we found our foe had fled during the night.

Now began a foot race for the mountains of West Virginia, in which Hunter abandoned to our small force of cavalry, which kept in close touch with him, much of his artillery, army transport wagons, and other equipment, besides many prisoners who could not keep their places in ranks, but fell into our hands. This march was very hard on the Confederates, who were equally as anxious to capture General Hunter as he was to escape. He had rendered himself so obnoxious to our authorities by his inhumanity that they were very desirous to get him. He was one of those who thought the white people of the South ought to be exterminated by fire and sword. Every morning we rose long before day and started in pursuit and marched until a late hour at night. But when we came in sight of the fires of his encampment, we were too tired to attack and he was out and gone some time during the night. This was the nature of his retreat until he finally escaped through the narrow mountain roads of West Virginia.

While his army occupied Lexington before he went to Lynchburg his soldiers went to the cemetery where Stonewall Jackson is buried, and many of them took a small quantity of dirt from the mound and put it in their pocketbooks. Others cut a small piece of wood from the flagpole at the head of the grave. Our cavalry who captured the prisoners found these souvenirs in their possession. Hunter burned the Virginia Military Academy at that place. I suppose his soldiers were as brave as any others, but our men had a great contempt for them on account of their commanding officer.

Late at night of the last day of the pursuit, General Early reluctantly returned to the Valley pike, where he rested his army all the next day. If he had orders from General Lee to capture Washington, D. C., and he had pushed on as rapidly as we had come from Richmond, he would have had ample time to march into that place.

Early moved leisurely down the Valley until he came to Martinsburg on the 3rd of July, where we drove off General Sigel, the "Flying Dutchman," and captured a large quantity of army stores. Here again we lost much valuable time in destroying the railroad. On the 6th we waded the Potomac and drove Sigel and his army into their impregnable fortified position on Maryland Heights, overlooking the Potomac and Harper's Ferry, Va. Not wishing to leave this considerable force in his rear without giving them a good reason to keep quiet and be good, General Early deployed Gordon's Brigade around the mountain and began a lively skirmish battle with the enemy. This consumed two days of valuable time, in which the enemy expected us to assault them and showed their apprehension by the free use of artillery ammunition, and at this place we lost some of our best soldiers, killed or wounded by shell fire.

Feeling that he had this idea well fixed in their minds, General Early marched his forces away from this mountain fortress after midnight of July 9th, en route for Washington. In all my experience as a soldier in the Confederate army, I never saw a night so dark. It was impossible to see any object ahead of us. The file of soldiers in front of the column marching two abreast, reached forth their hands and caught a few strands of the colonel's horse's tail to keep themselves in the narrow mountain path, and those in the rear were guided by the footfalls of those immediately in front; but after we reached the open country, we suffered no great inconvenience until daylight. At early dawn we passed by General Rodes's men sleeping sweetly under their blankets in the fields by the roadside, and we felt envious that we had been denied the privilege.

Further on we bivouacked, kindled little fires, and warmed up our coarse rations of bread and boiled beef. After we had eaten and rested perhaps an hour in all, we resumed our march as light hearted and jolly as if we had enjoyed a feast. On this march we felt sure that victory was ours now, since we were no more facing in breastworks the overwhelming numbers of Grant's army, and, with the utmost confidence in our noble John B. Gordon, we were willing to be led anywhere; though young, we were all veterans of many battles and thought we were superior in bravery, dash, and military skill to any force the enemy could bring to oppose us in the open country. Then we had an idea we were on our way to Washington, where we would march in, capture "Old Abe," and put an end to the war.

We were exceedingly anxious to get him and hold him responsible for the outrageous policy of his government in their conduct of the war on the Southern people. There were in our ranks many whose homes were burned and their mothers and little brothers and sisters turned out in the cold to live or die. They knew of other atrocities more shocking. Others had been in prison and knew what tortures their comrades there were suffering, dying by hundreds every day of disease, starvation, and cold. Knowing these things, all were ready to make any sacrifice to put a stop to them. Animated by these thoughts, we cared little for the hardships we were then undergoing, but marched forward resolved to do our best for our cause and country.

Some time during the morning, we heard the boom of cannon in front toward Frederick, but we paid little attention to it, as that was not unusual when we were on the march. The cavalry was always ahead in touch with the enemy and having minor engagements with their advanced forces. Though it was continuous as we advanced, we thought little or nothing of it, and when we were coming over the higher ridges west of the city, we could see clouds of white smoke of the artillery arising beyond the town.

Before we reached the city, the head of our column turned to the right and took a road that led off in a southerly direction. This we followed some distance and then turned toward the east, crossing a creek before we reached the river. At this creek, or the river, I remember we found General Gordon sitting on his horse, and as some of our comrades showed a desire to make some preparation before stepping into the water, he spoke in a commanding voice and said, "Plunge right in, boys, no time for taking off shoes," and into it we went. The bottom was very sticky mud, and we came out wet and heavy. After we got across the Monocacy, we found a large meadow, and as we advanced some distance we saw that some of our cavalry had been having a hot engagement with the enemy. I saw a cavalryman taking his saddle off of his horse lying dead or wounded. When this man saw us coming, he ran to us with his cavalry equipment, saying: "I'm glad you're come. We'll give them —— Yankees hell now. I want to go in with you boys." I did not pay any more attention to him, and do not know whether he did so or not.

Our brave cavalrymen under General McCausland had crossed the river at the ford where we came over and, after dismounting, made an attack in an open field on General Rickett's five thousand veterans in good position behind a fence. Twice they had charged the enemy and were badly cut up before we reached the scene.

After passing out of the meadow near the river, we saw before us at some distance a mountainous ridge. This was covered with timber, and the surface of the ground was covered with rocks, which made our advance over it difficult. Behind this Gordon's Brigade, now commanded by General Clement A. Evans, numbering not more than fourteen hundred, was formed. General Evans, misinformed as to the enemy's position on the other side of the mountain, rode along behind the regiments and told us that the enemy's left wing rested just over the hill. He instructed us to advance quietly until we had passed over the crest and when we had come in sight of the enemy, to bring a yell and fall on them and rout them as we had done so successfully in the Wilderness on the 5th of May, when we had routed General Grant's right wing, capturing two of his generals and doubling up his whole army.

But in this he was mistaken. General Rickett was over there facing toward us with five thousand veteran troops sent from Grant's army, one line in the open wheat field, and another in a sunken road in the rear, behind a high rail fence, and still another on the Georgetown Pike protected by high banks. Fourteen hundred ragged Confederates against five thousand Yanks! When the word was given, we moved forward according to instructions and, in spite of the rough nature of the ground, kept our alignment perfect. When we came in sight of the enemy's forces in the open field, we brought a yell and started for them. They replied with a well-directed volley that seemed to kill or wound every officer in the brigade and very many men in the ranks.

But this did not check our advance a minute. We dashed forward, and the enemy's line, as usual, broke immediately, and we pressed them back across the broken ground full of shocks of wheat on to the second line in the sunken road behind the fence. Here they made a determined resistance for quite a while, but we routed them out of this also. The ground from this place to the Georgetown Pike was much more level and perfectly open. Over this we drove them in a trot until they took refuge behind the banks of this road.

By this time our ranks were pretty thin — hardly a good skirmish line — but ranged along the higher ground we continued for quite a while to exchange shots at the heads of the enemy in the road below us. In the meantime the fighting was hot on the left toward the river and on the right at the Thomas house, where the enemy had a considerable force holding the residence, outhouses, and grove around the premises. The regiments of our brigade, which attacked this part of the enemy's line, were as good as any in the brigade, but they had to come up through the open field to the attack, while the enemy was protected by the buildings. Here again we lost some of our best soldiers until our artillerymen finally, with much effort, succeeded by some means in getting one gun across the river. This they placed in position at the corner of the Worthington residence and opened on the enemy at the Thomas house with such effect that their resistance ceased and gave way along the whole line.

In the center, where this scribe was trying to do his duty, the men on the firing line had melted away until by this time there were but three of us still keeping up the fight. When the last shot was fired by the enemy, they ran away and left us there, but not until we gave them a last parting salutation and the fight was over. Looking around, we were amazed by the sudden close of the engagement. Not a Confed or Yank was to be seen anywhere except three blue-clad fellows lying about a hundred yards away, too badly wounded to stand up. On the left of our line toward the river, where the enemy occupied the sunken road under the hill, our men were badly cut to pieces. They had to advance in the open, while the enemy was well protected and presented nothing to shoot at except their heads. The 61st Georgia, one of our best regiments, but now reduced to only 150 men, a regiment that had never failed to drive the enemy from any position, charged them several times, only to be shot to pieces in every attempt to dislodge them, and perhaps would never have done so, but, fortunately for them, when they had about lost heart, the Louisiana brigades of Hays and Nichols, originally ten thousand strong, but now reduced to only two hundred, seeing their friends slaughtered, boldly waded the river and attacked the enemy on the flank and in the rear. Once more taking heart, they joined in the final attack, which resulted in routing the enemy on that part of the line. The broken remnants of Lew Wallace's army, though double that of the Confederates engaged in this battle, fled, utterly routed, toward Baltimore. At no time during the fight, as far as I could see, did the enemy assume the offensive, but fled from one position of protection to another, closely pursued by the Confederates, until the close of the engagement.

But I must admit I could not see what was going on along the whole line. I could see pretty well from the center to the right at the Thomas house, but my view to the left, where there was much bitter fighting in progress, was obscured.

This battle, as far as Gordon's Georgia Brigade was concerned, was conducted by private soldiers, each man acting independently, as our officers, as I have already intimated, were shot down in the first volley fired by the enemy.

The loss on each side was about seven hundred. That of Gordon's Brigade was about five hundred in killed and wounded. Many of these brave young fellows had on their bodies the marks of many wounds received in previous battles. Peace to their ashes!

*****

An effort is to be made to make this battle field a memorial park to commemorate this event, which delayed our advance on Washington one day and thereby saved that city and perhaps Lincoln from falling into our hands. What the result on the war would have been had we succeeded, I will not attempt to say, but I know the sentiment which animated every soldier in Early's army. We were all exceedingly anxious to get Lincoln and hold him to account for the inhuman treatment of the Southern people and the outrageous punishment of our helpless prisoners in their hands. We were all exasperated on account of these things.

Gettysburg was on a much larger scale than Monocacy, and there are memorials all over the ground to commemorate the event, but the latter was even more important in consequence as to the result of the war than the former.

In conclusion, I wish to say that I am no hero; but when this battle ended so abruptly, two comrades and I were the only Confederates on the ground. We stood there on a bluff overlooking the Georgetown Pike as the last of our enemies ran away, and we hastened their departure by emptying our Enfields at them as a mark of our respect.

Everything now was quiet. Looking around us, we saw scattered everywhere over the field new U. S. army blankets, linen tent flies, knapsacks, guns, and other equipment cast aside by Rickett's men in flight to escape. After putting out a fire which was slowly burning in the wheat stubble and advancing toward the wounded Yanks already mentioned, and ministering to their needs, I sat down on the bank of the Georgetown Pike and awaited the return of our stragglers. I found that every man in my company, now reduced to only twelve, had been hit except one. We bivouacked that night on the roadside, and early the next morning set out for Washington. In another article, I will write up our march to that city and subsequent events.

Yes, by all means let the government make this place a memorial park. It will not only commemorate the salvation of the national capital, but will show to future generations the daring spirit of the Anglo-Saxon race. How a few of them routed a great army of their enemies, turned aside and waded a great river, attacked another army, bottled it up in a fort on top of a mountain, boldly crossed another stream, climbed a mountain, attacked a veteran army well posted, twice as large as itself, with reenforcements perhaps as numerous, routed them and threatened the national capital itself, and recrossed the Potomac into their own country. These achievements ought to be perpetuated to all time.

"Lest we forget — Lest we forget."

Union Officers

GENERAL LEW WALLACE
Courtesy, MOLLUS. Collection

GENERAL ERASTUS B. TYLER
Courtesy, Mrs. Agnew Patterson

CAPTAIN GEORGE E. DAVIS
CO. D 10th VERMONT VOLUNTEERS
Awarded the Medal of Honor for
Gallentry at Monocacy
Courtesy, MOLLUS. Collection

Confederate Officers

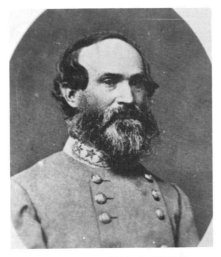

GENERAL JUBAL A. EARLY
Courtesy, Library of Congress

GENERAL BRADLEY T. JOHNSON
Courtesy, MOLLUS. Collection

GENERAL JOHN McCAUSLAND
Courtesy, Millers Photographic History

The Battlefield Today

Today the Monocacy River meanders peacefully through the battlefield that bears its name.

Courtesy, Theodore J. Johnson

Battlefield Monument erected July 1964 by the Maryland Civil War Centennial Commission.

Courtesy, Theodore J. Johnson

The Worthington House was behind Confederate lines during much of the battle. General Breckinridge observed the final Confederate assault from the front yard.

Courtesy, Brian Pohanka

The Thomas Farm "Araby", scene of the heaviest fighting at Monocacy. Ricketts' division battled Gordon's Confederates in the fields around the red brick house and barn, the 87th Pennsylvania taking position within the house and outbuildings.

Courtesy, Brian Pohanka

After defeating Hunter at Lynchburg, Early moves down the valley arriving at Winchester July 2 (1). There he divided his force, sending half of it north to Martinsburg (2) and the other half to Harpers Ferry (3). After an unsuccessful attempt at capturing Franz Sigel's force there, Early's men crossed the Potomac at Boteler's Ford. From Sharpsburg, McCausland's cavalry is sent to Hagerstown to confiscate military stores and levy a tribute on the town. Meanwhile Early's main force moves to Frederick where another tribute is levied. The Confederate advance toward Washington is temporarily blocked at the Battle of Monocacy (5). After defeating Lew Wallace there, on July 9, Early's force is near Rockville by the evening of the 10th (6). For two days the Confederates probe the defenses of Washington, re-crossing the Potomac at White's Ford (8). The army camped near Leesburg (9) on July 14.

Reprinted with permission from The Nautical and Aviation Publishing Company of America. Publishers of "A Battlefield Atlas of The Civil War," by Craig L. Symonds.

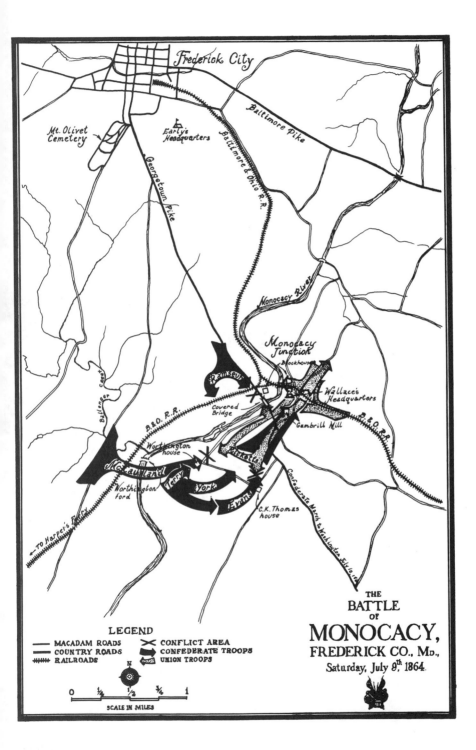

THE
BATTLE
OF
MONOCACY,
FREDERICK CO., MD.,
Saturday, July 9th, 1864.

The slope of Brooks Hill over which Gordon's and McCausland's troops advanced in their attacks on Ricketts' Federal Divison.

Courtesy, Brian Pohanka

"The Bivouac of The Dead"
Mount Olivet Cemetery, Frederick, Maryland

Confederate Monument
**In memory of those who fought at An-
tietam and Monocacy.**
Courtesy, Theodore J. Johnson

Confederate Section
**There lie dead from the Battle of Antietam
and Monocacy. Many are unknown.**
Courtesy, Theodore J. Johnson

Grave of G. W. Miller
8th Louisiana Regiment
Mortally wounded at Monocacy
Courtesy, Theodore J. Johnson

Grave of an unknown
Confederate casualty of the battle.
Courtesy, Theodore J. Johnson

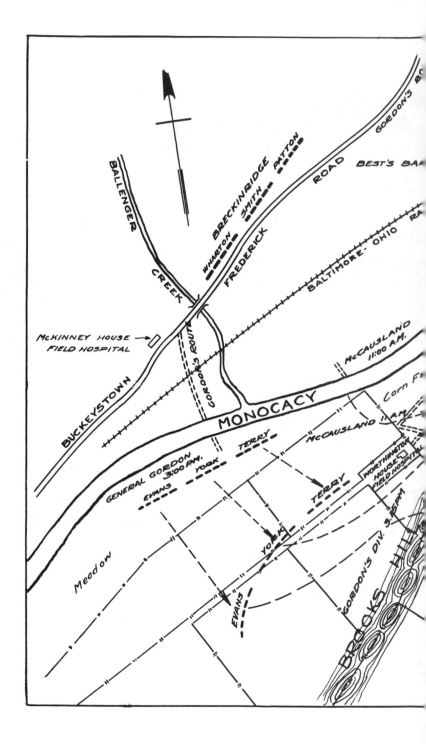

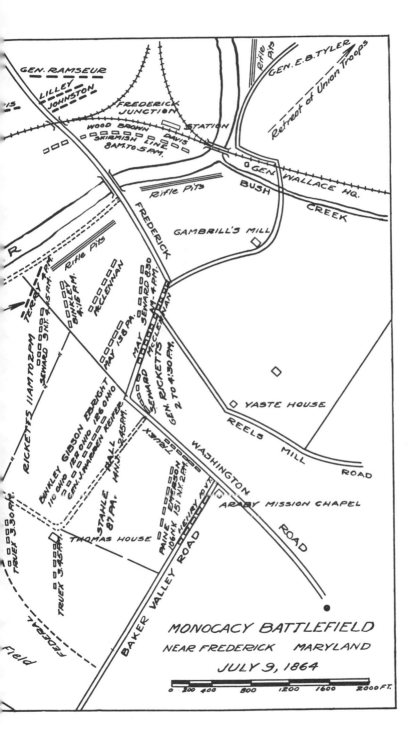

MONOCACY BATTLEFIELD
NEAR FREDERICK   MARYLAND
JULY 9, 1864

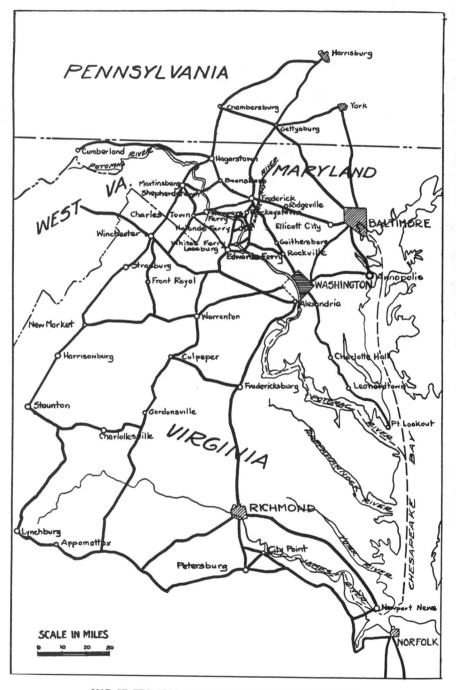

MAP OF THE TERRAIN INVOLVED IN EARLY'S INVASION.

The muffled drum's sad roll has beat
The soldier's last tattoo;
No more on life's parade shall meet
That brave and fallen few.
On Fame's eternal camping ground
Their silent tents are spread,
And glory guards, with solemn round,
The bivouac of the dead.

Theodore O'Hara, C.S.A.